Without Reservations

Without Reservations

Joey Altman
with Jennie Schacht

JOHN WILEY & SONS, INC.

Published by John Wiley & Sons, Inc., Hoboken, New Jersey

Published simultaneously in Canada

For general information on our other products and services or for technical support, please contact our Customer Care Department within the United States at (800) 762-2974, outside the United States at (317) 572-3993 or fax (317) 572-4002.

Wiley also publishes its books in a variety of electronic formats. Some content that appears in print may not be available in electronic books. For more information about Wiley products, visit our web site at www.wiley.com.

Interior design by Vertigo Design, NYC

LIBRARY OF CONGRESS CATALOGING-IN-PUBLICATION DATA

Altman, Joey.
Without reservations / Joey Altman with Jennie Schacht.
p. cm.
Includes index.
ISBN 978-0-470-13045-2 (cloth)
1. Cookery, American. 2. Cookery, International. I. Schacht, Jennie. II. Title.
TX715.A50244 2008
641.5973–dc22

2007024557

PRINTED IN CHINA

10 9 8 7 6 5 4 3 2 1

This book is dedicated to my wife, Jaemie, and my children, Johanna, Caleb, and Piper, for their love and support, and for making my life delicious.

CONTENTS

ACKNOWLEDGMENTS

There is a saying "Good chefs create, great chefs steal." While none of my recipes are actually pilfered, everything that I am and do is a result of all the great talents who taught and inspired me.

The work on this—my first—cookbook, began the moment I put something in my mouth and thought, "Boy, does this taste good—you should try it." Acknowledging everyone who has influenced me from that moment until now would take an impossibly large space. What I can say is that this book is the culmination of many years of work and a life that has been blessed by many generous and loving people who have taught, encouraged, and helped me along the way. They have had a profound influence on me and my cooking.

First, thanks to Linda Ingroia, my editor at John Wiley & Sons, for believing in me and helping me make this book much more than a collection of recipes. Sincere thanks also go to Ava Wilder, the production editor; Jeff Faust, the cover designer; and Alison Lew/Vertigo, the interior designer, for creating an accessible and beautiful book, as well as to Charleen Barila, Cecily McAndrews, David Greenberg, and Greg Mowery, for all their help.

To Carole Bidnick, my agent, for orchestrating all of the events and people that made the book possible.

To Jennie Schacht, my coauthor, for her amazing ability to capture my voice and articulate my instructions and cooking philosophy better than I ever could myself. Beyond writing, editing, rewriting, tasting, and critiquing, Jennie assembled and oversaw a small army of volunteer recipe testers whose feedback is the mortar that holds these recipes together. I offer my great appreciation to these testers, who generously volunteered their time and valuable feedback: Jane Boaz, Philip Cooper, Marilyn Davison, Dan Leff, Becky McIver, Jessica Reich, and Gwennyth Trice, and especially to Barbra Frank, Kathy Ko, Holly Krassner, and Linda Yoshino, who tested a large number of recipes with great enthusiasm.

Thanks to Frankie Frankeny, photographer extraordinaire, and food stylist Kim Konecny, for making the food look so mouthwateringly beautiful, and for being a blast to work with. To Christa Resing, the incredibly smart producer of my television show *Bay Café*, for not only making me bearable to watch on TV, but also for the use of her home and help in vetting many of the recipes.

I owe much thanks to Aliza Stern, the *Bay Café* culinary producer, for her talent and hard work making me look like a pro. To Art Takeshita, my cameraman of more than seven years, and a great friend and partner. To former *Bay Café* producers: the "If it's worth doing, it's worth overdoing!" Trisha Reece, for her huge vision and humor; and the master of style and substance, Bertrand Pellegrin, for giving me the best on-camera advice: "Mean it." To Danielle Daly, for being up for anything for the sake of good TV and a good meal. To KRON television executive producers Janette Gittler and Barbara Lane, for their lunacy in giving me a television show, and to their successor, Jim Swanson, for keeping me on the air.

Thanks to Kathleen Finch of Food Network, Paul David and Dave Dennison of David & David Productions, and my cohost Tori Ritchie, for the opportunity to "go national" with "Appetite for Adventure" and "Tasting Napa." To chefs Jean Yves Herledent, Bernard Constantin, Jean Brouilly, Bob Kinkead, Emeril Lagasse, Jeremiah Tower, Tim Ottaviano, and others along the way, for tolerating my many mistakes in their kitchens while I learned from them.

I can't thank enough my friends and colleagues at Diageo Chateau & Estate Wines Company—Philippa "Pip" Jones, Diana Morrison, Lynn Higgins, Maire Griffin, Tom Scott, Wayne Ryan, all of the winemakers, and everyone at BV's Rutherford House are some of the smartest, most talented, and fun people to work with in the wine industry. They have made my experience as a food and wine educator incredibly rewarding. They always have the perfect wine pairing for whatever I make!

Thanks to my Back Burner Blues Band-mates, Scott Warner, Gordon Drysdale, Mike Sweetland, Marc Baum, and Keith Luce, for their incredible friendship and an outlet to ROCK HARD! And to the San Francisco chefs, restaurateurs, sommeliers, wine and cheese makers, farmers, authors, and some really awesome home cooks who have come on my show to share their knowledge, passion, and pride in making a great meal, as well as the viewers who tuned in. I would not have succeeded on television without them, and so would not have had an opportunity to write this book.

Finally, a big thanks to the two who made everything possible—my dad, Michael Altman, for taking me out to great restaurants, teaching me to appreciate really great food and wine, and passing his food obsession on to me. And my mom, Natalie "Cookie" Altman, for her patience in allowing me to destroy her kitchen regularly and loving every burnt cookie, flat cake, and overcooked piece of everything she ever tasted from me. To the rest of my family and friends, thank you for showing me that everything tastes better if you're smiling when you eat it, and that cooking is an act of love.

INTRODUCTION
How I Became a Restaurant Chef

I started baking cookies and brownies when I was 8 years old because my mother knew better than to buy them for me. I soon learned that making breakfast for my family was a great creative outlet that made my parents happy. After taking my first restaurant job as a dishwasher when I was just shy of 14, I quickly realized the more fun jobs were in the kitchen. I moved from prep cook to line cook, thriving on the pressure of the dinner rush and intoxicated by watching faces in the dining room light up as they tucked into a meal I prepared for them.

I moved on to the kitchen of The Concord Hotel, an icon of the day in the Catskill Mountains, where we served 3,000 meals to hotel guests, three times every day. After graduating with honors from Sullivan County Community College's Hotel Restaurant Management program, I packed up and headed to France with a well-puffed ego. I quickly learned how little I knew as my eyes were opened to products that came straight from the farm or the docks. I apprenticed at three restaurants, each of which taught me the critical importance of selecting and respecting quality ingredients. I returned home with a newfound appreciation for the chef's craft.

My first stop back in the States was at Harvest in Cambridge, Massachusetts, where I worked with Bob Kinkead, a pioneer of New American cooking. From there I moved on to the kitchen of Commander's Palace in New Orleans, where the 28-year-old Emeril Lagasse was developing his passion for bold flavors. Next was San Francisco, the epicenter of cutting-edge cooking, where I had the privilege of working under Jeremiah Tower at Stars Restaurant.

In October 1998, at the age of 25, I was invited to be the opening chef at the Caribbean-inspired Miss Pearl's Jam House. The restaurant was located at the Phoenix Hotel, the local hangout for rock stars. The same year, I premiered my local television cooking program, *Bay Café*. More than 575 episodes, nearly 1,000 guest chefs, 2,500 recipes, and 3 James Beard Foundation awards later, I am still discovering how much there is to learn and love about food and cooking.

I still cook professionally, but having a wife and three children has taught me to adapt the lessons of the restaurant kitchen to the home. My busy schedule means that, like most people, I have limited time to cook. Yet my family and friends all expect me to turn out restaurant-quality food, even for casual weeknight dinners. And that's without a restaurant staff and commercial equipment! Over the years I've met the challenge, and this book shares what I've learned so that you, too, can cook like a restaurant chef at home, without fear or reservations.

Thinking Like a Chef

People love to eat in restaurants for two reasons: It's easier than cooking at home, and the food looks and tastes so good. Aside from having someone do all the work for you, restaurant-quality food and ambiance are within your reach, whether for a special celebration or an everyday meal. Sure, cooking great food requires a little time and effort. But following a few simple principles can elevate your home cooking from fine to sublime. In this book, I share what gives restaurant food that "Wow!" factor—from flavor to presentation—and hundreds of tips, tricks, and secrets to brighten your cooking.

These are the lessons I have learned over years of owning and cooking in restaurants, as well as working alongside nearly a thousand restaurant chefs on my television cooking program. These are the lessons I apply, day in and day out, in my own kitchen at home, for my family and friends. These are the recipes I use at the end of a long day, with a million things still on my mind to attend to and three kids each pleading with me to make something different for dinner.

I'll also show you ways to make cooking less work and more fun. You'll learn how simple it is to coax deep flavors from peppers just by roasting them, as in Pimentón Chicken with Piquillo Pepper Sauce. You'll unlock the door to unique combinations of just a few great ingredients in recipes like Cauliflower and Roasted Garlic Soup with Parmesan Croutons. You'll reproduce authentic ethnic flavors in your own kitchen with the likes of Thai Chicken-Coconut Soup. You will be cooking like a restaurant chef, without reservations, because the recipes are easy to follow and give you all the tips you need to be confident and get it right.

Just how is restaurant cooking different from what you typically prepare at home? Here are my guiding principles:

Bold flavors wake up the palate: Step into any good kitchen and you'll see the same scene: liberal use of ingredients that make foods taste fantastic. Does this mean you have to use a lot of fat to make food taste good? Absolutely not. Restaurant chefs do use butter and oil to enhance flavor, but they aren't afraid to use other bold ingredients, too. They don't shy away from garlic, chiles, onions, herbs, and spices. They season liberally with salt and pepper at all phases of cooking.

Layered flavors add nuance: When I want deep chile flavor, I don't stop with one type of chile. Instead, I combine several varieties, often some dried and some fresh, for flavor that keeps evolving as you eat.

Balance builds harmony: Balance makes a dish taste right. It comes from adjusting levels of sweetness, salt, acid (vinegar or lemon juice, for example), and other components until no one thing stands out like a sore thumb. Balance also comes from complementing and contrasting flavors and textures, like sweet with spicy, silky-smooth with crunchy, or even hot and cold.

Good technique elevates results: Technique does matter. Whether it's the way you cut your vegetables or boil your pasta, you can taste good technique in the final dish. In this book, I emphasize the techniques that matter without making the recipes difficult.

Quality ingredients enhance flavor: Good food is built on the best ingredients. By using great ingredients, you can just about step out of the way, letting the food speak for itself. Buy the highest quality ingredients you can afford and your cooking will already be so much better.

Artful presentations entice: Chefs know that we eat with our eyes. An attractive presentation actually makes food taste better. In many of the recipes I recommend side dishes and sauces found elsewhere in the book that complement a particular dish, suggest ways to compose the food on the plate, or advise a simple garnish to brighten the presentation. While my presentations aren't fussy, I do like a dish to look dressed and ready before it goes out. Use my presentation suggestions as a guide, but please, use your own creativity to decide what works for you.

Classics comfort: Familiarity is comforting. But that doesn't mean it has to be the same as the way you remember it from childhood. In my recipes, I put new twists and turns on classics to make them new again, while holding on to that familiar feeling that fills you with happy memories.

Do all these great ingredients and techniques make cooking difficult or fussy? No—when used skillfully, these principles make great ingredients better. Unless you are on a strict doctor-prescribed eating plan, you don't have to pass up the good stuff to maintain a healthy diet. You just have to keep things in balance. It happens naturally: If a dish is really flavorful, truly satisfying, you won't need to eat so much of it. You'll feel sated and happy—even fuller—eating smaller portions.

There's a French saying "In order to make an omelet, you have to crack eggs." That expression isn't so much about cooking as it is about the realities of life. You often have to create a bit of a ruckus before you can put things back together in a good way. In the kitchen, I think about it this way: You can't be afraid to kick up some culinary dust if you want to build a great dish. Sometimes that means a bit of effort. It doesn't mean you have to use every pot in your kitchen, start cooking days in advance, and go to twelve stores for ingredients. But it does mean that good cooking requires thinking about ingredients, flavors, and balance, and about having patience, doing some planning, and perhaps learning some new knife skills. Good food is built by layering flavors, by treating each ingredient in the way that brings out its best qualities. You can taste that complexity in the finished dish—as you eat, you notice a little something different in every bite.

Making Music in the Kitchen

When I'm not in the kitchen or with my family, you will probably find me strumming my guitar. Sometimes, when I play, I think about how making good food is like making good music. You may not be a musician yourself, but anyone who loves music can relate to the connections between music and food.

Chefs are control freaks who like to orchestrate your dining experience to make the most of it. We fine-tune the flavors on the plate like a recording engineer does on an album. A good recipe has to be in balance. In music the balance is treble, mid-range, and bass. We season and tweak flavors to create high notes in a dish–those things that strike you immediately when you put a bite of food in your mouth. These are the elements that bring other flavors to life–things that turn the lights on, making it possible to "see" the other flavors. Salt and citrus are prime examples. Then we balance those high notes with mid-range flavors that carry the bite as you eat it. These may include the main flavorings of a dish–the meat and vegetables. Finally, we create bass notes that stay with you after you swallow. These are the intense spices and flavorings–chiles, earthy mushrooms, hearty meat stock, rich cream, and tangy Gorgonzola cheese–that linger on the taste buds.

In cooking it's all about balancing salty, sour, bitter, sweet, and, some might add, that elusive savory quality the Japanese call *umami*. In music, you can change things by turning the volume up or down, adding harmonies, or changing the instrumentation. You can vary your cooking by complementing and contrasting textures and flavors–crunchy nuts, pungent herbs, caramelized onions. You might turn up the volume with salt, lime, or some tongue-searing habañero chiles. Or you may create softer notes with silky cream, a taste of honey, and gentle flavors that linger on the tongue long after the eating ends. What makes one song, or recipe, different from another is you–the cook or musician–and that special way you put everything together and serve it up.

In this book, I've selected recipes that have worked for me and chefs I've worked with for years. They are delicious, crowd-pleasing, and doable at home. For each recipe, I identify what makes it a standout in both a restaurant and at home, as well as the keys to what makes it work, what makes it special.

In the chapter that follows and throughout the book, I share tips about ingredients, tools, and techniques for creating bold, powerful, compelling–and always balanced–flavors in the kitchen. You'll find tempting photographs to inspire you, as well as how-to photos to help you follow the techniques I describe.

I love music as much as I love cooking, and as I cook I'm often thinking of musical analogies. When I think a musical note might help, I include it in the recipe so that it can help you think about cooking in a different way. By sharing how I think at the stove–and on stage–I hope to help you make your cooking rock!

How to Use This Book

This book tells you everything you need to know to prepare restaurant-style food at home without fear or reservations. These are the dishes I cook again and again in my own home. They are the weeknight meals I prepare for my own family and the recipes I use to create festive occasions with friends, fellow chefs, and musicians. The recipes have passed the hardest testers: my three children.

I developed many of the recipes in this book for my restaurants. Others I adapted from the wealth of recipes that restaurant chefs have shared with me and the audience on my television cooking show. What they all have in common is this: They are the staples of my home kitchen because I know I can count on them for great results, every time. They are recipes that are easy to prepare without the staff and equipment of a restaurant kitchen. I am sharing them with you so that you, too, can cook like a restaurant chef without hesitation. Here you will find everything you need to reproduce these dishes for your own family and friends at home.

We've built several tools into the book to make your cooking more delicious, less work, and more fun. First, we have incorporated icons for recipes that are Make Ahead or Easy Prep.

Make Ahead recipes, indicated by the [MAKE AHEAD] icon, are recipes where one or more elements can be made in advance. You won't have to leave your guests for long as you complete just a step or two to finish the dish right before serving.

[EASY PREP] Recipes that show the Easy Prep icon have a short list of ingredients or require little time to prepare. These recipe are perfect for every-night meals or a casual evening with friends. What's more, these recipes all taste like they must have involved considerably more effort.

Selected recipes also include Chef's Tips that let you in on those little tricks restaurant chefs know and love, and that you can use at home.

Don't Hold Back sidebars offer tips for exploring new ingredients (or learning more about ones you may already know), practicing or improving new skills with the right tools and techniques, and creating variations to adapt the recipes to your own taste or to ingredients available to you.

Except for the cocktails, sauces, and side dishes, each recipe includes guidance about pairing it with wine or other beverages.

Let's get cooking!

JOEY'S NO-BLUES PANTRY

WITH THE RIGHT INGREDIENTS and equipment on hand, you can turn a seemingly empty fridge into dinner in a heartbeat. A well-stocked pantry will save you hours hopping from store to store scanning grocery shelves in an effort to hunt down an ingredient or two for a recipe.

I often return home from the store or farmers' market with a mismatched basket of groceries that caught my eye: fresh-picked corn, tomatoes just off the vine, tender greens, a piece of farmstead cheese, a pristine fillet of local salmon. Hoping to prepare a meal with my bounty, I peruse my well-stocked pantry for inspiration. I'm free to take my provisions in many different culinary directions because I likely have everything I need, right there.

Keeping a supply of staples also comes in handy when guests drop by, or when you realize there's "nothing" in the house and you have to put food on the table. Sure, you could pull a pizza from the freezer, nuke a TV dinner, or call for take-out. But wouldn't it be nice to serve Thai Chicken-Coconut Soup? A garlicky Caesar salad? Coconut–Red Curry Seafood? Huevos Rancheros instead of scrambled eggs?

My No-Blues Pantry will insure that, when overcome with the urge to cook, you will have much of what you need already on hand. You don't have to stock up in one shopping trip. Going to Chinatown for dinner? Stop by a local grocery and look for some of the more exotic Asian ingredients. Pizza in Little Italy or making a stop at the local Italian deli? Pick up some Parmigiano-Reggiano, a bottle of good olive oil, canned San Marzano tomatoes, and a bottle of balsamic vinegar. Continue to add ingredients until your pantry is well stocked. When it's time to cook, just add a few main ingredients—a piece of chicken or fish, a steak, vegetables from the market—and you are ready to hit the stove.

SHOPPING ADVICE

Being a great chef begins with being a great shopper. A famous chef once shared with me his simple philosophy of cooking: "I buy the best ingredients I can find and try not to %$&# them up!" If you can afford it, it's worth spending a little more for quality. Especially in simpler preparations, a single ingredient–that peppery Italian extra-virgin olive oil, a sprinkling of briny sea salt, a well-marbled cut of meat–can make the difference between good and "Wow!"

You don't have to serve $30-a-pound diver scallops or $120-a-pound Kobe beef every day. But when shopping for a half liter of premium extra-virgin olive oil to use in a month's worth of meals, your investment of an extra $10 will pay off. If you are pumping gas at escalating prices but trying to save a few bucks on food, I have some advice for you: Walk a little more and eat better. You'll thank me later.

The following are some essential ingredients for your pantry. While some may be pricey or unusual, they are the stuff of full-throttle cooking without reservations because you have what you need to make a basic meal and even to experiment. They are the ingredients I have used in restaurants and at home. Even if you use only a small quantity in a recipe, once you have them you will find many uses for them in other recipes.

Properly stored in a cool, dry place away from direct light, or refrigerated if indicated, most of these have a reasonably long shelf life. (In the recipes, look for sidebars on ingredients that play a starring role.)

ESSENTIAL INGREDIENTS

Baking Powder and Baking Soda
Check expiration dates. Baking powder loses its effectiveness over time.

Bread Crumbs
Standard variety and flaky Japanese panko crumbs.

Butter
Use the best-quality butter you can find for recipes where butter is a major ingredient. "European-style" butters have a higher fat content, which means less water, more flavor. Unsalted butter gives you more control over the salt in a recipe.

Chicken Broth
Shelf-stable chicken, vegetable, and beef broths add flavor to soups, stews, and other dishes. Use low-sodium broth for more control over the salt in the recipe.

Chiles
I use a wide variety of fresh and dried chiles in my cooking. Sometimes I want the pure flavor of one variety in a dish, but more often, I combine several different types to

create layers of flavor that keep surprising me with something new as I eat. For fresh chiles, I love large green poblanos (the ones used for chiles rellenos), red and green jalapeños and serranos, and the ultra-hot tiny Thai bird chiles or habañeros.

Some of my favorite dried chiles are anchos, cascabels, guajillos, and pequins. (See also Chili Sauces and Pastes, page 10.)

When cutting chiles, consider wearing gloves to protect your hands and anything you touch afterward from their fiery oils.

Chocolate

Keep good-quality chocolate on hand and you will always be ready for dessert. Callebaut, El Rey, Ghirardelli, Guittard, Scharffen Berger, and Valrhona are all good brands. I prefer bittersweet chocolate, 62 to 72 percent cacao solids, for most baking. Chocolate chips are meant to hold their shape when baked, so it's best not to substitute them for solid chocolate.

Citrus

I keep fresh lemons and limes on hand all the time to balance with acid and to add punch to my cooking.

Cocoa

Cocoa is chocolate has had most of cocoa butter removed and is then ground into a powder. Dutch-process (alkalized) cocoa makes desserts appear darker, fooling us into thinking they have more flavor. Actually, nonalkalized cocoa has the bolder flavor; it's the one I choose for most cooking and baking. Good brands include Scharffen Berger and Ghirardelli. Guittard is a good choice for alkalized cocoa.

Cornstarch

I use cornstarch two ways. It makes a delicate and crunchy coating for deep-fried foods, either by itself, as in my Salt and Pepper Shrimp (page 46), or mixed with rice flour. It is also one of the most basic common ingredients to use to thicken sauces, gravies, pie fillings, and puddings.

Cream

Look for cream that has no additives such as carrageenan, monoglycerides, or diglycerides. While these may help increase volume or stabilize the cream when you beat it, they compromise the pristine taste of pure cream, and can get in the way of setting some desserts.

Eggs

When you can find them, fresh local eggs will have the best flavor. Eggs separate more easily when they are cold, but they create more volume when you beat them at room temperature. Always beat egg whites in a clean, dry bowl with clean beaters, as even a drop of fat from the yolk can prevent them from reaching their full potential.

Flour

I use all-purpose flour in most recipes. I prefer pastry flour for delicate baked goods because of its finer grain size and lower gluten.

Grains

I keep an assortment of grains on hand to pair with dishes according to my mood and what I am cooking. Some grains to consider keeping on your own kitchen shelf are couscous (both standard and the larger Israeli couscous), cornmeal (regular, coarse, or polenta), and quinoa (actually a seed but eaten as a grain). It's worth exploring the world of rice, which is available in ever-increasing varieties. I always keep four rice varieties on hand: long-grain white, fragrant basmati, jasmine, and Arborio or Carnaroli, the stubby grains that release their starch as you stir them to make creamy risotto.

Legumes and Pulses

I keep red and black beans, lentils, and cannellini beans in my pantry. Experiment with the vast assortment in the market and choose your own favorites.

Oils

I keep the following oils on hand. Because oils are volatile, buy only as much as you will use in a couple of months and store them in dark bottles in a cool, dark cabinet. Refrigerate nut oils after opening them. Check your oils frequently for freshness. Once you detect the slightest hint of rancidity, it's time to replace them.

TYPE	QUALITIES	USES
OLIVE OIL	With over 2,500 varieties available, olive oils are all over the map, with flavor and texture affected by the olive's variety, ripeness, the region and climate in which it was grown, and the methods used to produce the oil. Taste to find the ones you like best. Olive oil is graded by its level of defects such as bitterness, rancidity, and off notes. Start with the best you can afford.	**Extra-virgin:** This is what I use most of the time. I even cook with it. Rich and full-bodied, it's great for dressings, marinades, and sautéing. I keep a variety of extra-virgin oils on hand. I might choose a peppery oil to drizzle over grilled meats, a buttery-smooth one for a salad dressing, or a more grassy-herbaceous oil to pair with fresh mozzarella. **Virgin:** Use for more subtle olive flavor. **Pure:** Use when you prefer olive oil but want a more neutral flavor.

TYPE	QUALITIES	USES
CANOLA OIL	Canola oil comes from a hybrid plant known as rapeseed. Canola has one of the lowest ratios of saturated to unsaturated fat.	Its neutral flavor makes canola oil perfect for stir-fries and baking. I combine it with olive oil to tame the olive's assertive flavor in mayonnaise. Canola oil has a high smoke point, which makes it a great choice for deep-frying.
NUT OILS	**Almond:** This mild oil is a lovely change of pace from olive. **Hazelnut:** This amber oil has a distinctive nutty flavor. Use sparingly or mix with a milder oil to balance its assertive flavor. Look for French imports. **Peanut:** This oil's faint peanut flavor makes it a good choice for Asian dressings. **Walnut:** Light-colored and delicate, this oil has a subtle nutty quality. Many good examples are made in France's Perigord and Burgundy regions.	**Almond:** This is the oil I use when I want a fairly neutral flavor with just a hint of nuttiness. It's great for seared scallops or on vegetable salads. Its high smoke point makes it a good choice for sautéing and stir-frying. **Hazelnut:** This oil adds a nutty, exotic flavor to dressings, sauces, and marinades. I love it with peppery lettuce, bitter greens, and in warm duck salad. **Peanut:** My favorite for deep-fried appetizers like spring rolls or for whole crispy fried fish, peanut oil has a very high smoke point. **Walnut:** It is subtler than hazelnut oil, and perfect for salads that include walnuts or that would go well with them. I love it in a chicken salad with grapes, drizzled over warm goat cheese, or in pasta dishes.
TOASTED SESAME OIL	Toasted sesame oil is best drizzled on after cooking, or used in dressings or sauces. Its low smoke point means that it burns easily and can turn bitter with excess heat.	I use toasted sesame oil for an Asian nuance in dressings and marinades. It's essential in Chinese Chicken Salad, spicy peanut dressings, and stir-fries.
INFUSED OILS	Infused oils are made by steeping aromatics like herbs, chiles, zests, or roasted garlic in neutral oils. Purchase high-quality products in small quantities.	I love to finish spicy dishes with a few drops of chili oil. Rosemary oil is great for lamb and chicken dishes, while roasted garlic oil adds great flavor to pasta and vegetable salads.

Pasta

I keep an assortment of shapes and sizes on hand. Two of my favorites brands are Rustichella d'Abruzzo and De Cecco. With pasta and a can of tomatoes in the house, and a basil plant in the garden, dinner is never far away.

Salt

Salt may be the single most important element in cooking, bringing out the flavor in other ingredients. The flavor of salt varies subtly depending on its place of origin, and in some cases, what is added to it. Almost as important is the size of the crystal, which affects how fast it dissolves on the palate and its perceived "saltiness."

Kosher salt is my everyday salt. It's popular with chefs because of its clean flavor (pure salt), moderate intensity, and medium grain size, which lends itself to grabbing with the fingers—a chef's secret for feeling and controlling the amount of salt used. It's a practice worth cultivating at home.

When I want to add a bit of the briny, mineral taste of the sea, I turn to sea salt—finely ground for most things, coarse when I want crunch. For sprinkling on top of a dish just before serving, nothing beats *fleur de sel,* the "flower of the sea." Its uneven crystals deliver a slight crunch and a burst of sea flavor. One salt I never use is iodized salt, which has a disagreeable metallic flavor.

Sweeteners

I keep a good assortment of sweeteners on hand for their varied flavors. Start with granulated sugar, superfine sugar for easy dissolving, and dark brown sugar, honey, and maple syrup.

Tomato Products

I keep canned diced tomatoes on hand, as well as canned peeled whole tomatoes and tomato paste.

Vinegars

After salt, acid is the most important flavor element in a dish. Acid can come from citrus or other fruits, or from wine. Probably the most convenient place to find it is in vinegar.

Vinegar has myriad uses, from making pickles to deglazing pans, marinating meats, and adding tang to vinaigrettes, sauces, and even desserts. Add quality vinegars to your collection as you discover them. You might pay a little more for those that are rich in flavor, well balanced, and free from artificial coloring and flavoring, but you will use less because they contribute more flavor. Stored in a cool, dark pantry, most vinegars have a very long shelf life. Infused vinegars may lose their fresh flavors over time.

TYPE	QUALITIES	USES
WINE VINEGAR	Wine vinegars are typically moderate in acidity and mild to robust in flavor. The flavors of red and white wine vinegars vary with the grape varietals used. Their reasonable price means that you can keep a few different types on hand.	Because of their balanced and moderate flavor, these are my go-to vinegars for basic dressings, vinaigrettes, mayonnaise, and other sauces.
SHERRY VINEGAR	This aromatic vinegar is loved by chefs for its delicate sweetness. It is smooth and often a bit smoky. The best, made from Sherry wine from the Jerez de la Frontera region, is Spain's answer to Italy's balsamic. Aging in wooden casks adds beautiful complexity.	Chefs often use Jerez (Sherry) vinegar to deglaze pans, adding zip to their sauces. It's a natural with cheese, seafood, hearty meats, and other big-flavor ingredients.
BALSAMIC VINEGAR	True *balsamico* is made in Modena in the Emilia-Romagna region of Northern Italy. The healing "balsam" is made from unfermented grape must, generally from trebbiano and lambrusco grapes. The cooked must is aged in wood, sometimes for as long as 100 years. Over time, it is transferred from barrel to barrel, combining it with balsamic from earlier years. The balsamic you buy is actually a blend. Traditional balsamic must meet the quality standards of the consortium that tests and approves *balsamico tradizionale.* It is expensive, but it is so intense in flavor that you need to use only a few drops. Avoid commercially produced balsamic vinegars made with vinegar and caramel coloring.	Less expensive balsamic vinegars are great for salads that benefit from a sweet-tangy accent. I love them on salads with roasted fruits and meats. Aged fewer than 12 years, the thinner condiment is also perfect for meat glazes. A slightly more complex 12-year-old balsamico is perfect drizzled on a salad of simple mixed greens that have been lightly coated with extra-virgin olive oil. The longer-aged versions will fill your mouth with a bouquet of flavors from dark berry and chocolate to honey and plum. They are great drizzled over fresh mozzarella, panna cotta, or fresh strawberries, or sipped as an after-dinner digestif.
MALT VINEGAR	Malt vinegar is famous for sassing up fish and chips. Made from fermented barley, the distinctively lemony vinegar cuts through the richest batters and oils.	I use malt vinegar to enhance dishes with bold spices like chiles and allspice. I love it with spicy and smoky dressings, like those made with chipotle chiles.

TYPE	QUALITIES	USES
CIDER VINEGAR	Made from apple cider, this vinegar has a bright-tart taste I love. It's hearty enough to cut through the biggest and boldest flavors. Cider vinegars from small organic producers can sometimes be a little cloudy, but they often have more character.	Cider vinegar is essential for barbecue sauces, as well as dressings or sauces for roasted meats or chicken. It's a must in coleslaw and it's perfect for making spicy pickles. It's ideal with dishes incorporating cooked fruits—apples, of course, but also pears or cherries—or to cut the richness of nut oils and cheeses.
RICE VINEGAR	This mild, slightly sweet vinegar is used throughout Asia in sauces, dressings, and other cooking. It is essential for seasoning sushi rice. Seasoned rice vinegar has sugar and salt added, but chefs often prefer to add their own to taste.	Rice vinegar is necessary for Asian-style dressings and vinaigrettes, as well as Asian slaw, spicy shrimp salad, Chinese Chicken Salad, and other bright, spicy dishes.
INFUSED VINEGARS	Vinegars are easy to flavor by steeping herbs, fruits, or spices in them. The vinegar is sometimes heated to facilitate the infusion. In some vinegars, the flavoring elements are strained out, but you may also find herb sprigs and other flavor enhancers in your bottle.	These vinegars are perfect for adding subtle flavor to sauces and dressings. Tarragon-infused white wine vinegar is a natural with Béarnaise sauce, raspberry red wine vinegar with duck or quail salad, and fig balsamic for grilled meats and onions.
VINEGAR ALTERNATIVES	When you want a sour punch without the fermented flavor of vinegar, try a squeeze of lemon, lime, orange, or grapefruit. Pomegranate juice adds acid and sweetness, much like balsamic. Fruit juice oxidizes and becomes astringent within hours; your best bet is freshly squeezed.	Add lemon to vinaigrettes for a bright, summery taste. Lime matches well with Asian or Latin flavors, grapefruit and orange with exotic spiced dishes, and pomegranate juice with Middle Eastern flavors.

FLAVOR BOOSTERS

Anchovies

These little fish pack quite a punch! I love the salt-packed type, which should be soaked and rinsed before using. Sauté anchovies with garlic and red chile flakes for Italian pasta dishes. The fish disintegrate in the pan, leaving briny, deep-ocean flavor in their wake. These are a must for Caesar salad.

Capers

Capers are the unopened flower buds of a small Mediterranean bush of the same name that have been pickled in vinegar and salt. If they are dry-packed in salt, soak them in water, rinse, and drain before using. Capers add a wonderful, pickled mustard taste to many dishes. Probably their most famous pairing is with smoked salmon. The small nonpareil capers have the best flavor.

Chili Sauces and Pastes

Restaurant chefs know that heat is best when it's backed up by the flavor of the peppers it comes from. These sauces vary widely in their flavor mixes and heat levels. My favorites to keep on hand are:

Chinese Garlic Chili Paste: Coarsely ground chiles and garlic, for stir-fries, spicy peanut sauces, and other dishes that could use a kick in the pants!

Chipotle Chiles in Adobo: I can't sing the praises of these little devils loudly enough. (And I have a powerful voice!) The smoked, ripe jalapeño chiles are packed in adobo sauce, a tomato-based sauce with garlic, vinegar, spices, and sometimes sesame oil. I use these chiles in my Ranchero Sauce, Angry Pork, guacamole, and many other dishes that benefit from a spicy-smoky boost. Stir a little chopped chipotle and a bit of the sauce into sour cream, add a squirt of lime, and you have an easy, intensely flavored sauce for fish tacos or quesadillas. Once you've opened a can, you will find a million uses for the chiles inside.

Harissa: This Moroccan preparation is typically made with chiles, garlic, and spices. It is deep red and has a distinctive toasted spice flavor and a good hit of heat. Often sold in tubes, harissa is essential to Moroccan tagines and is a great addition to couscous.

Hot Sauces: There are more varieties of hot sauce on the market from all over the world than I could begin to count. My favorites are from the Caribbean, Latin America, Indonesia, and the United States. There are generally at least a dozen types in my fridge at any given time, with differing intensities and chile types, starting at "kinda hot" and topping out at "burn-a-hole-in-your-head-and-make-you-wish-you-were-never-born" hot. I'm a glutton for punishment.

Sambal Oelek: Sambal is an Indonesian pepper condiment, generally made with chiles, with many variations. Sambal Oelek (sometimes called Ulek) is made of crushed chiles with no garlic or other spices except sometimes a touch of salt or lime. When you want to add chile heat and flavor without affecting a dish's delicate flavor balance, this is the one to reach for. If you can't find it, substitute one of the other chili pastes made from nothing more than chile peppers, garlic, and salt; a splash of your favorite pepper sauce; or a pinch of red chile flakes. You can make your own sambal by pulverizing fresh red chiles with a pinch of salt in a mortar with a pestle or blender, adding just enough water to form a thick paste.

Sriracha: Named for the town in Thailand where it originated, this hot sauce is made from sun-ripened chiles blended with garlic, vinegar, and sugar. It is popular throughout Asia for its medium-hot, salty-sour-sweet flavor. You may have encountered the squeeze bottle of red sauce on the table of Thai, Vietnamese, and other Southeast Asian restaurants in the United States. It's a great way to kick up the chile flavor in any food with an Asian accent.

Chutney

Originating in South Asia, chutneys are condiments made from a variety of fruits and vegetables. One of the most popular is made with mango. The flavors are typically sweet, sour, aromatic, and spicy. I serve chutney alongside roasted or braised meats. It adds a complex, vibrant flavor to my Curried Chicken Salad.

Curry Pastes

Concentrated Thai and Indian curry pastes are made of varying blends of chiles with aromatic herbs and spices, making them dynamic and intense. Running from mild to intensely hot, the pastes add a spicy kick to stews, sauces, and curries. They are meant to be diluted, so be sure to add adequate quantities of broth or other liquid to the mix.

Dried Fruits

I use dried fruits to add texture and sweet flavor to couscous, chutneys, stuffings for poultry or pork, as well as desserts. I keep an assortment on hand, including dried apples, apricots, raisins, sour cherries, sweet cherries, peaches, and pears.

Dried Mushrooms

Dried mushrooms offer a gold mine of deep, earthy flavors. A good starting assortment should include porcinis, shiitakes, and morels. Add soaked mushrooms and their (strained) soaking liquid to intensify soups and sauces, or grind the dry mushrooms and use in place of, or in addition to, breading for a unique coating.

Fish Sauce

Known as *nuoc mam* in Vietnam and *nam pla* in Thailand, this fermented sauce is to Vietnamese cooking what soy sauce is to Chinese and salt is to Western cooking. It is included in practically all Vietnamese and many Thai recipes. Made from anchovies fermented with salt in huge wooden barrels, the best is clear and light in color. It has a strong and pungent aroma, but it mellows when added to other ingredients in dips, sauces, and stews for a deep, dark, robust salty flavor.

Hoisin Sauce

Hoisin is a Chinese sauce made from fermented soybeans, vinegar, sugar, and spices. It's used in stir-fries and barbecue marinades, and as a dipping sauce for Peking duck. I mix Koon Chun brand hoisin sauce with plum sauce as the base for my spicy hoisin BBQ sauce.

Mayonnaise

It's simple enough to make your own, but sometimes a spoonful of mayonnaise from the jar is the easiest way to add creamy texture to a sauce or salad dressing.

Miso

Miso is a Japanese paste made from fermented barley, rice, or soy beans. In addition to the ubiquitous miso soup found in Japanese restaurants, the intensely salty and pungent paste is used in sauces, spreads, marinades, salad dressings, and other preparations. When mixed with sugar, mirin, and sake, it makes in incomparable marinade for fish, most notably for black cod (see Miso-Marinated Black Cod, page 134), where it creates an outrageous sweet and savory glaze. There are many varieties of miso, starting with mild white, which borders on sweet, to the most pungent red varieties. I keep two or three on hand.

Mustard

The world of mustards can be daunting, with varieties from generic yellow mustard, to Dijon and whole grain, to mustards flavored with tarragon, honey, or ale that has been cooked down to a syrup. I keep whole-grain, Dijon, and Chinese hot mustard on hand.

Olives

We are fortunate that good-quality olives have become so readily available. Look for upscale grocery stores that stock an assortment in tubs and ask to sample one or two varieties each time you shop. Whole olives are a great way to stimulate the appetite at the start of a meal, while chopped olives offer yet another way to add briny, salty flavor to a variety of dishes. Minced olives make a flavorful tapenade for topping croutons or for whisking into a sauce to serve with fish or lamb.

Oyster Sauce

Oyster sauce is a dark, deeply flavored sauce used in Chinese, Thai, and Filipino cooking. The sauce is thickened with cornstarch and often gets its dark color from caramel coloring or burnt sugar. I use it in stir-fries and Asian noodle dishes. Look for the real article, actually made from oysters, rather than the imitation "oyster-flavored sauce." Lee Kum Kee is a reliable brand, especially their premium variety.

Pancetta

Pancetta is an Italian bacon from the pig's belly, or *pancia*. It is cured and lightly spiced but not smoked. You can sometimes find it packaged in slices, but often it is cut to order at the deli counter from a long, rolled log. If you purchase it from a log, you will generally want to ask the clerk to cut it into thin slices.

Parmigiano-Reggiano

When I use Parmesan cheese, I almost always use this Italian variety from the north of Italy for its deep, nutty taste. For best flavor, grate the cheese from a block of good-quality Parmigiano-Reggiano. Less expensive but still flavorful grating cheeses include Pecorino Romano, aged Sonoma dry Jack, and Asiago. You can purchase grated Parmesan cheese in tubs from many groceries, but make sure that the store is grating good-quality cheese, and buy just enough to use within a couple of weeks. Just please promise me you won't use the flavorless "cheese" in the shiny green can.

Pickled Ginger

This is served in Japanese restaurants to cleanse the palate between bites of sushi. The white and red varieties are the same except for added food coloring. A little bit of pickled ginger cut in thin slices can add fun and flavor to vinaigrettes and sandwich fillings. In a pinch, use minced pickled ginger instead of fresh in marinades and dressings.

Plum Sauce

Plum sauce is sometimes known as duck sauce because Western restaurants serve it with Peking duck, thinking it a traditional Chinese practice. Sweet from plums and other stone fruits, the sauce is enhanced with sugar, vinegar, chiles, and other flavorings. It's a good base for gingery and spicy dipping sauces, especially for fried Chinese foods.

Prepared Horseradish

I love the fresh, intense flavor and nasal-clearing qualities of freshly grated horseradish. Since I can't have it on hand all the time, I keep a jar of prepared horseradish in my refrigerator. Made from the grated root mixed with vinegar, salt, and sometimes red beets for color, horseradish packs a potent heat that, unlike chiles, doesn't linger. Horseradish combined with ketchup makes a great cocktail sauce, and the beet-tinted version is the classic accompaniment to gefilte fish. I use white horseradish to spike my Island Gazpacho, spoon it onto fresh oysters on the half shell, mix it with crème fraîche to serve with grilled steak or smoked salmon, and I never forget it in a Bloody Mary or in the tequila version, Bloody Maria.

Sour Cream

Sour cream is perfect for adding creamy texture and tangy flavor to dressings and sauces. While my wife likes a dollop on just about everything, her favorite use is a quick dip for chips made by stirring fresh salsa or barbecue spice rub into the sour cream.

Soy Sauce

Made from salted, fermented soybeans, this sauce is used throughout Asia but especially in Chinese and Japanese cooking. Japanese versions are typically lower in sodium than Chinese brands, which tend to be more robust and smoky. A wheat-free version called tamari is somewhat stronger in flavor.

Vanilla

Tahitian vanilla is soft and floral, while the pricier Bourbon vanilla is more intense and complex. I prefer to use whole beans in ice cream, custards, and sauces for their pure vanilla aroma and flavor. Refrigerate the beans in a closed container to use for special occasions. After steeping, store the thoroughly rinsed, scraped pods in a small, tightly sealed jar of sugar or rum to use a second time. When using extract, pass up "vanilla-flavored" extracts and flavorings with their artificial taste in favor of pure vanilla extract.

Wasabi Paste or Powder

Wasabi is a variety of green horseradish grown primarily in Japan. You are unlikely to find it outside of that country, although it is now being grown by specialty farmers in Oregon. Wasabi paste and powder in the United States are generally made from mustard and green food coloring, with other flavor additives. Both versions have a hot, sharp flavor that is felt more in the nasal passages than on the tongue, and that sensation dissipates more quickly than that of hot chiles.

Worcestershire Sauce

An English condiment created in the early 1800s by the Lea & Perrins Company, Worcestershire was supposedly inspired by Britain's involvement in India. It is a fermented mixture of malt vinegar, anchovies, tamarind, molasses, garlic, onions, and spices—many of my favorite flavors. Its salty-sweet, earthy, smoky qualities enrich many sauces, soups, and marinades. It is essential to a good Bloody Mary and is a great addition to Caesar dressing and to tomato and meat sauces.

Yuzu Juice or Yuzu Vinegar

Yuzu is a Japanese citrus fruit similar to a lemon, but larger and quite sour. Often the rind is used to flavor dishes that would benefit from any citrus rind, but it is easier to find bottled yuzu juice imported from Japan, which can be used in place of lemon juice. The O olive oil company makes a Yuzu rice vinegar that I love to use when I want the sweetness of Meyer lemon along with hints of other citrus and a sour punch.

THE SPICE CABINET

Spices provide unending opportunities for varying flavor. Purchase dried herbs and spices in small quantities and store them in a cool, dry, dark place. Kept above the stove they will quickly lose their flavor. To get the freshest flavor from your spices, purchase them whole and grind them as you need them in a spice grinder or a coffee mill used exclusively for spices. When adding spices to foods that won't be cooked, such as a dipping sauce or vinaigrette, you may wish to toast them first to bring out their fullest flavor.

Dried herbs lose their flavor more quickly than spices. Fresh herbs are often best, but when they are not in season or you want the more pungent flavor of dried herbs in long-cooked sauces, buy them in small quantities and replace them frequently.

These are my must-have pantry basics; they should be in every spice collection.

Allspice	Crystallized Ginger	Nutmeg
Anise	Cumin Seeds	Pink Peppercorns
Bay Leaves	Curry Powder	Red Chile Flakes
Black Peppercorns	Fennel Seeds	Saffron
Cardamom Pods	Fenugreek	Sage
Cayenne Pepper	Garlic Powder	Sesame Seeds
Chili Powder	Ginger	Smoked Spanish Paprika (Pimentón)
Chinese Five-Spice Powder	Green Peppercorns	
	Habañero Chile Powder	Sumac
Cinnamon (Sticks and Ground)	Hungarian Paprika (Hot or Sweet)	Thyme
		Turmeric
Cloves	Juniper Berries	Za'atar (Middle Eastern spice blend)
Coriander	Mustard Seeds	

ESSENTIAL EQUIPMENT

Keep these items on hand and you will be prepared for most any kitchen task. Your effort in cooking these out will save you time and effort later. You will have more fun in the kitchen, which will make you want to cook more often. In turn, your food will taste better because not only did you have the right tool for the job, you also had a good time cooking.

You can find many useful kitchen gadgets at gourmet cookware stores. For durable heavy-duty equipment at bargain prices, look to a restaurant supply store. Here are my essentials.

Baking Sheets

Keep both rimmed and flat baking sheets on hand. Use the rimmed sheets for anything that might spill or slip off. Flat sheets without sides allow greater air circulation for perfectly baked cookies and breads. Rimmed baking sheets range in size from about 15 by 10 inches to 18 by 13 inches. Choose the largest size that fits comfortably in your oven. Pans made from heavy aluminum help avoid buckling in a hot oven.

Blenders and Immersion Blenders

Traditional blenders are great for blending things to a fine purée. However, you can't beat an immersion blender (also known as a stick blender) for puréeing directly in a pot of hot soup or sauce. You remove the risk of having the blender spew hot liquid, and it saves time cleaning up. I find mine indispensable.

Cutting Board

Second to a knife is a good cutting board made from durable hardwood that won't warp. Bamboo is a great choice, with the plus that it's a sustainable wood. Another good hardwood is maple. The board should be as big as your counter can handle. My favorite is 24 by 18 inches, but if that's too big for your counter, just choose the largest that will comfortably fit.

Electric Mixers

A solid standing mixer makes easy work of creaming, whipping, and mixing, especially when long mixing is required, as you can step away while the mixing continues. The paddle attachment is perfect for creaming butter and other tasks when you don't want to add air, while the whisk attachment is the one for whipping air into egg whites or cream. A handheld electric mixer is handy for its portability.

Fine Mesh Strainer

Keep strainers in various sizes on hand for draining, straining, pushing soft foods through to assure a smooth purée, or removing any fine particles from a sauce or other mixture for the smoothest result.

Food Processor

Drier mixtures like pestos and tapenades blend better in a food processor than in a blender. A food processor is also the choice when you don't want to add air to the mix as an electric mixer would. (Even a blender adds a certain amount of air.)

Graters

I love my Microplane graters and zesters, which make easy work of many grating tasks from cheese to chocolate to lemon zest. These handheld graters in many sizes are modeled after a woodworker's rasp.

Knives

Your number-one kitchen essential should be a good, heavy chef's knife that feels good in your hand. Be sure to keep it sharp—run it over a steel each time you use it to keep its teeth aligned. That's right: Even knives that aren't serrated have little teeth on the edge that help them cut. When the teeth go out of alignment, the knife gets dull. I recommend taking your knives to a good sharpener twice a year to keep them in shape. Ask your local butcher or cooking equipment store manager for a recommendation.

My go-to knife is the Global santoku. It has great weight for cutting through denser vegetables and a comfortable grip. Because the handle is metal, though, it can become quite slick when I've been working with oils and other fats. I also love my MAC knives for their light weight and thin blades, which make easy work of slicing vegetables thin. Other essentials include a heavier chef's knife, a paring knife for peeling and other small tasks, a serrated knife for bread and soft foods, a boning knife for butchering, and a cleaver for cutting through heavy bones.

Mixing Bowls

Keep plenty of bowls on hand in assorted sizes for all your kitchen tasks. I generally prefer metal bowls, as they won't chip. However, glass and ceramic bowls also have their place. Smaller bowls are good for collecting your *mise en place* as you slice and dice vegetables and measure seasonings in preparation to hit the stove.

Saucepans and Skillets

Investing in good pots and pans will pay off in making your cooking more fun and less frustrating. Start with a few different shapes and sizes, adding more as you find you need them. You will soon find the ones you go to most often, as well as any gaps in your collection. Keep a stock pot, 12 quarts or larger, on hand for making stocks and large pots of soup. A good pasta pot (approximately 8 quarts) with a strainer insert is also useful.

Heavy saucepans and skillets allow for better heat distribution, meaning that your food will be less likely to scorch. That means easier cleanup, too. Look for pots and pans with ovenproof handles so that you can easily move them from stove top to oven. You can find good-quality, heavy saucepans made from anodized aluminum, stainless steel, and enamel-coated cast iron.

Nonanodized aluminum, unseasoned cast iron, and copper pans will all react with acids. For recipes that include acidic ingredients like citrus juices, vinegar, or tomatoes, be sure to use a nonreactive saucepan. For nonacidic ingredients, I keep cast-iron skillets in large, medium, and small sizes. Otherwise, anodized aluminum and stainless steel work well here, too. It's also worth having a nonstick skillet or two for ingredients that tend to stick.

Spatulas

Having a good set of heat-resistant silicone and metal spatulas makes cooking a pleasure. Use silicone spatulas for scraping bowls and stirring ingredients in a saucepan. Flat and offset metal spatulas are perfect for spreading batters in pans and to slide under things to loosen them from a baking sheet. It's also worth having a flat-edge bench scraper on hand to clear your work space and transfer foods from the cutting board to a bowl or skillet as needed.

Tongs

Tongs large and small are just the thing for transferring sturdy ingredients from one place to another, and for keeping ingredients moving in the pan as you cook them.

Whisks

Keep a few small and larger whisks on hand, including a good balloon whisk with a comfortable handle, for blending and whisking air into ingredients. Flat whisks reach more easily into the edges of pans, while a silicone-coated whisk is handy for use with nonstick pans.

Wooden Spoons and Spatulas

For sauces, certain soups, and some sautéed items, a wooden spoon or a straight-edged wooden spatula is indispensable. It is also a safe choice for nonstick surfaces.

OTHER TOOLS AND GADGETS

Citrus Squeezers

Mexican-style handheld citrus squeezers make easy work of extracting juice from lemons, limes, and oranges. Look for a heavy-gauge stainless-steel juicer, or enameled squeezers that come color-coded to those three types of citrus. (If you have room for only one in your utility drawer, the lemon yellow is most versatile.) Roll the fruit on a cutting board before squeezing, pressing it with your palm, to begin breaking down the internal cell walls and releasing the juice. After squeezing several citrus halves, put a couple of the spent rinds together back in the squeezer and press down to squeeze out any reluctant juice.

Mandoline Slicer

A traditional French metal mandoline, or the plastic Benriner slicer, is great for cutting thin slices of vegetables or semihard cheeses. Just be sure to use the guard to protect your fingers!

Mortar and Pestle

For some spices and other flavoring elements, nothing beats a stone mortar and a pestle for releasing flavor and grinding ingredients to a paste. I love my large granite one for making guacamole—I can serve it right in the mortar for a captivating presentation.

Ramekins

Ramekins and ceramic baking dishes are excellent for baking custards and other desserts. With the wide range of sizes, shapes, and colors available, they double as decorative serving dishes. To measure the capacity of a ramekin, fill it with water and then pour the water into a measuring cup. An 8-ounce ramekin will hold 1 cup; a 6-ounce one will hold ¾ cup. With custards and liquidy batters, you will generally want to leave ¼ inch of space at the top to avoid spills.

Ring Molds

These metal rings in various sizes are found in many upscale restaurant kitchens. They're great for creating neat plate presentations by placing foods inside one (rice, mashed potatoes, sautéed spinach), then lifting it off, leaving behind a perfect cylinder of the food.

Silicone Baking Mats

These mats have become readily available, and that's good news for home cooks. The mats clean up easily and roll up for easy storage. They are the perfect liners for baking pans to prevent sticking. Parchment paper is a good substitute.

A FEW FAVORITE KITCHEN TECHNIQUES

Crushing Peppercorns

Place the peppercorns on a flat surface and use the bottom of a heavy skillet to crush them, pressing and twisting the skillet until the peppercorns are the desired size. Alternatively, you can grind them as course or fine as you like in a spice grinder or coffee grinder.

Cutting Corn from the Cob

Lay the ear of corn flat on a cutting board and cut straight down with a large chef's knife to cut the kernels from one side. Roll the ear and continue to cut off all the remaining kernels.

Dicing Onions

Cut the onion in half through the root end and remove the peel. Lay one half cut side down on a cutting board with the root end facing you. Make 3 to 4 horizontal cuts into the onion, holding the knife parallel to the board and cutting almost all of the way through but leaving the root end attached. This will help to hold the onion together. Make 3 to 4 vertical (perpendicular) cuts into the onion, again leaving the root end attached. Now slice across the cuts to cut the onion into small dice and discard the root end.

Preparing Citrus Fruits

To remove the skin and pith from an orange or other citrus fruit, cut a slice from the top and bottom of an orange. Place the orange on a flat end on a cutting board. Using a sawing motion with a sharp paring knife, follow the curve of the orange from top to bottom, cutting behind the skin and all of the white pith. Continue cutting away strips until you have removed all of the peel and pith. Trim away any remaining skin or pith. The orange in now ready to cut into segments or rounds.

Trimming Scallions

Unless otherwise specified, simply trim the root end and about an inch from the top of the scallion and use all the rest.

COCKTAIL HOUR

GOING OUT TO A RESTAURANT is a freeing event. We are happy to let the chef and servers take care of us. Even at a casual neighborhood place, there is a sense of occasion and celebration. We are looking to relax, cut loose, splurge a little. And we want to be surrounded by that sense right from the start. Did I hear someone say, "Cocktail, anyone?"

The best restaurants understand that your first impressions—from the moment you walk in the door—will color your experience for the entire evening. A skilled server will appear immediately after you have been seated to ask whether you would like something to drink.

A well-crafted cocktail sets the stage for an enjoyable evening. Many restaurants are going beyond Martinis and Cosmopolitans to offer signature drinks that express the same creativity behind the bar as in the kitchen. Like chefs, bartenders like to showcase seasonal ingredients and follow—or start—flavor trends.

You can create that same experience at home by starting a meal with a great cocktail. It will signal the start of something special, assuring a fun and festive evening ahead. This chapter includes seven signature cocktails I have developed over the years. The Desert Rose was even awarded first prize at a San Francisco bartenders' competition. These cocktails aren't difficult to make, and they will set your evening off with a convivial bang.

HULA-VA SAKETINI

Sake drinks have become the rage in restaurants. Save your very best sake for contemplating on its own, but do use a good-quality sake for this drink. Light, fruity honjozo, junmai, or ginjo styles work well. Adjust the lime juice to make the saketini as tart as you like.

Makes 1 drink

4 ounces (½ cup) sake

2 ounces (¼ cup) pineapple juice

Juice of ½ lime

Ice

1 unsprayed orchid, for garnish (optional)

Shake the sake, pineapple juice, and lime juice with ice in a cocktail shaker. Strain into a chilled martini glass and garnish with an orchid, if desired.

DON'T HOLD BACK ■ EXPLORE NEW FOODS

Sake is the Japanese word for "alcoholic beverage." In English we equate it with rice wine. Actually, the fermented rice drink is brewed in a manner more similar to beer than to wine. Knowing which sake to choose can be tricky because the system used to classify it is complicated. Premium sakes are classified by the degree to which the rice grain is polished away and also by whether alcohol is added to fortify them. There are four main types of premium sake: honjozo, junmai, ginjo, and daiginjo. Honjozo has the least rice polished from the grain and is fortified. Junmai is made from rice only, never fortified, traditionally with at least 30 percent of the rice polished away. Ginjo has 40 percent to 50 percent of the rice polished away, and daiginjo more than 50 percent. Junmai added to the name of a Ginjo or daiginjo means that in addition to the level of polish, no alcohol was added in making it. Sakes range from about 12 percent to 18 percent alcohol. The best are served cold or at cool room temperature rather than warmed.

MOCHATINI

Cocktails aren't just for before dinner anymore. This drink is just the thing when the party continues after dinner into the night. Use vanilla-flavored vodka if you have it.

Makes 1 drink

Chocolate syrup (optional)

2 ounces (¼ cup) vodka

1 ounce (2 tablespoons) white crème de cacao

½ ounce (1 tablespoon) Tia Maria, Kahlúa, or other coffee liqueur

Ice

2 chocolate-covered espresso beans, for garnish (optional)

Drizzle the inside of a martini glass lightly with chocolate syrup, if using. Shake the vodka, crème de cacao, and Tia Maria in a cocktail shaker with ice. Strain into the martini glass. Top with chocolate-covered espresso beans, if desired.

THE DESERT ROSE

I developed this drink for a competition held at San Francisco's Rye Bar by the San Francisco chapter of the Bartenders Guild. Each month, ten of the city's best bartenders enter a cocktail using a spirit selected for that month. I'm a big fan of tequila, so when Jose Cuervo's Centenario was featured, I mustered up my courage to compete with San Francisco's master mixologists and entered the fray. Having once featured this lively competition on my television cooking show, *Bay Café,* I knew my drink-making skills would be put to the test. I relied on my chef's palate and it paid off—I took home the gold!

My favorite brand of pomegranate juice, widely available, is POM.

Makes 1 drink

Ice

2 large fresh mint leaves

2 ½ ounces (¼ cup plus 1 tablespoon) pomegranate juice

1 ½ ounces (3 tablespoons) white or silver tequila

1 ½ ounces (3 tablespoons) fresh lime juice

1 ounce (2 tablespoons) fresh tangerine juice

1 teaspoon superfine sugar

Fill a cocktail shaker half full with ice. Place the mint leaves over the ice, then pour in the pomegranate juice, tequila, lime juice, tangerine juice, and sugar. Cover and shake, then strain into a chilled martini glass.

DON'T HOLD BACK ■ EXPLORE NEW FOODS

Centenario is a reposado ("rested") tequila, which means that it was aged in oak barrels for at least two months but no longer than a year. You don't have to use that tequila to make this cocktail taste great, but do choose a blanco (white or silver, unaged), reposado, or añejo (aged one to three years) tequila made from 100 percent blue agave, without the caramel coloring, wood flavoring, and other additives sometimes used to make unaged tequilas pass for more mature ones.

BLOODY MARIA

This creative interpretation of the traditional Bloody Mary uses tequila in place of vodka. I've added horse-radish and substituted lime juice for lemon. This is the perfect accompaniment to Mexican breakfast, brunch, and lunch dishes such as Joey's Huevos Rancheros (page 56).

Makes 1 drink

1 ounce (2 tablespoons) tequila
(I use Cuervo Gold)

3 ounces (about ⅓ cup) tomato juice

Juice of 1 lime

½ to 1 teaspoon freshly grated
horseradish or prepared white
horseradish

Big pinch of celery salt (or a pinch
each of celery seed and salt)

A dash or two of hot sauce, to taste

Ice

1 rib celery

Put the tequila, tomato juice, lime juice, horseradish, celery salt, and hot sauce into a cocktail shaker or tall glass with several ice cubes. Cover and shake, or stir if in a glass. Taste and add more horseradish and/or hot sauce, if you like. If using a cocktail shaker, strain into a tall glass over fresh ice cubes. Add the celery as a stir-stick.

SUPER SUMMER SIPPER

The slight bitterness of Campari and grapefruit combine with the orange juice and a hint of mint for the most refreshing summer cocktail ever.

Makes 1 drink

2 ounces (¼ cup) fresh orange juice

2 ounces (¼ cup) fresh ruby red grapefruit juice

1½ ounces (3 tablespoons) Campari

Ice

Fresh mint sprigs, for garnish (optional)

CHEF'S TIP

For granita, make the drink in quantity and follow the technique used in Margarita Granita (page 244).

Shake the orange juice, grapefruit juice, and Campari in a cocktail shaker with ice. Pour the drink with the ice into an old-fashioned glass and garnish with mint, if desired. For an elegant presentation, strain the drink into a chilled martini glass and garnish with mint.

POMEGRANATE SANGRÍA

Pomegranate juice is the surprise here, adding tartness to balance the sweet Cointreau and Port in this deep red sangría. In keeping with the Spanish theme, use a Spanish wine such as a tempranillo, garnacha, Cariñena, or another full-bodied red wine. Ruby Port is generally the least expensive of the ports. It lends complexity and sweetness to the sangría. Since you won't be peeling the orange, use one that is organic, or at least unsprayed. You can make this sangría your own by adding other fruits such as berries, lemon, or lime.

Makes about 8 drinks

One 750 ml bottle red wine

One 15-ounce bottle pomegranate juice (scant 2 cups)

1 cup ruby Port

2 ounces (¼ cup) Cointreau

2 oranges, cut crosswise into ¼-inch slices

1 apple, quartered, cored, and cut into ¼-inch slices

Mix together the wine, pomegranate juice, Port, Cointreau, oranges, and apple in a pitcher. Smash the fruit a bit with the handle of a wooden spoon. Cover and refrigerate until cold, or for up to 24 hours. Serve in wineglasses, including some fruit in each serving.

JOE-HITO

This is my interpretation of the classic Cuban mojito, using ginger ale in place of soda for extra bite. Use a ginger ale made with real ginger if you can find it–Reed's Ginger Brew (I like the Original style) or Boylan Ginger Ale are good choices. I prefer this with dark rum, but you can also use light.

Makes 1 drink

2 or 3 sprigs fresh mint, plus more for optional garnish

Juice of 1 lime

1 teaspoon superfine sugar

Ice

2 ounces (¼ cup) rum

Ginger ale to fill the glass (about half of a 12-ounce bottle)

Put the mint, lime juice, and sugar into a tall, narrow glass and use the handle of a wooden spoon or a muddler to crush the mint and release its flavor. Add a few ice cubes and the rum. Add ginger ale to fill the glass. Garnish with additional mint sprigs, if desired.

GUESTS AT THE DOOR?

BEGAN COOKING FOR SELFISH REASONS. I wanted to be able to eat whatever I wanted, whenever I wanted it. I made it my career when I saw how happy my cooking made my friends and family. Cooking for people you care about is one of life's greatest joys, and one of the nicest (and most delicious) ways to let people know how much you appreciate them. I love having people over for meals or parties, where I spoil them with awesome food. It never feels like work because I know how much pleasure my guests will take in relishing the food and enjoying the festive atmosphere.

Entertaining has evolved into a multibillion-dollar business, with high-end caterers and party planners coordinating elaborate events. To me, entertaining is at its best when it's simple and sincere. Like a modern musician who delves into world music to bring alluring exotic sounds to the stage, I often choose dishes representing flavors from all corners of the globe. This can still be simple. My favorite recipes are the ones that reliably wow my guests and leave me plenty of time to spend with those guests.

In this chapter I share my favorite party foods, along with tips for hosting a great gathering. When the doorbell rings, you'll be ready with something extra special. Whether for brunch on a lazy Sunday, a celebratory cocktail party, or a formal dinner, the food will be part of the buzz.

PANINO of BRIE, FIGS, PROSCIUTTO, and ARUGULA

I make this hot, crisp, open-faced sandwich for practically every party because it's so easy and it's always such a hit. Guests who recognize what's coming get excited about the tangy cheese, earthy figs, and salty prosciutto the moment they see these go into the oven.

Focaccia is the oil- and herb-topped slab bread you may have enjoyed at your favorite Italian restaurant. Fougasse is its French cousin. A ciabatta (Italian slipper loaf) will also work. The bread should be about an inch to an inch and a half thick.

Makes 8 to 10 servings

What to Drink: The rich cheese, tangy balsamic onions, jammy figs, salty prosciutto, and peppery arugula make many pairings possible, from a cocktail to a red, white, or rosé wine. My top match is a sparkling wine.

2 tablespoons extra-virgin olive oil

1 red onion, halved crosswise and sliced thin

2 tablespoons balsamic vinegar

2 teaspoons chopped fresh thyme or 1 teaspoon dried, crushed

1 loaf fresh focaccia or other flat loaf (about 1 pound)

12 ounces ripe Brie cheese, at room temperature, cut into ⅛-inch-thick slices if it is too firm to spread (no need to remove the rind)

¼ pound thinly sliced prosciutto, about 8 slices

1 pint fresh figs, stemmed and cut into ¼-inch-thick rounds (save a few whole figs for garnish)

1 packed cup arugula leaves, rinsed and spun dry, plus a handful extra for garnish

Salt and freshly ground black pepper

1. Heat the olive oil in a heavy skillet over medium-high heat. Add the onions and cook, stirring frequently, until lightly caramelized, 5 to 10 minutes. Add the vinegar and continue stirring until the onions are almost dry. Stir in the thyme, remove from the heat, and set aside.

2. Use a long serrated knife and a sawing motion to slice the bread in half horizontally, as if for a giant sandwich. Place each half crust side down on a flat surface. Spread or arrange half the cheese on each side of the loaf.

3. Distribute the sautéed onions over the cheese and arrange the figs on top. Lay the prosciutto over everything. Use a wide spatula or your hands to gently press down on the toppings to help them adhere to the sandwich. (To make ahead, cover with plastic wrap and leave for up to 1 hour, or refrigerate for up to 3 hours.)

4. To finish, preheat the oven to 400°F with a rack set in a lower-middle position. Transfer the bread halves to one or two baking sheets and bake until the Brie is melted and beginning to bubble, 8 to 10 minutes.

5. Remove the loaves to a cutting board and let them rest for a minute or two. Scatter the arugula on top. Press down for a few moments to ensure that everything will stick together when sliced.

6. Use a long serrated knife to carefully cut the loaf in half lengthwise, then crosswise into 1- to 2-inch pieces. Place on a serving platter and decorate with additional arugula and whole figs.

DON'T HOLD BACK ■ MAKE IT YOURS

Try some of my favorite variations, or invent your own.

- *When figs aren't in season, substitute thin slices of apple, pear, or Fuyu persimmon.*

- *Instead of fresh fruit, spread the bread with fig jam before layering on the toppings.*

- *Instead of Brie, use any creamy, full-flavored cheese such as Camembert or goat cheese.*

- *In place of the prosciutto, try thinly sliced ham, smoked turkey, or, for a vegetarian version, use a smoked cheese such as smoked Gouda or mozzarella.*

- *In place of arugula, substitute watercress, radicchio, endive, or mixed greens.*

CURRIED CHICKEN in RADICCHIO CUPS

When making hors d'oeuvres, chefs will sometimes use good-quality store-bought products for quick flavor. I love to spice things up with exotic combinations like hot Indian curry and sweet mango chutney. Here, they combine in an alluring sweet heat that delivers a delicious adventure in every bite. Almonds add crunch and a nutty flavor.

Chicory balances the sweetness in the filling with a bitter bite. Some varieties of radicchio grow in a ball-shaped head that makes round lettuce cups, while the elongated Treviso variety, which looks like red Belgian endive, creates boat-shaped cups. You could use white or red endive, as well. If bitter flavors aren't your thing, use smaller leaves of red leaf or butter lettuce.

Makes about 48 lettuce cups, enough for 24 servings as a party hors d'oeuvre, 12 appetizer servings, or 6 to 8 entrée salads

What to Drink: Choose a wine with plenty of body and a little sweetness, such as a viognier or a rosé.

⅔ cup slivered almonds

One 3-pound roasted chicken, at room temperature

⅓ cup mayonnaise, plus more to taste

⅓ cup plain yogurt, plus more to taste

½ cup mango chutney, such as Major Grey's, plus more to taste

¼ cup fresh lemon juice, plus more to taste

3 tablespoons Indian curry paste, as hot as you like

Dried cranberries, halved grapes, or chopped apples (optional)

Sea salt and freshly ground black pepper

2 medium heads round or Treviso radicchio

1 bunch cilantro, picked apart into small sprigs

Small bunches grapes, for garnish (optional)

CHEF'S TIP

Skip a step and pick up a roasted chicken at your local market or poultry shop.

1. Preheat the oven to 350°F. Spread the almonds on a baking sheet and toast for about 8 minutes, until fragrant and golden. Set aside to cool.

2. Shred the chicken meat using two forks. Use a knife to cut pieces that don't shred easily. (Snack on or discard the skin and discard the bones.) Place the chicken into a large mixing bowl.

3. To make the dressing, pulse the mayonnaise, yogurt, chutney, lemon juice, curry paste, and almonds to a chunky texture in a food processor fitted with a metal blade. (Alternatively, you can mix this by hand, cutting up any large pieces of chutney, if needed.) Stir in the cranberries, if using.

4. Mix the dressing with the chicken, adding mayonnaise or yogurt if needed to generously coat the chicken. Season to taste with salt and pepper and additional chutney or lemon juice, if desired. (To make ahead, cover with plastic wrap and refrigerate for up to 3 hours.)

5. Cut the core from the radicchio and carefully pull apart the leaves. For the first few, you will need to roll back the edges to peel them off the head without tearing them. If you are using Treviso, cut off the bottom inch of the head and the leaves should easily fall apart. The larger leaves are best for plated presentations, while the smaller ones work well as finger food for hors d'oeuvres. Trim the largest leaves if needed to make them more manageable. (To make ahead, place in a resealable container with a damp paper towel over the radicchio, cover tightly, and refrigerate for up to 3 hours.)

6. To serve, spoon the chicken mixture into the radicchio cups and garnish each with a sprig of cilantro. After you have filled the leaves, stack any remaining ones, roll them up into a tight cigar shape, and cut crosswise into thin ribbons to use as a bed for your platter or entrée-size salad. Arrange the cups on the platter and garnish with additional ribbons of radicchio, cilantro sprigs, and small bunches of grapes, if you used them.

DON'T HOLD BACK ■ EXPLORE NEW FOODS

There are probably as many Indian curry combinations as there are regions in India—maybe more! Depending on the region, the blend might include garlic, ginger, coriander, cumin, tamarind, turmeric, fenugreek, coconut, cinnamon, or cloves. Tomato purée is sometimes added to bind the mixture. Kashmir curry from Northern India tends to be delicate and mild, while vindaloo blends Portugese and Indian cuisines with blazingly hot chiles and tamarind or vinegar. Many, many blends lie somewhere in between. You can make your own, but the prepared pastes make easy work of injecting complex flavor into a dish. Find a brand you like and experiment with different varieties; Patak's is a reliable one. If curry paste isn't available, substitute 1 tablespoon medium-hot Indian curry powder (such as Madras curry), adding a bit more mayonnaise or lemon if needed for additional moisture.

AHI TUNA POKE with WONTON CRISPS and WASABI CREAM

Chefs go wild reinventing the classics, and one of their favorites to play with is steak tartare. The French bistro standard is made of chopped raw beef, punched up with capers, garlic, and mustard. Chefs love to take this straightforward dish and create their own riffs using fish, lamb, or other meats. And as sushi has become increasingly popular, so has ahi tuna tartare.

Hawaiians have been making a version they call poke (POH-kay) using raw ahi (their word for "tuna") for a long time. Poke is traditionally made from chopped raw ahi tuna mixed with soy sauce, chiles, kukui nut (also known as candlenut, and roughly similar to macadamia), and seaweed. My version shows its Hawaiian spirit with the addition of pineapple and macadamia nuts, while wasabi recalls the sushi influence and balances the rich tuna and sweet pineapple.

The key to great poke is purchasing the freshest sushi-grade fish you can find. It should be deep red in color. Bring it home, preferably in a cooler, and get it right into your refrigerator to maintain its pristine texture and flavor.

This can be served as an hors d'oeuvre or as a first course.

Makes 24 hors d'oeuvres or 8 first-course servings

What to Drink: Serve with your favorite cocktail, an ice-cold beer, or a crisp, aromatic white wine with some richness. Pinot blanc and viognier are good choices.

CHEF'S TIP
Save a step by purchasing cored or cut fresh pineapple from the produce section of your local market.

1 tablespoon chopped macadamia nuts

½ cup vegetable oil

12 wonton wrappers, cut in half on the diagonal

⅓ pound sushi-grade ahi, trimmed of silverskin and cut into ¼-inch dice

2 tablespoons diced fresh pineapple

1 tablespoon finely chopped scallions

1 tablespoon minced red onions

1 tablespoon toasted sesame oil

1½ teaspoons grated fresh ginger

1½ teaspoons extra-virgin olive oil

1 serrano chile, seeded and minced

¼ teaspoon sea salt

1 lime

2 teaspoons wasabi powder mixed with 1 teaspoon water, or 1 tablespoon prepared wasabi paste

2 tablespoons mayonnaise

1. Preheat the oven to 350°F. Spread the nuts on a baking sheet and toast for about 6 minutes, until fragrant and golden. (Alternatively, you can toast them in a small dry skillet over medium heat.) Set aside to cool.

2. Heat the vegetable oil to 375°F in a wok or heavy deep skillet. It should sizzle immediately when you put in the end of a chopstick or the corner of a wonton. Gently lay the wonton halves in batches on the surface of the oil, dropping them away from you to avoid splashing oil on your hands.

3. Cook the wontons in a single layer, turning with tongs or a Chinese skimmer, until they are golden brown on both sides. Carefully transfer to a plate lined with paper towels. Once they are completely cool, you can store them in a cool, dry place for up to four days in a tightly covered container. (Alternatively, you can brush the wonton wrappers lightly on one side with vegetable oil and bake oiled side up on a baking sheet in a preheated 375°F oven until they are golden brown and crisp, about 5 minutes. If you press each into a mini muffin cup to bake, you will have little cups for your poke.)

4. Stir together the tuna, pineapple, nuts, scallions, onions, sesame oil, ginger, olive oil, serrano, and salt in a bowl. Refrigerate if you will not be using it immediately.

5. Just before serving, cut the lime in quarters and give 1 quarter a good squeeze over the tuna; stir to coat. Taste and adjust the salt and lime to taste. (Save any remaining lime for another use.) Stir together the wasabi and mayonnaise in a small bowl. Stir in 1 tablespoon water until the mixture is the consistency of a loose dressing.

6. Top a fried wonton with a spoonful of the tuna and drizzle with the wasabi mayo. Continue with the remaining wontons and poke, arranging them attractively on a platter or on individual appetizer plates. Serve immediately, while the wontons are still crispy.

DON'T HOLD BACK ■ EXPLORE NEW FOODS

Tuna sold by its Hawaiian name, ahi, is most often yellowfin tuna, which is among the leanest. But because ahi is not a standardized term, it may also be bigeye, which is a little richer and generally more expensive than yellowfin. Bluefin is the largest, generally most expensive, and considered by many seafood experts to be the best of the lot. Whichever variety of tuna you buy, be sure to purchase it in a market you trust and that has plenty of turnover, and ask the fishmonger what is best that day.

Wonton wrappers, also known as wonton skins, are available in the refrigerator or freezer section of many grocery and specialty stores, as well as in Asian markets. Wasabi paste or powder is also commonly available in supermarkets or Asian markets.

PRAWNS with ANCHO CHILE, TEQUILA, and LIME

I made this dish with singer-songwriter Sammy Hagar, aka "the Red Rocker" on my *Bay Café* television show. Hagar stirred up a couple of his signature mojitos using his Cabo Wabo Tequila on the sun-drenched deck of a waterside restaurant in Sausalito, north of the Golden Gate Bridge. After downing a couple of Cabo-jitos with these piquant prawns, we grabbed our guitars and gave the forty or so restaurant patrons an impromptu blues concert. It was an unforgettable moment.

While Hagar is a consummate rocker, his tequila has also garnered much respect. Anthony Dias Blue of *Bon Appétit* magazine named Cabo Wabo Tequila one of the top three tequilas in the world. The Rolling Stones carried off a dozen cases after their Hawaiian tour. I don't know whether they ever made these prawns, though.

Chefs like using tequila with chiles because their shared smokiness harmonizes well. Toasted dried chiles, puréed or minced, offer a simple way to infuse deep chile flavor into a dish. They're easy to make, so prepare a few extras and stow the remaining purée in the fridge to add a kick to other dishes. I keep some on hand to add to mayonnaise for chicken sandwiches, or to meat pasta sauces for a hint of smoky heat.

Makes 40 hors d'oeuvres

What to Drink: Match the tequila and lime with The Desert Rose (page 26), made with Cabo Wabo or your favorite tequila, or the Joe-Hito (page 32). Or enjoy with a cold Mexican beer or a glass of chilled crisp white wine.

1 dried ancho chile

20 medium shrimp (about 1 pound), peeled, tails removed

4 tablespoons (½ stick) unsalted butter

6 medium cloves garlic, minced

½ cup tequila, preferably *reposado*

¼ cup fresh lime juice

Sea salt and freshly ground black pepper

Avocado Salsa with Roasted Corn (page 206)

1 bag good-quality tortilla chips (you will need 40 unbroken chips)

About 40 cilantro sprigs, for garnish

1. Toast the ancho chile in a small dry skillet over medium-high heat, turning, until it is fragrant, about 3 minutes. Put into a bowl of warm water until it is soft, then drain and finely mince the chile, or purée it with just enough water to process it, about ¼ cup. Set aside.

CHEF'S TIP

Cook with liquor to impart
flavor without alcohol—
virtually all of the alcohol
burns off in cooking.

2. Line up the shrimp on a cutting board as if they were "spooning." Hold a long, thin-bladed knife parallel to the board and cut through the back of the first shrimp, continuing through all of them, to cut them in half lengthwise. Remove any veins.

3. Melt 2 tablespoons of the butter in a heavy skillet over medium-high heat. Add the shrimp and sauté until they are cooked through, about 1 minute. Add the ancho chile and garlic and cook for 1 minute longer. Remove the shrimp to a plate with a slotted spoon and set aside.

4. Add the tequila and lime juice to the skillet and boil briskly, stirring occasionally, to reduce the mixture to about a quarter of its original volume, about 15 minutes. Add the remaining 2 tablespoons butter a little at a time, stirring constantly, until it is well incorporated and the sauce is thick and smooth. Remove from the heat, add salt and pepper to taste, and return the shrimp to the sauce.

5. To serve, place a spoonful of the avocado salsa on a tortilla chip, top with half a shrimp, drizzle with a bit of the sauce, and garnish with a cilantro sprig. Repeat with the remaining shrimp, arranging them attractively on a platter. Serve warm.

SALT and PEPPER SHRIMP

This classic Chinatown dish shows how easily you can turn just a few ingredients into exciting dining. It's also a great lesson in making crispy food.

San Francisco's Chinatown is my favorite place for late-night eats. After a long night of playing music, my Back Burner Blues Band and I often make a visit to Yuet Lee, where Chef Timmy covers every square inch of our table top with his Hong Kong–style cooking. His food always satisfies the soul, but it's his Salt and Pepper Shrimp that make me weep. I adapted this from the version he prepared on my "Bay Café Eats Late-Night" episode. But it's good at any time of day.

There are several secrets to this recipe: A toss in baking soda sweetens the shell-on shrimp by neutralizing its fishy flavor. A quick blanching in boiling water, followed by cold water, rinses and refreshes them. Cornstarch and a quick pass through sizzling hot oil prepare the shrimp for a crunchy finish after the final stir-fry in flavorful seasonings. The result is crisp-tender shrimp with an explosion of intense, bright flavor in every bite.

Thai chiles, sometimes called bird chiles, are short and slender. Look for them in markets that specialize in Asian produce. They may be either red (fully ripe) or green; both are full of flavor and very hot. If you can't find them, substitute serrano or jalapeño chiles.

Head-on shrimp are best for this recipe. One of the advantages of preparing them this way is that you can eat the whole thing, shell and all, and the head is one of the most flavorful parts. If you can't find head-on shrimp or prefer your shrimp headless, purchase 2 pounds of 21/25 shrimp, which will be about twice as many shrimp. Avoid jumbo shrimp for this as their shells will be too tough.

Makes 8 generous appetizer servings

What to Drink: You just can't beat this with an ice-cold Tsingtao beer.

2 pounds medium-large head-on shrimp in their shells (24 to 32 shrimp)

2 teaspoons baking soda

1 tablespoon plus ½ teaspoon sea salt

1 quart peanut oil

3 tablespoons cornstarch

1 tablespoon minced Thai chiles

2 scallions, sliced thin on a diagonal

2 medium cloves garlic, minced

½ teaspoon freshly ground black pepper

1. Toss the shrimp in a bowl with the baking soda to coat them well. Cover and refrigerate for 20 minutes.

2. Bring 2 quarts water and 1 tablespoon of the salt to a boil in a large pot. Add the shrimp and blanch for 10 seconds. Drain and rinse under cool running water. Set aside.

3. Turn on your kitchen exhaust fan. You will need a wok or a pot large enough to hold the quart of peanut oil and deep enough to submerge the shrimp in a strainer into it. Heat the wok over high heat for 1 minute, then add the peanut oil and heat to 350°F. When you poke a chopstick in the oil, the oil should sizzle vigorously.

4. Place the shrimp in a stainless-steel or other heatproof strainer and sprinkle the cornstarch over them, tossing to coat them lightly. Toss again to remove any excess cornstarch. Carefully lower the strainer into the oil for 1 minute. Remove the strainer and let the oil drain back into the pot. Transfer the shrimp to a plate. (The shrimp can be prepared to this point up to an hour in advance.)

5. Carefully pour off all but 1 tablespoon of the hot oil into a large heatproof container. Return the wok to high heat and add the chiles, scallions, garlic, black pepper, and the remaining ½ teaspoon of salt. Cook, stirring continuously, for 45 seconds, then return the shrimp to the pan and cook, stirring to coat them with the seasonings, until they are dry and crusted, 1 to 2 minutes longer.

6. Transfer the shrimp to a heated platter and serve immediately.

PANCETTA-WRAPPED SEA SCALLOPS with GINGER–CITRUS BUTTER SAUCE

This recipe contrasts plump, sweet scallops with crisp and salty pancetta, then bathes them in a buttery sauce made lively with ginger and citrus. To serve as a plated appetizer, pair the scallops with a salad of arugula and endive with grapefruit and orange segments, drizzled with the sauce as a dressing.

Makes 16 hors d'oeuvres or 8 plated appetizers

What to Drink: This is a great match with a Vouvray from France's Loire Valley. Its steely mineral flavors balance the sweet ginger and citrus flavors in the dish.

1 cup fresh orange juice

½ cup white wine

⅓ cup fresh lime juice

1 tablespoon rice wine vinegar

2 medium shallots, minced

1 tablespoon minced fresh ginger

¼ pound (1 stick) unsalted butter, cut into 6 pieces, cold

Kosher salt and freshly ground black pepper

8 thin slices pancetta or bacon

16 day-boat sea scallops (about 1 pound), tough muscle strip discarded (see "Explore New Foods," page 127)

About 3 tablespoons extra-virgin olive oil

Minced red bell peppers and thinly sliced scallions, for garnish

1. To make the sauce, bring the orange juice, wine, lime juice, vinegar, shallots, and ginger to a boil in a large nonreactive skillet. Cook until reduced to about ½ cup.

2. Reduce the heat to low and whisk in the butter, 1 piece at a time, until the sauce is creamy. Season to taste with a pinch each of salt and pepper. Keep the sauce warm but not hot to prevent it from separating.

3. Separate the pancetta slices or unfurl them if they are cut from a rolled log. Cut into 16 pieces. (If you are using bacon, cut the strips in half crosswise.) Wrap each scallop with a piece of pancetta; it should go around the scallop roughly twice. Secure the pancetta with a toothpick.

4. Heat 1 tablespoon of the olive oil in a large heavy skillet over medium-high heat until it is hot. Brown the scallops flat side down in batches, about 3 minutes per side, taking care not to overcook them; they should remain plump and tender. (No need to brown the pancetta—it will cook from the indirect heat.) Add more oil to the pan as needed. Transfer the scallops to a platter as they are done. Season very lightly with salt and pepper.

5. Just before serving, drizzle the sauce over the warm scallops and garnish with the peppers and scallions.

GRILLED STEAK TEXARKANA HAND ROLLS

Hors d'oeuvres that taste and look great and are also easy to eat with your hands are party essentials. This one has bold flavor and a cool presentation that doesn't fall apart when you eat it. It's fun and surprising, and that's a big part of what good restaurants are about—engaging the imagination as well as the appetite. You can prepare the rub, grill the steak, and mix the chipotle mayonnaise in advance.

This recipe makes enough rub for two 1-pound steaks. Store the remaining rub in a tightly covered container at room temperature for future use.

Makes 20 hors d'oeuvres

What to Drink: Serve a cold beer or a spice-friendly wine such as a zinfandel, syrah, or merlot. Avoid wines that are too tannic or high in alcohol, which can clash with spicy foods.

Kosher salt

1 ½ teaspoons chili powder

1 ½ teaspoons garlic powder

1 ½ teaspoons sweet paprika

1 ½ teaspoons freshly ground black pepper

1 teaspoon cayenne pepper

1 pound flank steak, trimmed

1 tablespoon extra-virgin olive oil

½ cup mayonnaise

1 chipotle chile in adobo, minced, plus 1 teaspoon adobo sauce

2 firm ripe avocados

2 cups Salsa Cruda (page 203)

Ten 8-inch flour tortillas

20 small cilantro sprigs, for garnish

CHEF'S TIP

Make a tray of these shortly before your guests arrive and greet them with a nosh as you finish off other dishes.

1. If grilling the steak, heat the grill to high.

2. Make a spice rub by combining 1 tablespoon salt, the chili powder, garlic powder, paprika, black pepper, and cayenne in a small bowl.

3. Coat the steak with the olive oil and a liberal amount of the spice rub, using about half of it. Let stand for 5 to 10 minutes; the salt will draw out moisture from the meat, allowing the spices to adhere to the steak.

4. Grill or sauté the steak over high heat to your desired doneness, about 12 minutes for medium-rare on a grill. Transfer the steak to a plate for 15 minutes to let the juices settle. Transfer the steak to a cutting board and cut lengthwise in half, then cut into very thin strips across the grain, at a slight angle. Lightly sprinkle the cut meat with salt. Return the sliced steak to the plate to let it reabsorb some of its juices. Cover and store at room temperature for up to an hour.

5. Stir together the mayonnaise, chipotle, and adobo in a small bowl. Cover and refrigerate for up to 24 hours.

6. Cut the avocados in half and remove the pits. Use a large spoon to cut down into the avocado flesh close to the edge of the shell, scoop out a thin, long strip of avocado. Continue making parallel scoops into the avocado to make 10 pieces from each avocado half, or a total of 40 pieces. (The pieces will be shorter closer to the edges and longer in the middle.) Place the avocado pieces on a small plate.

7. To finish, warm the tortillas on the grill or in a dry skillet, turning to warm both sides. Stack them on a cutting board and cut them in half. Stack the two piles together on a plate and cover with a clean kitchen towel to keep the tortillas soft and pliable.

8. Arrange the tortilla halves in rows on a clean, flat surface with the flat edges facing you. Place a couple of steak strips on each tortilla at the 10 o'clock position. Drizzle with chipotle mayonnaise, then top with a small spoonful of salsa, 2 pieces of avocado, and a cilantro sprig.

9. Fold the tortilla half into a cone around the meat, rolling from left to right with the center bottom as the tip. Stack the cones on a platter with their points toward the center of the plate. Serve immediately with any remaining chipotle mayonnaise and salsa in bowls on the side.

DON'T HOLD BACK ■ MAKE IT YOURS

This recipe lends itself to many adaptations. You can swap out the steak with grilled chicken, tuna, or even slices of grilled vegetables. If you don't have chiles in adobo on hand, substitute your favorite hot sauce. I have a shelf lined with several in my refrigerator. The more you collect, the more uses you will find for them!

SPICY LAMB SLIDERS with CILANTRO-CUMIN YOGURT SAUCE

Restaurant chefs add whimsy to their menus with retro dishes and fun adaptations of classics. These mini lamb burgers look familiar, but one bite reveals their complex Middle Eastern flavors. The optional pomegranate seeds give them a lovely, jeweled look and additional crunch. Served with thinly sliced marinated red onions and sprinkled with the Middle Eastern spice mix called za'atar, they make a perfect party hors d'oeuvre.

Look for mini pita breads at your supermarket, health food store, or gourmet food shop.

Makes about 20 small burgers

What to Drink: Choose a Châteauneuf-du-Pape or any of the fruity Rhône varietals—syrah, grenache or cinsault.

2 tablespoons olive oil, plus a little for the baking sheet

½ cup minced yellow onion

½ cup pomegranate seeds (optional)

¼ cup pine nuts

1 tablespoon plus 1 teaspoon minced garlic

2 tablespoons chopped fresh cilantro

1 tablespoon chopped fresh mint

1½ teaspoons chopped fresh oregano

1½ teaspoons cumin seeds

1½ teaspoons chili powder

1 teaspoon cayenne pepper

Kosher salt and freshly ground black pepper

1 pound ground lamb

8 ounces ground pork

½ cup crumbled feta cheese

2 cups plain whole-milk yogurt

1 tablespoon ground cumin

1 medium red onion, halved top to bottom and sliced very thin

¼ cup fresh lemon juice

1 tablespoon za'atar

10 mini pita breads, split in half crosswise to make two small pockets

1. Preheat the oven to 450°F with a rack in the middle. Toast the cumin seeds in a small skillet until fragrant. Set aside. Sauté the yellow onions, pomegranate seeds, if using, pine nuts, 1 tablespoon of the garlic, and a generous pinch of salt in the olive oil until the onions are tender and lightly browned. Add 1 tablespoon of the cilantro and all the mint, oregano, toasted cumin seeds, chili powder, and cayenne. Cook for 1 minute longer, then transfer to a plate and refrigerate to cool it.

CHEF'S TIP

To get the seasoning mix
in a meat patty right,
sauté a bit as a test, then
adjust the seasonings
before cooking the rest.

2. Mix together the lamb, pork, and feta in a large mixing bowl. Stir in the cooled onion mixture along with a good pinch of salt and several grindings of black pepper until everything is well combined. Form a small patty from the mixture and sauté it in a little olive oil to test the seasonings, then adjust to taste.

3. Form 20 balls, then flatten them into patties and place them on a lightly oiled baking sheet about 1 inch apart. Bake until they are cooked through, about 12 minutes.

4. While the patties bake, stir together the yogurt, ground cumin, and the remaining 1 teaspoon garlic and 1 tablespoon of the cilantro in a small serving bowl. Add salt and black pepper to taste.

5. In another bowl, combine the red onions with the lemon juice and za'atar. Leave the onions to marinate for at least 5 minutes to soften. They will turn a bright fuchsia.

6. Just before serving, warm the pitas on a baking sheet in the oven for about 3 minutes. Place a warm lamb patty inside each pita pocket. Top each patty with a few strands of the marinated onions and about a teaspoon of the yogurt sauce. Serve the remaining onions and yogurt on the side.

CRAB CAKES with ROASTED POBLANO HOLLANDAISE

These restaurant-style crab cakes boast large pieces of crab, shrimp, and scallops for a brunch that feels like a special occasion. Coating them in the Japanese-style coarse, flaky bread crumbs known as panko and allowing them to stand a few minutes results in a perfect, crunchy crust that doesn't fall off when you dig into the crab cake. Mixing some of the bread crumbs into the crab mixture is the secret to cakes that hold together without being starchy.

This is the recipe I use when I want to pull out all the stops for my guests. It is always a treat for out-of-towners who have never experienced Dungeness crab. It makes a great brunch or lunch, or eliminate the hollandaise and serve miniature crab cakes as hors d'oeuvres.

Makes 6 servings

What to Drink: Try a domestic sauvignon blanc, or the French Sancerre or Quincy, a pinot grigio, or a sparkling wine.

1 pound crabmeat, coarsely chopped (fresh is best, but you can substitute good-quality canned crab)

½ pound shrimp, peeled, deveined, and coarsely chopped

½ pound medium sea scallops, coarsely chopped

¾ cup mayonnaise

½ cup minced scallions

½ cup minced celery

1 tablespoon whole-grain or Dijon mustard

1 teaspoon cayenne pepper

3 cups panko bread crumbs

Kosher salt and freshly ground black pepper

Vegetable oil, for the baking sheet

About 2 tablespoons melted unsalted butter, for brushing the cakes

Roasted Poblano Hollandaise (page 205)

1. Mix together the crab meat, shrimp, scallops, mayonnaise, scallion, celery, mustard, and cayenne in a large bowl until everything is well combined. Stir in ½ cup of the bread crumbs. Refrigerate for 10 minutes to allow the crumbs to absorb any liquid from the seafood.

2. Form the mixture into 12 balls, then press and turn the patties in your hands to smooth the sides and form uniform, hockey puck–shaped patties about ¾ inch thick.

3. Put the remaining bread crumbs into a bowl and, one at a time, put a crab cake into the crumbs and turn it to coat all sides, then cup it again in your hands, gently pressing the crumbs into the surface of the cake. Set the coated crab cakes, evenly spaced, on an oiled baking sheet for 20 minutes to allow the crumbs to adhere.

4. While the cakes sit, preheat the oven to 400°F. After the cakes have rested, brush the tops lightly with the melted butter, then bake until golden brown and cooked through, about 15 minutes. (Alternatively, you can sauté the cakes in a skillet in butter or oil.)

5. To serve, place 2 crab cakes on a plate and generously spoon the poblano hollandaise over them.

DON'T HOLD BACK ■ MAKE IT YOURS

These are equally at home morning, noon, or night. For brunch, top each crab cake with a poached or fried egg before cloaking with the hollandaise. Or make them into small cakes as a party hors d'oeuvre and serve the poblano hollandaise on the side for dipping.

Substitute lobster or halibut for some of the seafood if you like, or use all crab.

JOEY'S HUEVOS RANCHEROS

Over years of cooking for my in-laws, it's because of this dish that they say, "This is why we don't kick you out of the family." They're not big on complicated productions, but they do like a hearty meal with big, bold flavors. Prepare the Ranchero Sauce, Cumin-Lime Cream, and poached eggs before your guests arrive so that you can visit with them as you put the finishing touches on the *huevos*. Substitute fried eggs for poached if you prefer.

Makes 4 generous servings

What to Drink: Try a Bloody Mary or Bloody Maria (page 28) for breakfast; beer or a cool glass of chardonnay for Sunday supper.

One 15-ounce can refried black or pinto beans or 1½ cups canned or cooked beans

Vegetable oil

Eight 8-inch flour tortillas

1 cup shredded Monterey Jack cheese

1 tablespoon white or red wine vinegar

1 teaspoon kosher salt

8 large eggs

Ranchero Sauce (page 202)

Cumin-Lime Cream (page 195)

Cilantro sprigs, for garnish

CHEF'S TIP

To turn out perfect poached eggs in an instant, poach them up to two hours in advance, transfer to a bowl of ice water, then dip them into simmering water for about 30 seconds just before serving. Voilà!

1. Warm the refried beans, or heat the canned beans in a skillet with a little vegetable oil and smash them with a fork.

2. Spread a thin layer of refried beans on 4 of the tortillas and sprinkle the other 4 generously with cheese.

3. Heat a few teaspoons of the oil in a large skillet or griddle over medium heat. Place 1 cheese and 1 bean tortilla on the griddle. Whe the cheese melts, invert the cheese tortilla over the one topped with beans and cook the quesadilla, pressing gently with the back of a spatula, until golden on both sides. Transfer to a warm plate. Repeat with the remaining quesadillas, keeping them in a warm oven or covered with foil until they are all cooked.

4. To prepare the poached eggs, bring a generous amount of water (about 1½ quarts) to a simmer in a medium saucepan. Stir in the vinegar and salt. Break an egg into a small dish and gently slide it into the barely simmering water. Repeat with the remaining eggs. Cook until the eggs are done to your liking, about 2½ minutes for just-firm whites and runny yolks. (If preparing the eggs in advance, carefully transfer them to a bowl of ice water; dip them briefly into simmering water just before serving.)

5. To serve, cut each quesadilla into 6 wedges. For each serving, arrange the 6 wedges in a pinwheel fashion on a warm plate, points facing outward and bases of the wedges overlapping in the center. Top the quesadilla generously with the ranchero sauce, place two eggs on top, drizzle with the cumin-lime cream, and garnish with cilantro.

CHICKEN HASH with FRIED EGGS

Hash is a popular restaurant brunch item. It's a hearty dish, with a soft-crispy texture that is universally appealing. Here I use chicken instead of the traditional corned beef along with a flavorful blend of spices for a fresh-tasting hash that's easy to make at home.

Makes 4 servings

What to Drink: Serve with Bloody Marias (page 28), or a medium-bodied red wine such as a pinot noir or barbera.

¾ **pound new potatoes such as red, Yukon gold, or butterballs, cut into ¼-inch dice**

1 slice bacon, diced

1 small yellow onion, cut into ¼-inch dice

1 small poblano chile, seeded and cut into ¼-inch dice

1 small red bell pepper, seeded and cut into ¼-inch dice

2 medium cloves garlic, minced

½ teaspoon sweet paprika

½ teaspoon chili powder

¼ teaspoon cayenne pepper

1 whole chicken breast or 2 thighs, skinned, boned, and cut into ½-inch cubes

½ cup chopped scallions

¼ cup coarsely chopped cilantro leaves, plus a few sprigs, for garnish

¼ cup sour cream

1 to 2 tablespoons olive oil

4 large eggs

1½ teaspoons white wine vinegar

Kosher salt and freshly ground black pepper

Salsa Cruda, for garnish (optional; page 203)

1. Cook the potatoes in salted boiling water until they are tender. Drain and set aside.

2. Cook the bacon in a large heavy skillet over medium-high heat until crispy. Add the onions, poblano, bell peppers, garlic, paprika, chili powder, and cayenne. Cook for 2 to 3 minutes, stirring frequently, until the vegetables are nearly tender and begin to caramelize.

3. Add the chicken, half of the scallions, the cilantro, and the drained potatoes. Add half of the sour cream, stir, and cook, stirring occasionally, until the chicken is cooked through. Transfer the hash to a large bowl.

4. When it is cool enough to handle, divide the hash into 4 patties about 1 inch thick. If desired, refrigerate the patties, tightly covered, for up to 2 days before finishing.

5. Cook the patties in olive oil until they are heated through and crispy on both sides. Transfer to serving plates and drape with foil. Fry the eggs and place one on top of each patty. Dollop with sour cream and sprinkle with remaining scallions and cilantro. Serve with salsa, if using.

GARDEN GREATNESS

WHY IS IT THAT THE SALAD you toss together at home never has quite the same appeal as the one you recently relished at the neighborhood bistro or trattoria? Salad is easy, right? So what is it that chefs are doing that you're not?

The key lies in contrasting textures and flavors: snappy vegetables, seductive oils, tangy citrus or vinegar, pungent cheeses, piquant chiles and condiments, refreshing fruits, and aromatic herbs. Chefs play with these elements to create flavors that dance on the tongue, awaken the appetite, and satisfy that hot-weather urge for something cooling and light. Salads are one of the best ways to enjoy seasonal bounty.

These recipes are inspired by restaurant favorites from classic to contemporary. They include great starters as well as a few that are a meal unto themselves. With each, I offer tips for coaxing the best from seasonal ingredients. Mixed Greens with Roasted Pears is all about texture: Silky pears, soft cheese, and crunchy nuts will keep you coming back for another bite. Chinese Chicken Salad brings the restaurant classic home, with perfectly poached chicken and sesame-peanut vinaigrette on a bed of crunchy Napa cabbage. It's the perfect one-dish meal.

The secret to salad lies in stocking your pantry with flavorful oils and vinegars, along with accent ingredients that add zest to your greens. Rinse and soak your greens in cold water for a few minutes to rinse off grit and perk them up. Spin them dry so that the dressing doesn't get watered down. If you use seasonal ingredients and contrast textures and flavors, you will be well along the road to making great salads of your own.

MIXED GREENS with ROASTED PEARS, BLUE CHEESE, and SPICED PECANS

This salad appeared on the menu of my game-based restaurant, Wild Hare, for the entire four years we were open. Our customers wouldn't let us take it off. Comice, Anjou, or Bosc pears are good choices as they remain firm when roasted. (Firm Boscs will take a little longer to roast.) Blue cheese provides just the right salty-tangy punch. A flavorful goat cheese will also work. Be sure to include something that bites back in the salad mix. Anything from the chicory family will do—try curly or Belgian endive, escarole, radicchio, or frisée. The pecans can be made up to a few days in advance. If you like, double them and store the completely cooled nuts in a tightly sealed container to have on hand for snacking.

Makes 4 servings

What to Drink: Complement the salad's sweet and pungent flavors with a soft, lemony white wine such as an off-dry albariño or verdejo from Spain or a Loire Valley chenin blanc.

2 ripe but firm pears, peeled and quartered

½ cup plus 1 tablespoon extra-virgin olive oil

3 tablespoons balsamic vinegar

Fine sea salt and freshly ground black pepper

4 ounces (about 1 cup) pecan halves

2 tablespoons dark brown sugar

¼ teaspoon chili powder

¼ teaspoon cayenne pepper

1 medium shallot, minced

4 big handfuls (about 4 ounces) mixed baby greens (mesclun mix), rinsed and spun dry

4 ounces blue cheese such as Maytag or Roquefort

1. Preheat the oven to 350°F. Use a teaspoon measure to scoop the core from the centers of the pear quarters; discard. Place the pears in a salad bowl with 1 tablespoon of the olive oil, 1 tablespoon of the vinegar, and a pinch each of sea salt and pepper. Toss to evenly coat the pears, then transfer them cut side down to a rimmed baking sheet. (No need to wash the bowl; you can incorporate any remaining juices into the dressing.) Bake until a knife pierces the flesh all the way through with only a little resistance, about 25 minutes. Remove from the oven but leave the oven on. Cool the pears for 15 minutes, then cut them into ¼-inch-thick slices. Set aside.

2. While the pears roast, toss the pecans in a small bowl with the brown sugar, 2 tablespoons water, ½ teaspoon salt, the chili powder, and cayenne, stirring to dissolve the sugar and distribute the spices. Line a rimmed baking sheet with a silicone baking mat or baking parchment and spread the nuts in a single layer. (Alternatively, use a nonstick pan.) Bake until the nuts are light brown in the center when you bite into one, 8 to 10 minutes. Set aside to cool.

3. To make the dressing, mix the remaining 2 tablespoons vinegar with the shallots in the bowl you used to coat the pears. Slowly drizzle in the remaining ½ cup olive oil while whisking continuously to emulsify the dressing. Season to taste with salt and pepper.

4. Just before serving, add the greens and pear slices to the dressing. Toss gently with two large spoons or your hands until everything is well coated. Toss in the pecans. Place a mound of salad in the middle of each plate, taking care to distribute the pears and pecans evenly. Crumble the blue cheese over the salads and dust them lightly with freshly ground black pepper.

ARUGULA SALAD with GRILLED PEACHES, GOAT CHEESE, and MARCONA ALMONDS

This salad is proof that simple ingredients can be creatively combined to turn an everyday dish into much more than the sum of its parts. Grilling the peaches caramelizes the sugar and adds a smoky flavor that complements the toasty almonds. Peppery arugula and creamy, pungent goat cheese assure that there is something interesting in every bite, with flavors that continually play off one another to keep it interesting.

My friend and bandmate Scott Warner showcased this salad on my television cooking show *Bay Café*. The elegant simplicity blew me away. The Spanish almonds, sprinkled with sea salt, give a crunchy contrast to the smooth cheese and silky grilled fruit.

Use peaches that are ripe but still firm enough so that they won't fall apart on the grill. If peaches aren't in season, try grilling firm-ripe pears (Anjou or French Butter varieties work well), or Fuyu persimmons (the flat, firm variety). If the grilled Fuyus are too firm to mash into the dressing, just skip that step.

Makes 6 servings

What to Drink: The aromatic fruit and floral flavors of gewürztraminer, riesling, and viognier make them good choices.

4 medium peaches

½ cup plus 2 tablespoons extra-virgin olive oil

Kosher salt and freshly ground pepper

2 tablespoons balsamic vinegar

2 tablespoons Sherry vinegar

2 tablespoons minced shallots

9 ounces arugula (about 12 cups, loosely packed), rinsed and spun dry

6 ounces mild fresh goat cheese, broken up into small nuggets

⅓ cup Marcona almonds or homemade Marcona-style almonds (see "Step Up Your Skills")

Sea salt

1. Heat a gas or charcoal grill, or heat a stovetop grill pan over medium-high heat. Cut each peach in half with a paring knife, starting at the top and working around the peach. Twist the two halves in opposite directions to separate them, then pull out the pit. If the peach is stubborn, cut it into quarters and cut it away from the pit.

2. In a medium bowl, toss the peach halves with 2 tablespoons of the olive oil and a pinch each of salt and pepper. Grill the peaches cut side down until they soften and you begin to see grill marks when you turn one over, about 2 minutes. Use tongs to turn them and grill for another minute or two. The peaches should be softening but not falling apart.

3. Transfer the peaches to a plate to cool slightly, then remove the skin that pulls off easily–don't worry about completely peeling them. Set aside the softest peach half and slice the others into three to four thick wedges each.

4. To make the vinaigrette, whisk together the remaining ½ cup olive oil, the vinegars, and the shallot in a medium bowl. Mash the softest peach half into the dressing with a fork. Add salt and freshly ground pepper to taste. (To make ahead, tightly cover the vinaigrette and loosely cover the sliced peaches. Set aside at room temperature for up to 2 hours.)

5. Just before serving, put the arugula into a large bowl. Pour on about half the vinaigrette and toss, adding more dressing as needed to lightly but thoroughly coat the leaves. Add the peach slices, goat cheese, and almonds, and gently toss to combine. Center a mound of the salad on salad plates. Sprinkle a little sea salt over the top.

DON'T HOLD BACK ■ STEP UP YOUR SKILLS

Marcona almonds are a particular varietal of the nut native to Spain. They are larger–and some say sweeter and more flavorful–than the almonds grown in the United States. They are typically blanched, fried, and salted to bring out their toasty flavor and a seductive crunch. You can easily make a reasonable approximation of the addictive nuts at home.

Coat a cup of blanched whole almonds (they should be very fresh, flavorful, and crunchy) with ½ cup extra-virgin olive oil and roast them in a single layer on a rimmed baking sheet in a 350°F oven until lightly browned, about 12 minutes. Strain the nuts and reserve the oil; you can use it in place of some of the oil in the vinaigrette. Drain the nuts on several layers of paper toweling and sprinkle lightly with fine sea salt. Once cool, store the nuts in an airtight container for up to 3 weeks.

STRAWBERRY SPINACH SALAD

If you have never had fresh strawberries in a savory dish, this salad will be a delicious discovery. As Italians have known for a long time, sweet-tart balsamic brings out the sweetness in strawberries. I've taken the classic pairing a step further by adding briny feta and crunchy pine nuts for texture and contrast in this perfect summer picnic salad.

If you can find it, a mild Bulgarian feta has just the right salty-pungent balance and creamy-crumbly texture for this dish. If not, any feta will work. Look for genuine balsamic vinegar from Modena, Italy, made with only grape must, no added vinegar or caramel coloring. White balsamic has a similar sweet-acid balance to the more common dark version, but is less concentrated and intense. If it's not available at your market, substitute a white wine vinegar and add a small pinch of sugar to the dressing.

Makes 4 servings

What to Drink: Rosé is the perfect complement to the rosy strawberries in this salad.

½ cup pine nuts

1 pint ripe strawberries, rinsed and stemmed

2 tablespoons white balsamic vinegar

1 tablespoon balsamic vinegar

¼ cup extra-virgin olive oil

Kosher salt and freshly ground black pepper

8 ounces baby spinach leaves, rinsed and spun dry

1 small red onion, halved and sliced thin

½ cup crumbled feta cheese

1. Preheat the oven to 350°F. Spread the pine nuts on a baking sheet and toast about 8 minutes, until fragrant and golden. (Alternatively, you can toast them in a small dry skillet over medium heat.) Set aside to cool.

2. To make the dressing, dice 2 large or 3 small strawberries; slice the remainder. Mash the diced berries with a fork in a small bowl. Whisk in the vinegars, oil, ½ teaspoon salt, and ¼ teaspoon pepper.

3. In a salad bowl, toss together the spinach, onions, pine nuts, strawberries, and half of the feta cheese. Toss with enough dressing to coat the salad. Season to taste with salt and pepper. Distribute the salad among four plates and top with the remaining feta.

Pick the best-quality strawberries. In your local store, strawberries may not seem so red and ripe. They must be picked before they are fully ripe to weather the journey to your neighborhood. For red, ripe strawberries at their peak, shop locally, preferably at your local farmers' market or farm stand. Although it's not a foolproof test, the best strawberries generally have deep color. Lift a basket, check to be sure the bottom berries are not crushed and dripping, then inhale deeply. You should feel like you've been transported to a strawberry field.

OVEN-ROASTED BEET and ORANGE SALAD

Citrus makes beets shine, which is why you will frequently see orange paired with beets on restaurant menus. You can make a simple vinaigrette by combining vinegar or citrus with oil. What makes this one interesting is the complexity you get from a variety of acid components: lemon juice, orange juice, and Champagne vinegar. Orange zest takes it one step further by incorporating the flavorful oils in the skin. Extra-virgin olive oil and a little shallot soften the citrus and vinegar to round out the flavors.

Every so often, an obscure ingredient rises to become the darling of chefs. In the late 1980s it was sun-dried tomatoes. In the '90s, ahi tuna jumped from the sushi bar onto the menu of every corner bistro. In 2000, the lowly beet leapt into favor. It seemed there was a roasted beet in every salad. Chefs returned to their roots (literally!) en masse to tell the story of the sweet, earthy vegetable, with a firm texture and a rainbow of beautiful colors, that's perfect for dressing up a salad. This one is my signature beet salad from my restaurant Wild Hare.

If you can find them, use a mix of red, gold, and the exotically striated Chioggia (pronounce it key-OH-jah and you will be ahead of most chefs!) beets for the prettiest presentation and lots of variety on the plate. Blood oranges are typically available from December through March. If they are not in season, substitute an additional two navel oranges.

Makes 4 servings

What to Drink: A citrusy sauvignon blanc strikes the right note for this salad.

½ cup pine nuts

3 large beets (about ¾ pound)

½ cup plus 3 tablespoons extra-virgin olive oil

Kosher salt and freshly ground black pepper

1 tablespoon finely chopped shallots

1 tablespoon finely grated orange zest

⅓ cup fresh orange juice

2 tablespoons fresh lemon juice

3 tablespoons Champagne vinegar or white wine vinegar

2 navel oranges, skin and membrane removed, flesh cut into ¼-inch-thick rounds

3 blood oranges, skin and membrane removed, flesh cut into ¼-inch-thick rounds

2 heads Belgian endive, cut on a diagonal into ½-inch-thick pieces

1 bunch watercress, rinsed, spun dry, and separated into smaller branches

4 ounces soft goat cheese, crumbled (about 1 cup)

¼ cup loosely packed mint leaves, cut into thin ribbons

1. Preheat the oven to 350°F with a rack set near the middle. Spread the nuts on a baking sheet and toast about 6 minutes, until fragrant and golden. (Alternatively, you can toast them in a small dry skillet over medium heat.) Set aside to cool. Leave the oven on.

2. Remove the greens from the beets, leaving about 1 inch of stem. (Discard the greens or save for another purpose.) Rinse the beets in cold water and pat dry with a paper towel. In a medium bowl, coat the beets with 3 tablespoons of the olive oil and season lightly with salt and pepper. Line a baking sheet with foil. Place the beets in a single layer on the baking sheet and roast until you can easily pierce them with a paring knife, about 1 hour. Larger beets will take longer; remove each beet to a plate to cool as it finishes cooking. When the beets are cool enough to handle, rub off the skins using a kitchen towel you don't mind staining. Cut the peeled beets into ¼-inch-thick rounds; set aside.

3. While the beets are roasting, stir together the shallots, zest, orange and lemon juices, and vinegar in a small bowl. Whisk in the remaining ½ cup olive oil in a thin stream to incorporate it into the dressing. (To make ahead, cover the cooled beets and set aside at room temperature for up to 2 hours, or cover tightly and refrigerate for up to 3 days. For the vinaigrette, cover tightly and refrigerate for up to 24 hours.)

4. Just before serving, alternate the orange and beet slices in a wide circle on each of four salad plates. Drizzle liberally with the vinaigrette. In a medium bowl, toss the endive, watercress, goat cheese, pine nuts, and mint with enough of the remaining vinaigrette to lightly and evenly coat the salad. Season to taste with salt and pepper. Place a heaping handful of the greens in the center of each citrus circle. Grind a dusting of pepper over each. Serve immediately.

DON'T HOLD BACK ▪ STEP UP YOUR SKILLS

Get perfect zest with a Microplane, one of my favorite kitchen tools. This line of kitchen graters is adapted from the woodworker's rasp. The long one used for zesting, with its small slits, makes easy work of creating piles of fluffy zest, removing only the flavorful outer citrus rind without the bitter white pith beneath. Microplane also makes a spice grater that is perfect for cinnamon or nutmeg, a ribbon grater for cheese, and coarse and fine graters for many other uses.

CRAB-STUFFED AVOCADO with SPICY CITRUS-MANGO SALAD

Great-looking food really whets the appetite. This salad is a great way to create something that looks beautiful on the plate without a lot of effort.

Because of its starring role, use only fresh crab or an exceptionally good canned version. Choose avocados that have some give when you press them gently but are still rather firm. When you pull off the stem, you should see green underneath. I like Hass avocados for their firm, flavorful flesh. In summer you can often find chive flowers at farmers' markets or upscale produce stores, or perhaps in your garden.

Makes 4 servings

What to Drink: A refreshing sauvignon blanc, pinot grigio, or riesling is perfect with the citrus and seafood.

4 navel oranges

1 mango, ripe but not squishy

2 red Fresno or serrano chiles, seeded and minced

2 tablespoons minced red onions

¼ cup finely chopped chives

¼ cup plus 2 tablespoons extra-virgin olive oil

2 tablespoons fresh lime juice

1 tablespoon rice wine vinegar

Fine sea salt and freshly ground black pepper

8 ounces crab meat

2 teaspoons fresh lemon juice

2 medium avocados, ripe but firm, cut in half, pits removed

1 English or hothouse cucumber, peeled and sliced very thin

Sea salt

Chive flower petals, for garnish (optional)

1. Remove the peel and all the pith from 1 orange (see page 20). Cut the orange into ½-inch rounds, cutting away and discarding the tough center core pieces. Repeat with the remaining oranges. Stack a few orange slices at a time and cut into ¼- to ½-inch strips, then crosswise into dice, until you have cut all the oranges into dice.

2. Peel the mango, then place it on one of its short ends and cut off the large "cheeks" from each side of the pit. Turn the mango and cut off the shorter sides and any remaining flesh. Cut the flesh into ¼-inch dice.

3. Combine the diced oranges, mango, chiles, red onions, and half of the chives in a medium bowl. Add ¼ cup of the olive oil, the lime juice, and vinegar. Toss gently but thoroughly to coat. Season to taste with salt and pepper. Refrigerate for 30 minutes or up to 4 hours to allow the flavors to mingle while you prepare the remaining ingredients.

4. Mix together the crab meat, the remaining chives, the remaining 2 tablespoons olive oil, and the lemon juice in a small bowl with a fork. Season to taste with salt and pepper.

5. To assemble, use a large spoon to scoop each avocado half from its shell in a single piece. Lay an avocado half cut side down at the center of an 8-inch piece of plastic wrap set on a cutting board. Using a very sharp thin-bladed knife, slice the avocado crosswise into even ⅛-inch-thick slices, being careful not to cut through the plastic. Turn the avocado cut side up.

6. Lay a second piece of plastic wrap on top of the avocado, then gently press with even pressure to spread the slices as evenly as possible. Remove the top piece of plastic and place one-quarter of the crab mixture in the middle of the avocado fan. Gather the corners of the plastic wrap in the center above the crab; the avocado slices will begin to wrap around it.

7. Now lift the package off the cutting board and, cupping one hand around the bottom, gather up the ends of the plastic wrap and twist them to tighten the plastic around the avocado and coax it into a ball. Repeat with the remaining 3 avocado halves. Refrigerate the wrapped avocado-crab packages for up to 2 hours.

8. To serve, make a ring of cucumber slices on each of four plates, leaving about a 2-inch opening in the center of each ring. Mound the citrus-mango salad in the center of each plate. Carefully remove the plastic wrap from each avocado half and place it seam side down on top of a salad. Drizzle vinaigrette and juices from the bottom of the salad bowl over and around the avocado and cucumber slices. Sprinkle lightly with sea salt and garnish with chive flower petals, if using.

SWEET and SPICY WATERMELON SALAD

Chefs are masters at turning common ingredients into something unexpected. This salad brings together cold, crunchy watermelon with the flavors of fish sauce and chiles to create a salad that is at once refreshing and exciting. Lime and mint bring everything together—these flavors are a natural pairing with both the Thai flavorings in the dressing and the fruit.

This salad includes a few exotic ingredients, but don't fret if you can't find them in your local Asian or gourmet market—I've given suggestions for more common ingredients you can substitute. This is how chefs continually adjust their menus, adapting their recipes using what's available at the time. Sometimes, it's the way they discover new combinations they might like even better than what they had in mind.

Fish sauce is a key ingredient, and fortunately it is easy to find in most areas. Use a good-quality Vietnamese or Thai fish sauce. I like Tiparos, Tra Chang, Golden Boy, and Squid brands. If blackberries aren't in season, omit them or substitute raspberries. You can also use another melon, or a mix of melons, in place of the watermelon. The only inflexible rule is that it should be very cold.

Makes 6 servings

What to Drink: Try a refreshing cocktail such as my Super Summer Sipper (page 29) or The Desert Rose (page 26). A rosé with a touch of sweetness, or a riesling, also match well.

½ cup unsweetened flaked coconut

6 tablespoons fresh lime juice

¼ cup yuzu-flavored or regular rice wine vinegar

2 tablespoons palm sugar or light brown sugar

2 tablespoons fish sauce

1 red Fresno or serrano chile, cut in half, seeded, and minced

½ teaspoon black peppercorns, crushed (see page 19)

A large wedge of watermelon, rind removed, seeded, and cut into 1-inch dice (about 4 cups)

½ small red onion, cut into thin strips

1 ½ cups fresh blackberries, gently rinsed and laid out to dry on paper towels

A handful of fresh mint leaves, roughly chopped

1 small bunch watercress, rinsed and spun dry, heavy stems removed, and picked apart into sprigs (chop coarsely if the leaves are larger than bite size)

½ cup roasted salted peanuts, chopped

1. Preheat the oven to 350°F. Spread the coconut on a baking sheet and toast for 5 to 6 minutes, until fragrant and golden. (Alternatively, you can toast it in a medium dry skillet over medium heat.) Set aside to cool.

2. In a small bowl, stir together the lime juice, vinegar, sugar, fish sauce, chiles, and peppercorns until everything is well combined and the sugar dissolves. (To make ahead, refrigerate the dressing, tightly covered, for up to 6 hours. The other ingredients can also be prepared and set aside for up to 6 hours in advance; tightly cover and refrigerate the melon and onions in separate containers.)

3. Shortly before serving, in a large bowl, gently toss together the melon, onions, blackberries, and mint. Toss with the dressing until well coated. To serve, mound a handful of watercress on each plate and top with the salad. Garnish with toasted coconut and chopped peanuts and serve immediately.

CHINESE CHICKEN SALAD

MAKE AHEAD

There aren't many salads on a Chinese restaurant menu, but this one, that many do make, rocks! It's refreshing and zingy at the same time. It makes a perfect lunch or supper when you're in the mood for something light but satisfying.

Cutting the cabbage into bite-size pieces makes the salad easy to eat. The dressing keeps things exciting with bright salt and vinegar on a toasty base of peanuts and sesame oil. This Chinese restaurant classic is easy to make at home.

Makes 6 to 8 lunch entrée servings

What to Drink: Refresh the palate with a cold beer.

CHEF'S TIP
Poach chicken gently with aromatics to keep it moist and flavorful for a salad.

2 boneless, skinless chicken breast halves or thighs, about 6 ounces each

3 coins fresh ginger, about ¼ inch thick, plus 1 tablespoon finely grated fresh ginger

2 whole scallions, plus 3 scallions, sliced thin on a diagonal

Kosher salt

¼ cup toasted sesame oil

¼ cup peanut oil

2 tablespoons rice wine vinegar

Juice of 1 lime

2 tablespoons dark brown sugar

1 tablespoon natural-style peanut butter

1 tablespoon minced garlic

1 tablespoon minced shallots

1 teaspoon sambal oelek or red chili paste

Freshly ground black pepper

1 head Napa cabbage

½ cup roasted peanuts, coarsely chopped

¼ cup sesame seeds, lightly toasted

1 bunch cilantro, coarsely chopped

1. Put the chicken, ginger coins, whole scallions, and 2 teaspoons salt in a medium saucepan. Cover generously with cold water, bring to a boil, then reduce the heat to simmer for 10 minutes. Remove the pot from the heat, cover, and set aside for 5 minutes. Remove the chicken to a plate to cool. When it is cool enough to handle, use your fingers or two forks to shred the meat. If you used thigh meat, you may need to cut the meat into bite-size pieces. Set the chicken aside. (To make ahead, cover and refrigerate the chicken for up to 5 hours.)

2. While the chicken cooks, combine the sesame and peanut oils, vinegar, lime juice, brown sugar, peanut butter, the 1 tablespoon grated ginger, the garlic, shallots, sambal oelek, and ½ teaspoon salt in a blender. Add pepper and additional salt to taste. Set the dressing aside. (To make ahead, cover and refrigerate the dressing for up to 24 hours.)

3. Remove the outer leaves of the cabbage and cut off and discard about 1 inch at the bottom. Remove and discard the core. Rinse the leaves and spin dry, then cut the cabbage in half lengthwise, then crosswise into slices ⅛ to ¼ inch thick.

4. Just before serving, put the cabbage in a large salad bowl along with the peanuts, sesame seeds, cilantro, the sliced scallions, and the shredded chicken. Pour about two thirds of the dressing over the salad and toss gently, adding dressing as needed to lightly coat everything. Mound the salad on dinner plates to serve.

DON'T HOLD BACK ■ STEP UP YOUR SKILLS

For a more authentic Chinese restaurant taste and added crunch, top the salad with fried cellophane noodles. Heat about an inch of peanut oil to 375°F in a wok or large saucepan over high heat. Test the oil by dropping in a single noodle strand; it should immediately puff and turn golden. Add a 2-ounce package of bean thread noodles to the oil, a handful at a time, nudging them into the oil using a Chinese strainer or tongs just until the noodles puff and begin to turn golden. Carefully transfer the noodles as they puff to a plate covered with paper towels. Top the salad with the fried noodles just before serving.

MY FAVORITE CAESAR

You can create authentic Caesar flavor with the right balance of tart lemon, salty-fishy anchovies, Parmesan, and garlic. Because ingredients and tastes vary, I start with a formula that will work for most; you can tweak it to your own taste.

It would seem that a secret law was passed in the last ten years requiring every restaurant to put a Caesar salad on the menu. In some states, they must offer to top it with grilled chicken. This has lead to a number of versions with questionable resemblance to the original. The classic tableside presentation is dramatic, but I like the creamier texture I get by making the dressing in a food processor.

Quality makes a difference here. Buy a block of the best Parmigiano-Reggiano you can afford and grate it yourself. Alternatively, purchase date-stamped grated Parmesan cheese in a tub from a shop you trust. Use anchovies packed in olive oil or salt. For salt-packed anchovies, soak them in cool water for 15 minutes, rinse, and pat dry before using.

I use extra-virgin olive oil in almost everything, but here, equal parts canola and olive oil in the dressing keep the flavors in balance.

Makes 6 servings

What to Drink: Choose a cocktail or beer over wine, which will compete with the strong flavors in this salad.

½ loaf day-old Italian bread, cut into 1-inch cubes (about 4 cups)

1 cup extra-virgin olive oil

3 large cloves garlic, minced

½ cup plus 1 tablespoon freshly grated Parmesan cheese, plus shaved, shredded, or freshly grated Parmesan cheese, for garnish

¼ cup fresh lemon juice

2 tablespoons red wine vinegar

2 egg yolks

3 to 6 anchovy fillets, plus 4 for optional garnish

1 tablespoon whole-grain mustard

1 teaspoon Dijon mustard

¾ cup canola oil

2 romaine hearts, cored, leaves separated, rinsed, and spun dry

Salt and freshly ground black pepper

1. Preheat the oven to 375°F. In a large mixing bowl, combine the bread cubes with ¼ cup of the olive oil, about one third of the garlic (it's not necessary to be exact here), the 1 tablespoon Parmesan, and a pinch each of salt and pepper. Toss to evenly coat the cubes. Spread the croutons on a rimmed baking sheet and bake until golden brown, 10 to 12 minutes, turning the croutons once with a spatula as they bake. Transfer the pan to a rack to cool.

2. While the croutons bake, place the lemon juice, vinegar, ½ cup of the Parmesan, the egg yolks, 3 of the anchovies, the remaining garlic, and whole-grain and Dijon mustards in a food processor fitted with a metal blade. Purée until smooth. With the motor running, gradually drizzle in the canola oil and then the remaining ¾ cup olive oil until the dressing is thick and creamy. Taste and add another anchovy, lemon juice, salt, or pepper, if you wish. (To make ahead, refrigerate the dressing in a tightly sealed container for up to 2 days.)

3. To serve, toss the croutons with a tablespoon or two of the dressing to lightly coat them. Toss the romaine leaves in a large mixing bowl with just enough dressing to coat them well. Arrange the leaves all in the same direction on a platter or in a large, flat serving bowl. Sprinkle with the croutons and dust liberally with Parmesan. Garnish with additional anchovies, if desired.

DON'T HOLD BACK ■ STEP UP YOUR SKILLS

As a fun alternative to the croutons and cheese that top the salad, I like to bake Parmesan crisps. Mound tablespoonfuls of grated or finely shredded Parmesan cheese on a nonstick baking sheet, spacing the mounds about 2 inches apart. Bake in a preheated 400°F oven for 8 to 10 minutes, or until the cheese just begins to turn golden. (Too long and the cheese will turn bitter.) Remove from the oven and let cool a couple of minutes to firm up before gently transferring the crisps with a wide spatula to a flat surface lined with paper toweling. They'll be crispy once they're completely cool.

DON'T HOLD BACK ■ MAKE IT YOURS

Everyone seems to have an opinion about the perfect amount of anchovy in a Caesar salad. Anchovies vary in size and flavor and people vary in their taste for them. In a traditional Caesar, anchovy adds a distinctive flavor that shouldn't overpower the salad. Start with the lesser amount and sample by dipping a leaf of romaine into the dressing. Blend in additional anchovies, one at a time, until the dressing is to your liking. For real anchovy lovers, drape an anchovy or two across each serving.

LIQUID LOVE

SOUPS ARE AMONG A CHEF'S most adaptable courses. Whether sipping spicy Thai Chicken-Coconut Soup to soothe a cold, spooning up earthy Roasted Eggplant and Lentil Soup to satisfy a raging hunger, indulging in elegant Lobster Bisque to fan the flames of romance, or cooling off with Island Gazpacho on a hot day, soup is liquid love in a bowl.

Too often, we have the urge to pick up a can of soup or a prepared soup from an upscale grocery store. While those choices may come in handy, soup is one of the easiest and most satisfying things you can make at home. These recipes will encourage you back into the kitchen to express yourself. A fringe benefit is that soup can be made in big batches and enjoyed all week long. In fact, many of them improve once the flavors have had a chance to meld and mellow for a day or two.

Good soup relies on a unique combination of ingredients, along with techniques that maximize flavor and texture. When it works, you can't resist dipping your spoon back into the bowl for more. These soups each have a distinctive edge that will have your family and friends prodding you to divulge your secret.

ISLAND GAZPACHO

Chefs love to tinker with classic recipes, looking for new twists that don't lose sight of the dish's inherent qualities. In this recipe, gazpacho—the classic Spanish cold tomato soup—takes on an island flavor from tropical fruits and vegetables.

I served this at my Caribbean-inspired restaurant, Miss Pearl's Jam House, as soon as tomatoes were in season each year. Its color and textures are so vibrant, its flavors so fresh and bright, that it tastes like a tropical vacation. Put on some reggae music, don your sandals, and you will be having a good time, mon!

Everything should be at its peak of ripeness for this dish. In the height of tomato season, substitute fresh tomato juice for bottled by puréeing about 10 ripe tomatoes in a blender and straining them to make a quart of juice.

Makes 10 to 12 servings

What to Drink: The acid and vegetal character of a sauvignon blanc will balance the fruit and vegetables. For a richer wine, try an aromatic viognier.

½ **each red and yellow bell pepper (or one whole of either), seeds and veins removed**

1 Anaheim chile, seeds and veins removed

1 poblano chile, seeds and veins removed

2 hothouse or English cucumbers, peeled, cut in half lengthwise, seeds discarded

1 small red onion

1 small jicama root, peeled

1 mango, peeled and seeded

1 papaya, peeled and seeded

8 small red tomatoes, cored, halved, and seeded (reserve juice)

4 small yellow tomatoes, cored, halved, and seeded (reserve juice)

1 quart tomato juice

1 cup fresh lime juice

¼ cup extra-virgin olive oil

¼ cup finely chopped cilantro

2 jalapeño chiles, seeded and minced

1 teaspoon minced garlic

1 teaspoon freshly grated horseradish

Kosher salt and freshly ground black pepper

10 mint leaves, cut into thin ribbons, for garnish

1. Cut the bell peppers, Anaheim and poblano chiles, cucumbers, onion, jicama, mango, papaya, and tomatoes into 1/8-inch dice, putting them into a large bowl or container as you cut them. (Alternatively, cut the red and yellow peppers, Anaheim and poblano chiles, cucumbers, onion, and jicama into large chunks and put them into a food processor fitted with a metal blade. Pulse just a couple of times until the mixture looks

like confetti, with everything in small pieces. Transfer the mixture to a large bowl or container. Cut the mango and papaya into ⅛-inch dice and add to the bowl. Pulse the tomatoes in the food processor until they are in small pieces and add to the bowl.)

2. Stir in the tomato juice, lime juice, olive oil, cilantro, jalapeños, garlic, and horseradish. Strain and stir in the reserved juices from the seeds. Add salt and pepper to taste.

3. Refrigerate until cold, for about 2 hours or up to 1 day. Serve the gazpacho in bowls topped with julienned mint.

DON'T HOLD BACK ■ STEP UP YOUR SKILLS

This is a great recipe for honing your knife skills. Cutting by hand is the best way to achieve the satisfying harmony and stunning visual presentation that comes from cutting all the ingredients into a precise dice. But don't let the knife work or time commitment scare you off—you can make a really good gazpacho using a food processor, too.

THAI CHICKEN-COCONUT SOUP

Like many good restaurant recipes, this soup, known in Thai restaurants as *Tom Kha Gai,* balances richness (coconut milk) with exotic, aromatic flavors. The keys to its authentic Thai taste are kaffir lime leaves, lemongrass, and galangal root. Look for them fresh in Asian produce markets, or you can sometimes find kaffir lime and galangal frozen. Use the dried versions only if you can't find anything else. Remove these tough aromatics before serving if you like, but it is more authentic to leave them in the soup, where diners can suck the alluring flavors from them as they eat.

Chef-owner Pathama Parikanont of San Francisco's Thep Phanom restaurant has shared many of her recipes as a guest on my television show, but it was years earlier, when I asked to spend some time in her restaurant kitchen, that she entrusted me with her secrets. I learned a lot from her insanely good cooking, but it's her method for making this soup that I have used most. You can make this your own by adding corn, shrimp, squash, or your own personal twist.

Vary the heat from mild to incendiary; nothing beats a blistering bowl of Tom Kha Gai for kicking a winter cold. For a heartier soup, mound steamed jasmine rice in bowls before ladling in the soup.

Many restaurants use canned straw mushrooms in this soup, but I prefer the texture of fresh. I prefer chicken thigh meat for its moist texture and full flavor. I like Chaokoh brand coconut milk for its sweet, delicate flavor. If you can't find the wonderfully hot and full-flavored tiny Thai chiles, substitute a jalapeño or two, seeded and cut thin on a diagonal.

Makes 6 servings

What to Drink: I enjoy this with a gewürztraminer. It brings the Thai flavors forward in the soup and softens the heat of the chiles.

2 stalks fresh lemongrass, bottom 4 inches only

1 tablespoon vegetable oil

1 medium onion, cut into very thin strips (not rings)

12 ounces boneless, skinless chicken thigh meat, cut into bite-size pieces

1 cup sliced button mushrooms

2 cups low-sodium chicken broth

6 small red Thai chiles, slightly crushed, or more to taste

4 kaffir lime leaves, torn into a few large pieces

One 1-inch cube galangal root, cut into 1/4-inch-thick slices

One 14-ounce can unsweetened coconut milk

Up to 1/3 cup fish sauce

Up to 4 tablespoons fresh lime juice, plus lime wedges, for garnish

3 scallions, sliced thin, for garnish

Cilantro sprigs, for garnish

1. Cut the lemongrass into 2-inch lengths and bruise them by bashing with the spine of a heavy chef's knife to help release their flavor. (To do this, turn the knife upside down, holding it by the handle, and bruise them with the back of the blade.)

2. Heat the oil in a large saucepan over medium-high heat. Add the onions and sauté until they begin to soften. Add the chicken and mushrooms, stir, then add the broth, chiles, lime leaves, galangal, and lemongrass. Bring to a boil, then reduce the heat and simmer for 10 minutes. Add the coconut milk, bring back almost to the boil, then lower the heat and simmer for another 2 minutes. Stir in ¼ cup fish sauce and 3 tablespoons lime juice. Add more fish sauce and lime juice, a little at a time, to taste.

3. Serve immediately, garnished with scallions and cilantro sprigs, and lime wedges on the side.

ASPARAGUS BISQUE with SHIITAKE MUSHROOMS and PARMESAN "FOAM"

Foam? At the dinner table? Yes, this sauce, whisked to a frothy mass like the topping on a cappuccino, is all the rage at restaurants. The use of culinary foams was popularized by chef Ferran Adrià of El Bulli restaurant in Spain, who uses a whipped cream canister to froth up sauces and other flavoring elements in his restaurant. It's a creative way to add another layer of flavor and texture to the soup. The technique I use here is adapted to the home kitchen, and it's sure to impress your dinner guests.

A bisque is a thick soup enriched with cream, often made with shellfish but sometimes with puréed vegetables. In this vegetarian version we borrow a technique from the Lobster Bisque on page 94. There we roast the lobster shells you might otherwise have tossed out, for an intensely flavored soup. This time, we use the asparagus stalks. One person's kitchen trash can be another's treasure!

Once you've mastered this bisque, try making it with other vegetables. Zucchini, carrots, English peas, or fava beans would all be delicious.

Makes 6 to 8 servings

What to Drink: Sauvignon blanc stands up to the asparagus's vegetal flavors while cutting the richness of the soup. Cream and Parmesan cheese seal the match.

2 pounds medium asparagus

Kosher salt

2 tablespoons (¼ stick) unsalted butter

2 large leeks, trimmed, dark green part removed, sliced thin, rinsed to remove any grit, and drained

1 clove garlic, chopped fine

3¼ cups heavy cream

¼ pound fresh shiitake mushrooms, stems removed, caps sliced thin

1 tablespoon extra-virgin olive oil

Freshly ground black pepper

¼ cup freshly grated Parmesan cheese

1. Cut the tough bottoms from the asparagus and set aside. Cut off the top inch (tips) and set aside separately. Cut the remainder of the stalks into ½-inch pieces.

2. Bring 2 cups water and 1 tablespoon salt to a boil in a large saucepan. Reduce to a gentle boil, drop in the asparagus tips, and blanch for 15 seconds. Use a mesh strainer or slotted spoon to scoop them out. Set aside.

3. Cook the tough asparagus stalk bottoms in the boiling water for 5 minutes. Drain off the water into a bowl and discard the stalks.

4. Melt the butter in the saucepan over medium heat. Add the leeks and garlic and cook, stirring frequently, until they soften, about 10 minutes. Add 3 cups of the cream

and the reserved asparagus water. Bring to a boil, then reduce the heat and simmer for 5 minutes.

5. Add the reserved asparagus stalk pieces and cook 2 minutes longer. Use an immersion or traditional blender to purée the soup, processing in batches in the blender, if necessary.

6. Sauté the shiitake mushrooms in the olive oil in a small skillet until they soften, release their juices, and then reabsorb them. Add the reserved asparagus tips. Season lightly with salt and pepper.

7. Just before serving, heat the soup until it is very hot but not boiling. Heat the remaining ¼ cup cream with 2 tablespoons water in a small deep saucepan to just below a boil. Stir in the Parmesan. Use an immersion blender at high speed to froth the mixture by completely submerging the blade in the mixture and moving it around the pot until the mixture is very foamy. (Alternatively, you can whip the mixture furiously with a fine-wired balloon whisk.)

8. Ladle the soup into bowls. Spoon the foamiest part from the top of the Parmesan foam as you would for a cappuccino, topping each bowl of soup with a generous spoonful. You may want to whisk the Parmesan mixture again if needed to generate more foam. Garnish with the sautéed mushrooms and asparagus.

CAULIFLOWER and ROASTED GARLIC SOUP with PARMESAN CROUTONS

Sometimes we go out to a restaurant just for the comfort of having someone else cook for us. But soups are easy enough to make at home, and creamy, rich soups made from vegetable purées can be the most comforting of all.

My favorite part about this recipe is the way all that comfort contrasts with the crunchy croutons and bold cheese. It assures that every bite offers the enticement to return for more.

For over fifteen years I shied away from cauliflower in my restaurants, thinking it bland and uninteresting. It was this dish that showed me how wrong I was, and it has since become one of my favorite vegetables, professionally and at home.

Makes 8 to 10 servings

What to Drink: Choose a medium-bodied chardonnay to match the cream and garlic.

2 large heads garlic, plus 1 clove, minced, for the croutons

¼ cup extra-virgin olive oil, plus 2 tablespoons, for the croutons

¼ loaf day-old Italian bread, cut into ½-inch cubes (about 2 cups)

3 tablespoons freshly grated Parmesan cheese

1 tablespoon chopped flat-leaf parsley

Kosher salt and freshly ground black pepper

1 medium leek, trimmed, dark green part removed, cut into ¼-inch dice, rinsed to remove any grit, and drained (about 1½ cups)

2 tablespoons (¼ stick) unsalted butter

1 medium head cauliflower, outer leaves and core discarded, cut into large florets

2 cups heavy cream

1. Preheat the oven to 375°F. Cut across the tops of the 2 garlic heads to expose the tops of the cloves. Place the garlic heads in a small baking dish and coat with 2 tablespoons of the olive oil. Cover with foil and bake until very soft, about 40 minutes. Let cool for 5 minutes, then squeeze the heads from the bottom to push the roasted garlic into a small bowl. Set aside.

2. While the garlic is roasting, make the croutons. Toss the bread cubes with the remaining ¼ cup olive oil, the minced garlic clove, the Parmesan, parsley, and a good pinch each of salt and pepper. Spread the croutons on a rimmed baking sheet and bake until golden brown, 8 to 10 minutes, turning the croutons with a spatula after about 5 minutes. Transfer the pan to a rack to cool. (The fully cooled croutons can be stored in a covered container at room temperature for up to 2 days.)

3. While the croutons are baking, cook the leeks in the butter in a large saucepan over medium heat, stirring frequently, until they are just tender but not browned, about 5 minutes. Add the cauliflower, cream, roasted garlic, a large pinch of salt, and 6 cups water. Bring the soup nearly to a boil over high heat, then reduce the heat and simmer until the cauliflower is very soft, 15 to 20 minutes.

4. Use an immersion or traditional blender to purée the soup until it is smooth. Taste and adjust the salt and pepper to taste. (To make ahead, cool and refrigerate the soup, tightly covered, for up to 2 days. Reheat before serving.)

5. To serve, ladle the soup into bowls and top with croutons.

BUTTERNUT SQUASH SOUP with TAMARIND-GLAZED CONFIT DUCK

This rich, elegant soup offers something exciting in every bite. I start by roasting the squash to intensify its sweet, earthy flavor, then add an unexpected tang with tamarind. The chewy morsels of duck provide a taste and texture bonus. Giving each ingredient its own special treatment creates layers of flavor that unfold as you eat.

The juxtaposition of the creamy, sweet soup and chewy-savory duck makes the soup shine, but don't be put off—the soup is satisfying on its own for an easy weeknight supper. As a shortcut, look for confit duck in the prepared food section of upscale markets.

The opportunity to use tamarind is a lesson in itself—once you are familiar with it, you will find yourself adding its sweet-pungent flavor to other dishes, as well. You can start by brushing any remaining tamarind glaze on chicken or fish before broiling or grilling.

Makes 6 to 8 servings

What to Drink: A riesling with a hint of sweetness or a soft, fruity pinot noir pair nicely with the squash, tamarind, and duck.

1 medium butternut squash (2 pounds)

Olive oil

4 tablespoons (½ stick) unsalted butter

1 medium yellow onion, diced or chopped fine

1 tablespoon minced fresh ginger

1 jalapeño pepper, seeded and minced

4 cups low-sodium chicken broth

½ cup heavy cream

Pinch of freshly grated nutmeg

Kosher salt and freshly ground black pepper

½ cup Laxmi brand tamarind concentrate, or ¼ cup tamarind paste simmered in ½ cup water and strained (see "Explore New Foods," page 147)

1 tablespoon honey

1 tablespoon cider vinegar

1 clove garlic, minced

1 teaspoon minced shallots

2 Confit Duck legs (page 155)

Chives or scallions, sliced thin, for garnish

1. Preheat the oven to 350°F. Cut the stem from the squash and split the squash in half lengthwise. Scoop out the seeds and discard. Place the squash cut side down on an oiled baking sheet or pan. Bake until tender, 45 to 60 minutes. Set aside to cool.

2. Melt the butter in a large saucepan over medium heat. Add the onions and ginger and cook, stirring frequently, until the onions soften, 5 to 10 minutes. Add the jalapeño and cook a few minutes longer. Use a spoon to scrape the flesh from the squash and add it to the pot. (Discard the skin.) Add the chicken broth and 2 cups water; simmer for 15 minutes.

3. Use an immersion blender to purée the soup until smooth. (Alternatively, you can purée the soup in a traditional blender, then return it to the pot to finish.) Add the cream and nutmeg. If the soup is very thick, thin it with additional broth or water. Season to taste with salt and pepper. Cover the soup and keep warm over low heat. (To make ahead, cool and refrigerate the soup, tightly covered, for up to 2 days. Reheat before serving.)

4. To make the tamarind glaze, simmer the tamarind, honey, vinegar, garlic, and shallots in a small nonreactive saucepan over medium heat until reduced and thickened, about 10 minutes. (The glaze can be refrigerated, tightly covered, for up to 2 days.)

5. Remove the skin and pull the meat from the duck legs. Place the duck meat in a small skillet with ¼ cup of the tamarind glaze. Stir over medium-low heat until the duck is warm to the touch. (Alternatively, combine the duck and glaze in a small baking dish and heat in a preheated 350°F oven for about 10 minutes.)

6. Just before serving, ladle the soup into bowls, garnish with the duck meat, and drizzle with some of the remaining glaze. Garnish with chives.

ROASTED EGGPLANT and LENTIL SOUP with MINTED YOGURT

Chefs use plenty of butter and cream for sure, but they also know how to make elegant and satisfying foods without them. Eggplant, lentils, and olive oil give this soup its satisfying texture and rich flavor, while mint and yogurt add bright notes. I've kept the spices on the mild side to let the eggplant and lentil flavors speak for themselves. If you prefer a stronger statement, spice it up with a little curry or red chile flakes as you sauté the vegetables. Yogurt drizzled over the soup as a garnish adds another healthy kind of richness.

Use a fruity, full-flavored olive oil as it adds considerably to the flavor of this soup. Unless you are on a strict diet, use whole-milk yogurt as they would in the Mediterranean or Middle East. It's creamier and less acidic than lower fat versions.

Makes 6 to 8 servings

What to Drink: A cold lager beer is a great complement. Pinot noir brings out the soup's earthy flavors.

2 large globe eggplants (about 1½ pounds), tops removed, cut lengthwise into 4 pieces each

Extra-virgin olive oil

Kosher salt

1 large yellow onion, chopped (about 2 cups)

2 medium carrots, cut into ¼-inch dice

2 ribs celery, cut into ¼-inch dice

2 tablespoons minced garlic

½ teaspoon ground cumin

1 cup French green lentils, rinsed

2 Roma tomatoes, seeded and cut into ⅛-inch dice

2 scallions, sliced very thin

¼ cup chopped flat-leaf parsley

1 cup plain whole-milk yogurt

1 tablespoon minced shallots

1 tablespoon chopped fresh mint

Freshly ground black pepper

1. Preheat the oven to 375°F. Place the eggplant pieces on a baking sheet and brush liberally with olive oil on both sides, using ¼ to ⅓ cup total. Sprinkle lightly all over with salt. Bake until the slices are a deep golden brown, about 50 minutes. Set aside to cool, then scrape the meat out of the skin with a spoon and reserve (discard the skin).

2. Sauté the onions, carrots, celery, and garlic in ¼ cup olive oil with a generous pinch of salt (about a teaspoon) in a large heavy saucepan over medium-high heat until the onions are lightly caramelized, about 10 minutes. Add the cumin, stir 1 minute to bring out its flavor, then add the lentils, another generous pinch of salt, and 8 cups water.

3. Bring to a boil, then reduce the heat and simmer until the lentils are completely tender, about 30 minutes. Add the reserved eggplant and simmer for 15 minutes longer. Use an immersion or traditional blender to purée the soup until completely smooth. (To make ahead, cool and refrigerate the soup, tightly covered, for up to 2 days. Reheat before serving.)

4. While the soup simmers, stir together the tomatoes, scallions, and parsley with a pinch of salt in a small bowl. In another small bowl, stir together the yogurt, shallots, mint, and a pinch each of salt and pepper. Taste and adjust the seasonings of the soup and condiments.

5. Serve the soup in bowls with a drizzle of the minted yogurt and a sprinkling of the diced tomatoes.

LOBSTER BISQUE

This is a riff on the classic French soup that gets its intense lobster flavor from the shells, which you might normally discard. It's a great lesson in eking out every possible bit of flavor from a lobster.

When he was a guest on my cooking program, *Bay Café,* Jasper White of Lobster Shack shared this trick for removing the meat from the cooked lobster's walking legs: Snap them off, line them up on a cutting board, and push a rolling pin firmly over them. The meat will pop right out, like toothpaste from a tube. Set it aside for a garnish or enjoy it as a well-deserved treat for the chef.

You can save a step here by purchasing a cooked lobster, so long as it's fresh. Or substitute a pound of shrimp or prawns for the lobster, reserving the shells to use in the recipe.

If fresh tarragon isn't available, substitute ½ teaspoon dried tarragon in the recipe and use celery leaves for garnish.

Makes 6 servings

What to Drink: Enjoy this elegant soup with a rich chardonnay with enough acid to balance the cream.

1 live lobster, about 1½ pounds

Kosher salt

2 tablespoons (¼ stick) unsalted butter

1 medium white onion, cut into ¼-inch dice

1 large leek, trimmed, dark green part removed, sliced thin, rinsed to remove any grit, and drained

2 ribs celery, cut into ¼-inch dice

1 medium carrot, cut into ¼-inch dice

½ teaspoon cayenne pepper

1 cup tomato purée

1 cup brandy

2 bay leaves

1 large sprig fresh tarragon, plus additional chopped tarragon, for garnish

2 cups clam juice

1 quart heavy cream

½ cup Arborio rice

1 medium russet potato, peeled and cut into ¼-inch dice

Freshly ground black pepper

1. Preheat the oven to 375°F.

2. Fill a pot large enough to easily hold the lobster about three-quarters full with water and add about a tablespoon of salt–enough so that it tastes like the sea. Bring the water to a rapid boil. Set a large bowl of ice water by the stove. Quickly plunge the lobster head-first into the boiling water and cook for 6 to 7 minutes. (See page 96 for an alternative method.) Use large tongs to carefully transfer the lobster from the pot to the ice water.

Use rice to add body
to cream soups. The
starch dissolves easily
so it disappears into the
finished soup. Try Arborio
rice for its high starch
content or substitute
short- or long-grained
white rice.

3. After 5 minutes, drain the ice water and hold the lobster over the empty bowl to catch its juices as you separate the lobster. (These juices provide a deep shellfish flavor that makes this soup special.) Use kitchen shears to cut the shells and a kitchen towel to protect your hands. Begin by separating the body from the tail by twisting them apart. Cut the soft undershell of the tail, pull the pieces apart, then pull and wiggle out the lobster-tail meat. Set the meat aside in a bowl. Remove the claws and arms from the body and lay them on a cutting board. Use the heel of a large chef's knife to cut into the thickest part of the claw, then twist the knife to crack the claw open and extract the meat. Snip one side of the arm with shears and remove the lobster nuggets. Set aside this meat with the tail. Remove and set aside all the remaining meat.

4. When you have removed all the lobster meat, cut it into bite-size pieces, cover, and refrigerate until needed. Put the shells on a baking sheet and roast them until they just begin to brown, about 10 minutes.

5. Melt the butter in a stockpot over medium heat. Add the onions, leeks, celery, carrots, and cayenne. Stir and cook until the vegetables are tender, about 10 minutes. Add the lobster shells and the juices collected in the bowl, the tomato purée, ¾ cup of the brandy, the bay leaves, and tarragon. Stir and gently push down the shells with a large wooden spoon as the soup cooks for 5 minutes.

6. Add the clam juice, cream, rice, potato, and 6 cups water. Bring to a boil, then reduce the heat and simmer for 40 minutes, stirring occasionally. Use tongs to remove and discard the large pieces of lobster shell. Use an immersion or traditional blender to purée the soup. (Note: If using a traditional blender, you may need to purée the soup in batches, working carefully to avoid splashing the hot soup.)

7. Strain through a fine mesh strainer into a large saucepan. Bring to a simmer and season to taste with salt and pepper. (To make ahead, cool and refrigerate the soup, tightly covered, for up to 2 days. To serve, warm over medium heat until very hot but not boiling.)

8. Just before serving, stir the remaining ¼ cup brandy into the simmering soup. Place some of the chopped lobster meat and a few tarragon leaves into soup bowls and ladle the bisque over them. Serve immediately.

Some people are a bit nervous to immerse a live lobster into boiling water. Does it hurt the lobster? Studies have found that lobsters feel no pain when you put them up to boil. The lobster dies almost instantly when it goes into a pot of rapidly boiling salted water, even though the tail may continue to twitch for a minute or so as a result of involuntary muscle contractions. That twitching can cause them to splash boiling water, which could hurt the cook. I prefer the following method for preparing a lobster to boil.

Lay the lobster on a cutting board, holding the lower body with one hand wrapped in a towel. Leave the rubber bands around the claws in place. With the other hand, plunge the point of a large heavy chef's knife into the lobster's head about an inch below the eyes, with the blade pointing toward the top of the head. When the tip of the knife reaches the board, rotate the blade down toward the board to cut between the eyes, from the top of the head to the throat. Although it is believed that lobsters feel no pain, this is thought by many to be the fastest, safest, most humane way to kill them.

CHICKEN SOUP THREE WAYS

Chefs are masters at "repurposing" kitchen basics to create a changing menu of great dishes. Here, I take a simple soup and turn it into three great meals.

Everyone should know how to make basic chicken soup, then vary it for different moods and menus. Here is a simple master recipe plus three cultural interpretations to get you started. With most of your work finished the first day, you can turn out these variations in short order.

THE BASIC CHICKEN SOUP

Makes about 6 quarts, enough for 8 servings of each soup variation

What to Drink: Try the Matzo Ball Soup with a French Chablis or other chardonnay with little or no oak. For the Mexican Tortilla Soup, try a pinot grigio. A gewürztraminer or riesling complements the jalapenos in the Egg Drop Soup. A light-bodied beer hits the spot with any of these.

One 4-pound roasting chicken, giblets removed (discard or save for another use), rinsed

2 large yellow onions, cut into ¼-inch dice

6 ribs celery, leaves trimmed, ribs cut into ¼-inch dice

6 medium carrots, cut into ¼-inch dice

8 cloves garlic

3 tablespoons kosher salt

1 teaspoon coarse-ground black pepper

3 bay leaves

1. Combine the chicken, onions, celery, carrots, garlic, salt, pepper, and bay leaves in a large stock pot. Add about 7 quarts cold water to generously cover, leaving at least 2 inches at the top of the pot. Bring the soup to a boil, then reduce the heat to simmer and cook, partially covered with a lid, for 1 hour. Add more salt and pepper to taste.

2. Leave partially covered to cool for 1 hour, then transfer the chicken to a large bowl. Pull off and discard the skin and pull the meat from the bones with your fingers or two forks. Discard the bones. Shred or cut the chicken into bite-size pieces. Refrigerate in a covered container until you are ready to make the variations, for up to 3 days.

3. Strain the soup, discarding the solids, and refrigerate in a covered container. When the soup is cold, skim off the fat (schmaltz) with a large spoon and refrigerate it separately to use in the Matzo Ball Soup (page 98) or for cooking potatoes.

CLASSIC CHICKEN and MATZO BALL SOUP

My great-grandmothers Rose and Esther and my grandmothers Dottie and Gertrude all made light, flavorful matzo balls. But did any of them show me how? No, I've had to figure it out on my own. Here are my secrets for light, fluffy matzo balls:

- Cook through, but don't overcook, as it will make them heavy.
- Don't make them too big—they expand as they cook.
- For flavorful matzo balls, cook them in a flavorful broth.
- Schmaltz (rendered chicken fat) adds rich, authentic flavor. Vegetable oil works well, too.

4 large eggs

½ cup club soda or unflavored seltzer

3 tablespoons fat (schmaltz) or vegetable oil

2 tablespoons finely chopped flat-leaf parsley, plus additional, for garnish

½ teaspoon kosher salt

¼ teaspoon freshly ground black pepper

1 cup matzo meal

2 quarts chicken stock

12 ounces cooked, shredded chicken meat (about one third of what you pulled from the chicken)

1. Whisk the eggs in a medium mixing bowl to break them up. Whisk in the club soda, schmaltz, parsley, salt, and pepper. Stir in the matzo meal just to blend. Cover and refrigerate for 1 hour.

2. Bring the chicken stock to a boil in a large saucepan. Reduce to a simmer. Wet your hands, pick up about 2 tablespoons of the matzo dough, and roll it between your palms to form a ball. Drop the balls into the simmering broth as you make them, and simmer, covered, for 30 minutes.

3. For each serving, ladle 2 matzo balls with about a cup of broth into a large, shallow bowl. Garnish with some of the shredded chicken meat and additional chopped parsley.

MEXICAN CHICKEN TORTILLA SOUP

This warming soup is just as comforting as the Jewish favorite Chicken and Matzo Ball Soup. For extra-spicy kick, add a little more chipotle.

Two 6-inch corn tortillas

¼ cup vegetable oil

Pinch of kosher salt

2 quarts chicken stock

2 ripe avocados

12 ounces cooked, shredded chicken meat (about one third of what you pulled from the chicken)

2 Roma tomatoes, halved, seeded, and cut into ¼-inch dice

2 jalapeño chiles, halved, seeded, and thinly sliced

1 teaspoon finely chopped chipotle chile in adobo (optional)

1 small bunch cilantro, picked apart into small sprigs

Crumbled queso fresco, for garnish (optional)

2 limes, cut into 4 wedges each

1. Cut the tortillas in half, then cut the halves crosswise into thin strips. Heat the vegetable oil in a small skillet. When it is hot enough to sizzle when you drop in a tortilla strip, add all the tortillas and fry, stirring occasionally, until golden brown. Use a slotted spoon to transfer the tortillas to a plate lined with paper towels. Sprinkle the strips with a little salt and set aside.

2. Bring the chicken stock to a boil in a medium saucepan. Cut the avocados in half lengthwise, remove the pits, and use a spoon to slice and scoop out long pieces of avocado. Divide them evenly among eight soup bowls. Add the chicken meat, tomatoes, jalapeños, and chipotle, if using, to the soup and simmer for 3 minutes. Ladle the soup over the avocado slices in the bowls. Garnish with the tortillas strips, cilantro sprigs, and a little cheese, if desired. Serve each bowl with a lime wedge to squeeze over it.

CHINESE EGG DROP SOUP

When I was a kid, my family frequented a Chinese restaurant in Monticello, New York, called Canton. The kitchen would send out small bowls of egg drop soup at the start of each meal. I loved watching the pieces of egg floating like snow in a snow globe. But what I loved best was the great flavor and the comforting feeling of that soup. For this version, I've pumped it up to make it a meal.

2 quarts chicken stock

12 ounces cooked, shredded chicken meat (about one third of what you pulled from the chicken)

2 large eggs, whisked

1 cup button mushrooms, sliced thin

2 jalapeño chiles, halved, seeded, and sliced thin

4 scallions, trimmed and sliced thin on a diagonal

A small handful each of fresh cilantro, basil, and mint, chopped

2 limes, quartered

Soy sauce

Bring the chicken stock and chicken meat to a boil in a large saucepan. Reduce to a simmer and stir the soup as you drizzle in the beaten egg. Divide the mushrooms, jalapeños, scallions, cilantro, basil, and mint among eight bowls. Ladle the soup into the bowls. Serve each bowl with a lime wedge to squeeze over it. Offer soy sauce to be drizzled in to taste.

NOODLES AND BEYOND

PASTA IS ONE DISH just about everybody feels comfortable making at home. Just as Deep Purple's "Smoke on the Water" was the first song I learned as a novice guitar player, pasta was among my earliest forays into the kitchen. But while pasta may seem pedestrian, it can be extraordinary. How fantastic that a simple dough made from flour, egg, and oil can produce such a variety of dishes. In this chapter I show you how to make the kinds of pasta dishes you love in restaurants.

It all starts with great noodles. Some dishes lend themselves to dry pasta, others to fresh. Fresh noodles are tender and silky. If there is a shop in your area that makes fresh pasta, take advantage of it.

The assortment of dried pasta available on grocery shelves has improved dramatically, with many fine brands now imported from Italy. My favorites are Rustichella d'Abruzzo, De Cecco, Latini, and Martelli. These rustic, toothsome pastas with their craggy, sauce-grabbing edges hold up to a range of sauces, from light and delicate to rich and bold.

For great texture in the finished dish, cook your pasta just until it is al dente. Translated as "to the tooth," the Italian term means that your pasta should be cooked through but with something left to bite into. To infuse flavor into the noodles, add about a tablespoon of salt to a large pot of boiling water. The water should taste like the sea.

The sauce brings the dish together. It may be as simple as tossing just-cooked pasta with chopped perfectly ripe tomatoes, hand-torn fresh basil leaves, a good drizzle of your very best olive oil, and a sprinkling of salt and freshly ground pepper. The Quick-and-Easy Tomato Sauce that tops the Stuffed Shells with Fun-Tina takes this one step further, quickly cooking the sauce.

Pasta loves rich, creamy sauces, too. Check out my version of classic carbonara. Or try Kabocha Squash Spaetzle (with shiitake mushrooms and arugula) for a dish where the noodle itself is the center of attention.

One of my favorite tips from an Italian guest chef on my television program is to save a little of the pasta cooking water for finishing your sauce. Use the pasta water to add flavor and body to the Perfect Carbonara or Stuffed Shells with Fun-Tina.

Combine good-quality pasta with fresh local produce, extra-virgin olive oil, and other flavorful additions. Pasta will shine at the center of your plate and you will be a pasta novice no more.

PERFECT CARBONARA

There's a reason certain dishes never go out of style. This classic Italian pasta is so rich and flavorful, it's worth the occasional indulgence–and not just when you're dining out. It's a simple dish I turn to for comfort and satisfaction on a chilly night. The egg yolks and cream coat the pasta with silky richness, while pancetta adds texture and salty flavor.

Seek out good-quality dried pasta for this dish (see page 102 for some of my favorites). I like pancetta best here, but you can also use bacon, keeping in mind that it will give the dish a smoky flavor, as bacon is generally smoked while pancetta is not. For best flavor, grate the cheese from a block of good-quality Parmigiano-Reggiano. Alternatively, purchase grated cheese in a tub from a store that grates good cheese in-house.

Makes 6 servings

What to Drink: A full-bodied chardonnay or viognier without strong tropical fruit flavors pairs well with this rich dish. A pinot noir or syrah will also work.

1 pound spaghetti

8 ounces pancetta or good-quality bacon, cut into ¼-inch squares

Up to 1 tablespoon extra-virgin olive oil, as needed

2 large egg yolks

½ cup heavy cream

2 tablespoons chopped fresh flat-leaf parsley

½ cup freshly grated Parmesan cheese

Freshly ground black pepper

1. Bring a large pot of generously salted water to a boil. Add the spaghetti and cook until it is al dente, 8 to 10 minutes. Add 1 cup cold water during the last minute to slow the cooking.

2. While the pasta is cooking, heat a large skillet over high heat. If you are using bacon, you probably will not need the olive oil. If you are using pancetta, which is leaner, you may want to start it in a little olive oil until it begins to render its own fat. Cook the pancetta, stirring, until it lightly browns. Reduce the heat to low.

3. Whisk together the egg yolks and cream in a small bowl.

4. When the pasta is ready, drain (do not rinse) and transfer it to a large pasta bowl. Pour the hot pancetta over the pasta, then pour the egg and cream mixture over. Toss the pasta with the sauce using two large forks, then add the parsley, half of the cheese, and a few grindings of pepper. Continue to toss vigorously to coat the pasta and allow it to absorb the sauce. Sprinkle the remaining cheese over the top and serve immediately.

Some ideas to get you thinking about adding your own twist to this classic:

- *For an elegant and aromatic feast, drizzle with white truffle oil as you toss.*

- *Mince 2 cloves garlic and add with a generous shake of red chile flakes as you cook the pancetta.*

- *Sauté 1 cup sliced wild mushrooms with the pancetta to add earthiness.*

- *Toss in a handful each of cherry tomatoes and fresh blanched English peas or good-quality thawed frozen ones at the end, along with some torn fresh basil leaves.*

STUFFED SHELLS with FUN-TINA and TOMATO SAUCE

Sometimes the secret to a truly flavorful dish lies in harmonizing just a few simple ingredients. In this Italian restaurant standard of cheese-filled pasta and tomato sauce, Italian fontina lends its wonderfully nutty taste, creating flavors that morph and meld with every bite. Splurge on locally made fresh whole-milk ricotta, if you can find it.

When my bandmate and fellow Bay Area chef Gordon Drysdale was making a pizza blend using primarily fontina cheese mixed with mozzarella, Parmesan, and herbs, I joked that he was turning fontina into fun-tina. This dish pays homage to his child- and adult-friendly blend. For variety, add sautéed chopped mushrooms, diced roasted red peppers, or cooked spinach (squeezed dry and chopped) to the cheese filling. A green salad and a loaf of crusty bread (garlic bread is even better) are all you need to round out the meal.

Makes 6 to 8 servings

What to Drink: Choose a Chianti or other light-bodied, full-flavored Italian red wine.

Olive oil to coat pan

8 ounces grated fontina cheese (about 1½ cups)

One 15-ounce container ricotta

6 ounces grated mozzarella cheese (about 1 cup)

¼ cup chopped fresh flat-leaf parsley, plus more for optional garnish

¼ cup chopped fresh basil leaves

Salt and freshly ground black pepper

8 ounces dried jumbo pasta shells (about 24 shells), cooked in salted water until al dente and drained

1 recipe (about 3½ cups) Quick-and-Easy Tomato Sauce (page 201)

½ cup freshly grated Parmesan cheese, plus more for optional garnish

1. Preheat the oven to 350°F. Coat a 13 by 9–inch baking pan with olive oil.

2. Stir together the fontina, ricotta, mozzarella, parsley, and basil in a medium mixing bowl with a wooden spoon until well combined. Add salt and pepper to taste. Spoon the filling into the shells until they are just full, 2 to 3 tablespoons per shell. Place them open side up in the pan.

3. Blanket the shells with most of the sauce, leaving about ½ cup for finishing. Sprinkle the Parmesan over the top. (To make ahead, cool the dish, cover tightly, and refrigerate for up to 1 day. Bring back to room temperature and preheat the oven before proceeding.)

4. Bake until everything is hot and bubbly, about 25 minutes. Serve family style, 3 or 4 shells to a plate, spooning the reserved sauce around the pasta. Sprinkle with additional chopped parsley and Parmesan, if desired.

DUCK CANNELLONI with PORCINI MARSALA SAUCE

Though it takes a bit of effort, this showstopper will impress the most demanding foodie in your life. It offers the perfect blend of earthy flavor and rich texture, with the wine sauce adding brightness that keeps the dish from becoming heavy. Make it a day ahead and you won't miss out on visiting with your guests.

Restaurants often make fresh pasta, adjusting the size, shape, and ingredients to fit a particular recipe. For a beautiful presentation, we roll fresh herb leaves into the pasta.

If you haven't prepared Confit Duck, you can roast 6 whole duck legs in a covered baking dish at 300°F until they are quite tender, about 2 hours. Or substitute sautéed mushrooms for the duck and vegetable broth for the chicken broth for a decadent vegetarian pasta.

Balance this rich dish with a simple green salad for a satisfying meal.

Makes 6 servings

What to Drink: Duck and pinot noir were made for each other. This dish also pairs well with zinfandel, Chianti Classico, aglianico, or amarone.

1 recipe Fresh Homemade Pasta (page 112) or 12 ounces fresh store-bought pasta in large sheets (approximately 9 by 6 inches)

Olive oil to coat pans

6 Confit Duck legs (page 155)

1 large yellow onion, cut into ¼-inch dice

3 tablespoons rendered duck fat or unsalted butter

1 tablespoon minced garlic

1½ cups chicken broth

¾ cup heavy cream

3 tablespoons minced mixed fresh herbs (any combination of rosemary, parsley, oregano, thyme, sage, basil), plus more for garnish

¾ cup freshly grated Parmesan cheese, plus more for garnish

Salt and freshly ground black pepper

Porcini Marsala Sauce (page 204)

1. Bring a large pot of generously salted water to a boil. If you are using store-bought pasta sheets, cut them in thirds crosswise. You will need a total of 12 pasta sheets, each approximately 6 by 3 inches. Cook the pasta, 3 pieces at a time, for just 1 minute, waiting a few seconds before putting in the second and third pieces to avoid their sticking together.

2. Carefully lift out the pasta sheets with a flat mesh strainer and transfer them to a bowl of ice water for 1 minute, then carefully lay the sheets out on a lightly oiled baking sheet or a piece of plastic wrap. Repeat until you have cooked the 12 pasta sheets. (Tightly wrap and refrigerate any remaining uncooked pasta for another use.)

3. Pull the meat from the duck legs, shredding or cutting it into bite-size pieces. Discard the skin and bones.

4. Sauté the onions in the duck fat in a large skillet over medium heat until they soften and begin to brown. Add the garlic, broth, cream, and duck meat. Simmer until almost no liquid remains in the pan. Stir in the herbs and ½ cup of the Parmesan until well combined. Season with salt and pepper to taste.

5. Transfer the duck filling to a bowl and cool for 10 minutes, then refrigerate for at least 30 minutes.

6. Preheat the oven to 375°F with a rack set near the middle. Lightly oil a 13 by 9-inch baking pan.

DON'T HOLD BACK ■ STEP UP YOUR SKILLS

This recipe calls for rolling fresh home-made pasta with a pasta machine. If you don't have one, you can roll each piece of pasta with a rolling pin on a flat surface to a thin sheet approximately 12 inches long by 3 inches wide.

7. To assemble the cannelloni, cover a flat work surface with plastic wrap and place a sheet of pasta on it with a short side facing you. Mound about 2 tablespoons of the filling in a long cigar across the pasta sheet about an inch from the edge. Using the plastic wrap as a guide, lift the bottom of the pasta up and over the filling, then continue rolling to make a tube. Use the plastic wrap to gently but firmly compact the filled pasta roll. Remove the roll from the plastic and place in the baking pan. Repeat with the remaining pasta and filling to make 12 cannelloni.

8. Top the cannelloni generously with the Porcini Marsala Sauce and sprinkle with the remaining Parmesan. (To make ahead, cool the dish, cover tightly, and refrigerate for up to 24 hours. Bring back to room temperature and preheat oven before proceeding.)

9. Bake until hot and bubbly and the sauce has reduced somewhat, about 30 minutes.

10. Serve 2 cannelloni per plate, sprinkling additional herbs and Parmesan over the top.

FRESH HOMEMADE PASTA

1½ cups all-purpose flour, plus more for kneading and rolling

½ teaspoon kosher salt

2 large eggs

1½ teaspoons extra-virgin olive oil

A handful of whole fresh tender herb leaves such as chervil, parsley, or chives (optional)

1. Pulse the flour and salt a few times in a food processor fitted with a metal blade. With the motor running, add the eggs and olive oil through the feed tube. Continue processing until the mixture balls up around the blade. You may need to stop and start the food processor a few times, or shift the dough around in the bowl, until the stiff dough smoothes out and processes more easily.

2. Once the dough has formed, process for 3 minutes longer to develop the gluten in the flour. (The gluten makes the dough stretchy, which will help you later when you roll it.) Remove the dough from the food processor and knead a few times by hand on a floured board. Press it into a flat disk, wrap in plastic wrap, and set aside for 30 minutes at room temperature.

3. Divide the dough into 4 equal pieces. Flatten each piece into a small rectangle that will fit through your pasta machine (see "Step Up Your Skills," page 110). Lightly dust the rollers of the pasta machine with flour.

4. Roll one piece of dough through the pasta machine at the #1 setting. (Keep the remaining dough covered with a tea towel to prevent it from drying as you work.) Fold the dough in thirds lengthwise, like a letter, and roll it again. Adjust the setting up a notch to the #2 position and roll the dough through the machine twice; no need to fold.

5. Roll once at the #3 setting, then sprinkle the lower half of the sheet with a few of the herb leaves, if using. Fold the top half over, and press to seal. Put the sheet back through the pasta machine, back at the #2 setting once, as you have just made it thicker. Then roll once at the #3 setting, once at #4, and once at #5.

6. You will have a thin sheet of pasta approximately 18 inches long and 3 to 4 inches wide. Cut the sheet crosswise into 3 equal segments about 6 inches long, lay them flat on a baking sheet, and cover with a kitchen towel while you repeat with the remaining pasta dough.

SHRIMP and ROASTED CHILE PASTA GRATIN

Pasta is a culinary chameleon that adapts beautifully to almost anything. Here, I give pasta a Southwestern flair with roasted poblano chiles, chipotles, and queso fresco. Shrimp makes it special. Queso fresco is a mild fresh Mexican cheese. You can substitute a mild feta, but it's saltier. If tomatoes are not in season, substitute ½ cup drained canned diced tomatoes.

Makes 4 to 6 servings

What to Drink: The bright, crisp flavors of a Spanish garnacha rosé cuts through the richness yet has enough body to stand up to these bold flavors.

1½ teaspoons unsalted butter, plus extra for the pan

8 ounces dried ziti or penne pasta

1 poblano chile

1 medium clove garlic, minced

½ to ¾ cup heavy cream

8 ounces small shrimp, peeled and deveined, rinsed, and drained

1 chipotle chile in adobo, drained and minced

1 medium tomato, seeded and chopped (about ½ cup)

Salt and freshly ground black pepper

¾ cup crumbled queso fresco

¼ cup freshly grated Parmesan cheese

1. Bring a large pot of generously salted water to a boil. Preheat the oven to 350°F. Butter a 9-inch square baking dish.

2. Cook the pasta until it is al dente, about 8 minutes, depending on the size and thickness of the pasta. Drain and set aside in a large bowl.

3. Roast the poblano chile over an open flame or under the broiler, turning frequently to char the skin all over. Place the chile in a bowl and cover with a plate for 5 minutes to steam. Rub off the charred skin with your fingers. (Do not rinse, as you will wash away flavor.) Cut the chile open lengthwise and pull out the stem along with the seeds and veins. Cut the chile into thin strips.

4. Melt the 1½ teaspoons butter in a skillet over medium heat. Add the garlic and cook for 1 minute, then add ½ cup of the cream and the shrimp, chipotle, and poblano. Cook, stirring occasionally, for 3 minutes. Stir in the tomatoes. Season to taste with salt and pepper. Add the mixture to the bowl of pasta along with the queso fresco, 2 tablespoons of the Parmesan, and up to ¼ cup of the cream as needed to keep the mixture moist.

5. Transfer to the baking dish and sprinkle the remaining Parmesan over the top. (To make ahead, cool the dish, cover tightly, and refrigerate for up to 3 hours. Bring back to room temperature and preheat the oven before proceeding.)

6. Bake until lightly golden, about 20 minutes. Let stand for 5 minutes before serving.

KABOCHA SQUASH SPAETZLE

In their unyielding effort to keep dishes new and exciting, chefs are always in search of new starches to dress up a meal. This easy-to-make dumpling is a great change of pace from pasta, rice, or potatoes.

German for "little sparrow," spaetzle are small dumplings or noodles. The dough is often rolled into logs and cut into small pieces, but I find the easiest method is to force a softer dough through the holes of a large, flat cheese grater. The dumplings are boiled briefly before adding them to soups or other dishes. Chefs like to pan-fry them in butter to crisp them. Borrowing a lesson from pumpkin gnocchi, you could toss in a few fresh sage leaves as you sauté them.

Made with the Japanese pumpkin known as kabocha squash, these are a lovely orange with a faint sweetness that perfectly complements duck, pork, and other meats. Kabocha squash has fairly dry flesh when cooked. You can substitute butternut squash or a baking pumpkin such as the sugar pie variety—or even canned pumpkin, adjusting the amount of flour to the moisture content of the squash.

Makes 8 servings

What to Drink: Earthy and sweet flavors allow this dish to go white or red. Consider an aromatic white (viognier, pinot blanc) or a lighter-bodied red wine (pinot noir, grenache).

1 medium kabocha squash (about 2 pounds) or 3 cups mashed cooked pumpkin

4 large eggs

¼ cup extra-virgin olive oil, plus a drizzle to coat the cooked spaetzle

½ teaspoon sea salt, plus more for water and seasoning

¼ teaspoon freshly ground black pepper, plus more for seasoning

¼ teaspoon freshly grated nutmeg

2 to 2½ cups all-purpose flour

2 tablespoons (¼ stick) unsalted butter

1 cup sliced shiitake mushrooms (stems removed first)

2 cups loosely packed arugula leaves, rinsed, spun dry, and roughly chopped

1. Use a large chef's knife to halve and peel the squash. Remove the seeds and discard. Cut the squash into roughly 2-inch cubes. Put into a large pot with about ½ inch of water. Cover and cook until tender, about 15 minutes. Drain and let cool a few minutes.

2. Purée the squash in a food processor fitted with a metal blade. Measure out 3 cups and return to the food processor along with the eggs, the ¼ cup olive oil, salt, pepper, and nutmeg. (Reserve any remaining squash for another use.) Process until completely smooth, scraping down the bowl once or twice with a rubber spatula.

3. Add 1 cup of the flour and continue processing, adding more flour if needed, to make a mixture that is about the consistency of a thick muffin batter. The amount of flour needed will depend on the moisture content of the squash.

4. Bring a large pot of salted water to a boil. Use a rubber spatula to push ½ cup of the dough at a time through a large-holed cheese grater so that the batter falls in "fingers" into the boiling water. Stir gently with a wooden spoon to break up any clumps of spaetzle until they rise to the top and are tender, 30 seconds to 1 minute.

5. Use a fine mesh strainer to scoop out and transfer the spaetzle to a large bowl of ice water. Repeat with the remaining dough. Drain the spaetzle thoroughly, put in a bowl, and toss with a little olive oil just to coat them. (Once they are cool and oiled, the spaetzle can be refrigerated in a resealable plastic bag for up to 3 days and finished just before serving.)

6. Just before serving, melt the butter in a large skillet over medium heat until it just begins to turn golden. Add half of the shiitakes and sauté until they begin to soften, about 2 minutes. Add half of the spaetzle and sauté until they turn golden in places, about 5 minutes longer. Transfer to a large shallow serving bowl and cover loosely to keep warm. Repeat with the remaining shiitakes and spaetzle. Toss the arugula into the hot spaetzle until it is wilted. Season to taste with salt and pepper and serve family style.

PAD THAI MY WAY

EASY PREP

This is arguably the most popular dish served in Thai restaurants in America. When at home I easily turn out *Pad Thai* as good as one of my favorite restaurants, I feel like I've uncovered a national secret. With its complex blend of well-balanced flavors, Pad Thai exemplifies what good cooking strives for. The dish blends all the basic flavor elements—salty, sweet, earthy, fermented, and bright—with no one element standing out. The continuing dance of flavors is complemented by soft, chewy noodles, crunchy peanuts, and refreshing sprouts.

With its myriad ingredients, some of them foreign to many American kitchens, this dish can be intimidating. But while some ingredients are not pantry mainstays, most are available in the Asian food aisles of larger supermarkets, and certainly in Asian markets and online. Your culinary scavenger hunt will be rewarded with an exotic and delicious meal. For the rice sticks, look for medium-width noodles sometimes labeled with their Thai name, *sen lek.* Dried shrimp can be found in small plastic bags. If you prefer, you can use prepared savory baked tofu in place of the firm tofu.

Makes 6 servings

What to Drink: Serve with a cold Thai beer or an aromatic white wine with a touch of sweetness such as gewürztraminer or riesling.

8 ounces dried rice stick noodles

¼ cup vegetable oil

2 medium cloves garlic, minced

¼ cup small dried shrimp, soaked for 10 minutes in warm water, drained, and rinsed

8 ounces medium shrimp (21 to 25 per pound), peeled and deveined

8 ounces chicken thigh or breast meat, cut into bite-size pieces

¼ cup sugar

3 tablespoons Laxmi brand tamarind concentrate (see "Explore New Foods," page 147)

¼ cup fish sauce

1 teaspoon hot paprika or ¼ teaspoon cayenne pepper

1 small block firm tofu, drained and cut into 1 by ½-inch strips (about ½ cup)

2 large eggs, beaten

4 scallions, trimmed, white and green parts cut into 1-inch lengths

1 cup fresh mung bean sprouts

½ cup roasted peanuts, chopped medium-fine

A handful of cilantro sprigs

1 lime, cut into 6 wedges

1. Soak the rice noodles in room temperature water for 30 minutes. Drain and set aside.

2. Heat a large skillet or wok over medium-high heat for 5 minutes. Add the vegetable oil, then the garlic, dried and fresh shrimp, and chicken, stir-frying until they are just cooked through. Add the drained noodles and stir-fry until they turn from opaque white to almost translucent, reducing the heat if they stick.

3. Add the sugar, tamarind, fish sauce, and paprika, continuing to stir and cook until everything is well coated. Stir in the tofu.

4. Turn the heat to high, push the noodles to one side of the pan, and add the eggs to the other side, scrambling them with a spatula until they are gently set. Stir the eggs into the mixture, along with the scallions, and continue to cook over medium heat until most of the liquid has evaporated, about 2 minutes.

5. Immediately transfer the Pad Thai to a large shallow serving bowl. Top with the bean sprouts and peanuts, tossing them into the noodles. Garnish with cilantro sprigs and serve with lime wedges for squeezing over the top.

OCEANS OF FLAVOR

W ITH SUCH A WIDE VARIETY of flavors and textures, seafood offers great opportunities for creativity in the kitchen. And while it requires some attention, fish is one of the easiest meals to get on the table quickly. In this chapter I share a few simple principles to put you at ease as you expand your seafood repertoire.

Start by purchasing the freshest fish you can find. If there isn't a good selection in your area, substitute the best alternative available for the particular variety featured in a recipe. Shop at a market with plenty of turnover and a knowledgeable staff who can tell you what's fresh and local, or at least the best of their selection. If you're concerned about the sustainability of fish varieties that may be overfished or caught in ways that might harm the habitat, learn about which species make the best choices. The Monterey Bay Aquarium in California sponsors Seafood Watch, a program that produces regional guides for purchasing seafood. Ask your fishmonger whether they keep these on hand, or check the Web site at www.seafoodwatch.org. Many fish markets now have extensive labeling to guide you.

With fish, it's essential to get the cooking time right. Fish have less connective tissue and shorter muscle fibers than meat. That means they become tender fast, but it also means they are not so forgiving. When overcooked, fish and shellfish can quickly turn from moist and tender to rubbery or dry.

Some fish, such as salmon or tuna, are most tender and moist when a bit underdone. Others, such as halibut or black bass, should be cooked through but not a minute longer. Restaurant chefs often sear fish on the stove top in an ovenproof skillet and finish it in the oven. The oven heat surrounds the fish, assuring it cooks through before the outside overcooks. As a rule of thumb, fillets will generally be done in about 10 minutes per inch of thickness, depending on the cooking method and heat level. Whole fish may take a bit longer.

It's easy to know when fish is ready. The flesh goes from translucent to opaque (except for those best served while still translucent at the center), and most fish will flake when nudged with a fork or poked with a paring knife. Your job is to catch the transition—as it goes opaque or is just beginning to flake. Keep in mind that the residual heat will continue to cook the fish even after you remove it from the oven or stove.

Press a fingertip gently on the surface of the fish and you will soon learn what it feels like when raw, partially cooked, and cooked through. That's how most chefs gauge doneness, and once you learn it, it's one of the most reliable ways to judge when your fish is ready.

With mussels and clams it's even easier. They should always be closed to start. When they pop open, they are cooked. If they don't open, return them to the heat briefly to make sure they are fully cooked. If they still don't open, toss them—they weren't good to begin with.

The recipes in this chapter guide you through everything you need to know, with plenty of ideas for preparing and serving your fish swimmingly.

SAKE-STEAMED MUSSELS

This classic bistro dish is ridiculously easy to make at home. Use a light, fruity sake—one you like well enough to drink; but save your best sake for sipping alongside.

Make sure to check your mussels for any dead ones. Ones that are open and won't close when you tap them should be discarded.

Makes 8 appetizer or 4 entrée servings

What to Drink: Sake is a natural match, but this also pairs well with a mineraly white wine such as Sancerre or Quincy (sauvignon blanc).

8 large shallots, cut into thin slices

2 tablespoon minced fresh ginger

¼ pound (1 stick) unsalted butter

Kosher salt

2 cups sake

Freshly ground black pepper

4 pounds mussels, rinsed and debearded

4 scallions, cut into thin slices

Baguette or other crusty bread, for serving

1. Sauté the shallots and ginger in the butter with a pinch of salt in a large saucepan over medium heat until the shallots soften, about 5 minutes. Add the sake, another generous pinch of salt, and a few grindings of black pepper. Stir and bring to a boil. Add the mussels, cover, and steam, shaking the pan occasionally, until the mussels open, about 5 minutes. (Discard any mussels that do not open.)

2. Divide the mussels and broth among four large shallow bowls (eight for appetizer servings), sprinkle with the scallions, and serve with plenty of crusty bread for dunking.

BEER-BRAISED CLAMS

What's the most memorable part of a meal in a restaurant or at home? Generally, it's whatever you started and finished the meal with. Psychologists call the effect "primacy and recency." Chefs know this intuitively. This simple recipe gets a meal off to a fun and celebratory start. Why go out when it's so easy to do at home?

There are two main groupings of clams: hard shell and soft (which is actually thin and brittle). I like the medium to large hard-shell cherrystone clams for this dish, but you can use other varieties such as the smaller littlenecks, or the larger quahogs (pronounced KOH-hogs), found in abundance in Cape Cod, New Jersey, and Rhode Island. Westerners can look for the small Pacific littleneck or larger manila clam.

Make sure your hard-shell clams are tightly closed when you buy them. (Soft-shelled clams do not close completely.) If you tap an open shell and it doesn't immediately clamp shut, discard the clam; it's dead. A live soft-shell clam should show signs of life by retracting or moving when you touch its siphon.

Clams are high in protein, which means that they can seize up and become tough when cooked over direct heat or for too long. The following braising method gives them a beer and butter buffer, assuring a tender result. Serve these in bowls with lightly toasted slabs of rustic bread for dipping, or over al dente linguine.

Makes 12 appetizer or 6 entrée servings

What to Drink: Beer is perfect, of course, but these are also nice with an unoaked chardonnay or pinot grigio.

CHEF'S TIP

Ask your fishmonger whether the clams have been purged to coax out any grit hiding inside. If not, put them in a large bowl of cold water with a tablespoon of salt and 2 tablespoons of cornmeal, refrigerate for an hour or 2, then rinse well and drain. Reduce the salt in the recipe slightly to make up for the salt the clams will absorb during purging.

6 pounds cherrystone clams, scrubbed, purged, and rinsed if needed (see "Chef's Tip")

Two 12-ounce bottles light-colored beer, such as a hefeweizen (wheat beer) or lager

½ pound (2 sticks) unsalted butter

3 tablespoons minced shallots

3 tablespoons minced garlic

1½ teaspoons kosher salt

½ teaspoons freshly ground black pepper

Chopped flat-leaf parsley, for garnish

Baguette or other crusty bread, for serving

Put the clams in a large stock pot. Add the beer, butter, shallots, garlic, salt, and pepper. Cook over medium-high heat, covered, until all the clams have opened, about 5 minutes. (Discard any clams that do not open.) Transfer the clams and broth to large shallow bowls. Sprinkle with parsley and serve with crusty bread.

THAI GRILLED PRAWNS with EMERALD NOODLES

This dish is awesome for grilling and serving in the backyard with friends. The marinade's bright and spicy flavors contrast perfectly with the herbaceous, nutty noodles. It's also great made with grilled fish. The dressed noodles can be served either hot or at room temperature.

Makes 12 appetizer or 6 entrée servings

What to Drink: Serve with Thai iced tea or a cold Asian beer on a hot summer day. Other good choices include a kabinett riesling, gewürztraminer or other aromatic white wine with a touch of sweetness.

36 large shell-on shrimp (about 2 pounds)

½ cup chopped fresh mint

½ cup chopped cilantro

½ cup chopped fresh basil

2 serrano chiles, sliced thin

½ cup extra-virgin olive oil

3 tablespoons fresh lime juice

2 tablespoons fish sauce

1 tablespoon minced garlic

1 tablespoon sugar

1 teaspoon kosher salt

12 ounces capellini or angel hair pasta

2 cups Emerald Sauce (page 199)

Have on hand twelve 10-inch wooden skewers

CHEF'S TIP

Grill shrimp with shells on for more flavor. Cutting through the back of the shell makes it pop off for easy eating.

1. Bring a large pot of salted water to the boil. Preheat the grill to medium-hot. Put the skewers in a pan of water to soak.

2. Use a serrated knife to cut the shrimp lengthwise along the back of the shell, stopping short of cutting all the way through, to butterfly them.

3. Rinse and drain the shrimp and put them in a large bowl. Add ¼ cup of the mint, ¼ cup of the cilantro, and the basil, chiles, olive oil, lime juice, fish sauce, garlic, sugar, and salt. Toss well to coat. Remove the skewers from the water and thread 3 shrimp on each skewer through both the head and tail ends to hold them in their natural *C* shape.

4. Cook the capellini in the boiling water until al dente. Drain, rinse with cool water, drain again, and transfer to a large bowl. Coat with the emerald sauce, tossing with two spoons until the noodles are evenly coated. Set aside. (The pasta is best served at room temperature.)

5. Grill the shrimp over medium-hot heat until they are cooked through, 3 to 4 minutes per side. Use a fork to spiral the noodles, making a nest at the center of each plate. Serve 2 shrimp skewers crisscrossed atop the noodles for an entrée, or 1 for an appetizer. Garnish with the remaining mint and cilantro.

COCONUT–RED CURRY SEAFOOD

Clay pots have been used for cooking in many parts of the world over the ages. The traditional method of cooking in unglazed earthenware creates full-flavored, succulent food, protected from the oven's harsh heat and kept moist by the evaporation of the water the pot was soaked in before cooking. This dish mimics that effect using everyday equipment found in the home, with bold flavor developing in a short time in a single pot. All you need to accompany it is steamed jasmine rice.

Thai curry paste, coconut milk, and kaffir lime leaves are responsible for the stew's Thai flavor. You can now find Thai curry pastes in many supermarkets. Thai Kitchen and Mae Ploy are popular brands. My favorite brand of coconut milk is Chaokoh. Thai basil is especially aromatic, but if you can't find it, substitute common basil.

Makes 6 servings

What to Drink: The seafood, coconut milk, and curry work well with an off-dry white wine, such as a riesling, albariño, viognier, or Vouvray (chenin blanc).

2 teaspoons vegetable oil

1 small red onion, cut into ¼-inch wedges

2 tablespoons Thai red curry paste

One 14-ounce can unsweetened coconut milk

1 cup chicken broth or water

3 tablespoons fresh lime juice

2 tablespoons fish sauce, plus more to taste

3 kaffir lime leaves

⅔ pound mussels, rinsed and debearded (see headnote, page 122)

⅔ pound jumbo shrimp, peeled and deveined

⅔ pound skinless, boneless sea bass or other firm white fish, cut into 1-inch chunks

⅔ pound large sea scallops, tough muscle strip discarded (see "Explore New Foods," page 127)

3 medium Roma tomatoes, quartered lengthwise

Kosher salt (optional)

⅔ cup Thai basil leaves, roughly torn

⅔ cup cilantro sprigs

Steamed jasmine rice, for serving

1. Heat the vegetable oil in a large heavy saucepan over medium heat. Add the onions and sauté until they soften, about 5 minutes. Stir in the curry paste; cook and stir a few minutes to release its flavors. Stir in the coconut milk, chicken broth, lime juice, fish sauce, and kaffir lime leaves until everything is well combined. Bring to a boil.

2. Add the mussels to the pot, then the shrimp, followed by the sea bass, and finally the scallops. Scatter the tomatoes over the top. Cover and simmer until the mussels open, about 10 minutes. Taste and add fish sauce or salt if needed. Stir in the basil and cilantro just before serving.

3. To serve, place a mound of jasmine rice in large shallow bowls and ladle the seafood and sauce over the rice.

DON'T HOLD BACK ■ EXPLORE NEW FOODS

Like many shellfish, scallops are sold by variety and weight. The largest are generally the most expensive, but they are also the sweetest and most flavorful. Restaurant chefs and their suppliers talk about them in terms of the number per pound. The 10/20 size have 10 to 20 scallops to a pound and are the largest. Scallops may go from this largest size to 30/40 or sometimes even tiny 100s. Sea scallops tend to be larger, while bay scallops are typically small.

Scallops may be dredged or caught by divers or from day boats—boats that go out only for the day; thus the notation of "diver scallops" or "day-boat scallops" on many restaurant menus. These more expensive harvesting methods also do less

damage to the environment than dredging, which stirs up the delicate ocean or bay habitat.

Scallops are sold fresh, frozen, or frozen and thawed. Because they are delicate, they are often shucked and frozen immediately after being caught. For the best flavor and texture, choose scallops that are ivory to cream colored, pink (from their natural diet), or light beige. Avoid pure white scallops, which may have been treated with phosphates to plump them up for sale. Scallops sitting in a milky liquid also may indicate phosphate treatment. The best scallops will be dry, almost tacky. They should smell of the ocean—a sweet and briny aroma. Avoid any seafood with an unpleasantly strong fishy or sour smell.

SEARED SEA SCALLOPS with CORN RISOTTO

Chefs must economize to stay in business. They learn to find creative ways to use every last bit of what they buy. The payoff for the diner is deep flavor. In this case, the corn kernels, cobs, and "milk" are all used for a risotto with multilayered corn flavor.

Arborio and Carnaroli are two Italian rice varieties with short grains and lots of starch. When you cook them, slowly stirring in hot broth, they give up their starch, creating a creamy sauce for the rice grains, which maintain just a bit of bite at the center. Thanks to risotto's growing popularity, you can find these starchy rices where other grains are found in most supermarkets.

Makes 6 servings

What to Drink: Pair this rich dish with a crisp, bright pinot grigio or sauvignon blanc.

3 ears of corn, husks and silk removed

7 tablespoons unsalted butter

Sea salt and freshly ground black pepper

1 cup chicken broth

5 tablespoons extra-virgin olive oil

1 medium yellow onion, minced

1½ cups Arborio or Carnaroli rice

1 cup white wine

24 large sea scallops (about 1½ pounds), tough muscle strip discarded (see "Explore New Foods," page 127)

½ cup grated Parmesan cheese

A few drops black or white truffle oil (optional)

½ cup basil leaves, cut into thin ribbons

1. Cut the kernels from the ears of corn (see page 19), then scrape the cobs with the heel of the knife into a bowl to extract the "corn milk." Set aside the cobs and corn milk. Sauté the corn in 2 tablespoons of the butter in a large skillet over medium-high heat for 2 minutes. Season with salt and pepper and set aside.

2. Bring the chicken broth and 4 cups water to a simmer in a large saucepan. Add the reserved corn cobs to the pot. Keep at a simmer as you prepare the risotto.

3. Sauté the onions in 2 tablespoons each of the olive oil and butter in a heavy medium saucepan over medium heat, stirring occasionally, until the onions are tender and light golden. Add the rice and stir with a wooden spatula until it is well coated, then continue to cook and stir another minute or two to toast the rice.

4. Add the wine and continue to stir until it is absorbed. Ladle in about 1 cup of the hot broth and stir, keeping the mixture at a lively simmer, until it is almost absorbed: When

you run your spatula along the bottom of the pan, it should briefly clear a path before the risotto fills it back in. Continue to add the broth, about 1 cup at a time, stirring and waiting until the last ladleful is almost completely absorbed before adding the next.

5. When most of the broth has been absorbed and the rice is nearly tender (about 15 minutes total cooking time), prepare the scallops. Heat a large skillet over medium-high heat until it is very hot. Add the remaining 3 tablespoons each olive oil and butter.

6. Pat the scallops dry and season them with salt and pepper. Sauté them in the hot oil mixture, turning once, until they are golden and just cooked through, 60 to 90 seconds per side. Remove the scallops to a warm plate and drape with foil. Move the skillet to a cool burner.

7. To finish the risotto, stir the reserved corn kernels and corn milk into the risotto. Add another ladleful of broth and stir until it is almost absorbed. Continue cooking and adding broth until the rice is tender with just a bit of resistance at the middle but not at all chalky or hard. Stir in the Parmesan. Season to taste with salt and pepper.

8. Divide the risotto among warm shallow bowls, placing 4 scallops on top of each serving. If you are using it, add the truffle oil to the skillet and mix to combine it with the scallop pan juices. Drizzle the buttery pan juices over the scallops and garnish with basil.

SEARED HALIBUT with QUINOA, ARUGULA, and MEYER LEMON–GINGER VINAIGRETTE

Chefs love to introduce their customers to new ingredients and flavors. This recipe combines an unusual grain with simply cooked fish and a bright vinaigrette for a mix of rich peppery, citrus, and toasty flavors that excite the palate with something a little different in every bite. It's a pretty presentation, perfect for a dinner party. The quinoa will definitely be a conversation starter.

We are fortunate in California to have Meyer lemons growing in our yards nearly year-round. Originally from China, the sweet fruit (for a lemon) is thought to be a cross between a common lemon and an orange or mandarin. It is one of the best-loved ingredients of California Cuisine, as it adds bright citrus flavor without being sour or bitter. If you can't find them in your area, substitute half lemon juice and half orange juice.

You can prepare the quinoa and the vinaigrette a few hours in advance. Prepare the fish, then toss together the salad just before serving. For a taste of luxury and an alluring aroma, drizzle just a few drops of a good-quality white truffle oil over the fish just before serving.

Makes 4 servings

What to Drink: Serve with a mineraly, aromatic white wine such as a pinot grigio or grüner vetliner.

¾ cup quinoa

¾ cup extra-virgin olive oil

6 tablespoons Meyer lemon juice, or 3 tablespoons each lemon and orange juice

¼ cup minced shallots

2 tablespoons minced chives

1 tablespoon minced fresh ginger

Kosher salt and freshly ground black pepper

Four 6-ounce halibut fillets

4 large handfuls baby arugula, rinsed and spun dry

1. Preheat the oven to 400°F.

2. To prepare the quinoa, thoroughly rinse under cold running water in a fine mesh strainer. Put the quinoa into a medium heavy skillet with 1 tablespoon of the olive oil. Toast over medium heat, stirring frequently, until you begin to smell its fragrance, about 3 minutes. Add 1½ cups water, bring to a boil, cover, and cook over medium heat until the quinoa has absorbed the water, about 12 minutes. Remove from the heat, fluff with a fork, cover again, and set aside.

3. To make the vinaigrette, whisk together ½ cup of the olive oil and the Meyer lemon juice, shallots, chives, and ginger in a small bowl. Season to taste with salt and pepper. Set aside.

4. Season the halibut on both sides with salt and pepper. Heat a heavy ovenproof skillet over medium-high heat. When it is hot, add 2 to 3 tablespoons of the olive oil to generously coat the pan. When the oil is hot, lay the halibut in the skillet skin side up. (Even if the fish is skinless, you will want the presentation side down in the pan.) Sear for 3 to 4 minutes, then transfer the skillet to the oven until the fish is just cooked through, about 7 minutes longer. Remove from the oven and let rest for 5 minutes before carefully releasing the fish from the pan with a thin spatula.

5. While the halibut cooks, toss together the arugula, quinoa, and about half of the vinaigrette in a medium bowl. Adjust with additional vinaigrette, salt, and pepper to taste.

6. Just before serving, mound the arugula-quinoa salad in a middle of each of four plates and top with a halibut fillet, turning the fish over to serve with the seared side up. Drizzle additional vinaigrette over the fish, with some falling on the plate surrounding the salad.

DON'T HOLD BACK ■ STEP UP YOUR SKILLS

Quinoa is an ancient seed originally grown in the Andes mountains of South America. More recently, it has become popular for its nutritional value. In fact, the United Nations has classified it as a "super crop" for its high protein content, which has been estimated at 12 to 18 percent. It is now widely available in supermarkets, natural food stores, and specialty food shops. Though it is treated as a grain, it is more accurately a seed. Always rinse quinoa before cooking to remove its natural outer coating, which can taste bitter.

GRILLED MAHI MAHI with RED PEPPER RICE and POBLANO-BANANA SAUCE

Restaurant patrons often scoff at a server's suggestion that their fish will be at its best a bit underdone. Instead, they ask that it be cooked medium or even medium-well, then wonder why it's dry. Most fish is best cooked just until it's done and no longer, and mahi mahi is no different. But because it is a lean fish it can quickly become dry if overcooked. Be sure to take it off the heat when it is just done, or even a few moments sooner. The residual heat will continue to cook it a bit more and you will be rewarded with a deliciously moist piece of fish.

Mahi mahi is sometimes sold as dolphinfish (although it's not related to dolphin) or dorado. If it's not available, good substitutes include bluefish, grouper, pompano, striped bass, or tuna.

I came up with this dish at my popular Caribbean restaurant, Miss Pearl's Jam House, in San Francisco. I wanted to show tropical fruit's evocative savory side by showcasing the breakfast-dominated banana in a spicy-sweet sauce for a dinner entrée. It easily wins over cynics wary of Caribbean cooking and fruity food.

Makes 6 servings

What to Drink: The tropical notes in Vouvray and semillon are a perfect match for the banana and poblano.

Six 6-ounce skinless, boneless mahi mahi fillets, about 1 inch thick

3 tablespoons olive oil

Kosher salt and freshly ground black pepper

Scallions cut on a diagonal, or cilantro sprigs, for garnish

Poblano-Banana Sauce (page 200)

Red Pepper Rice (page 232)

1. If using a grill, preheat it to medium-high.

2. Coat the fish with the olive oil and season with salt and pepper. Cook the fish on the grill, or in a skillet over medium-high heat, until it is just cooked through, 5 to 7 minutes per side.

3. Make a pool of the poblano-banana sauce on each of six plates, spreading it with the back of a large spoon. Mound the rice in the center of the plate over the sauce, then top with a fish fillet. Drizzle more sauce over the fish and around the rice. Garnish with scallions.

MISO-MARINATED BLACK COD with SESAME SPINACH

This Japanese method for preparing fish has been around for a long time, but it became trendy after superstar chef Nobu Matsuhisa made it famous. The sweet-salty marinade and moist, flaky fish has broad appeal, even to people who don't think themselves fans of fish. My simple interpretation will make even the snobbiest of your seafoodie friends swoon.

This recipe uses yellow miso, which is on the milder end of the flavor spectrum. White miso will also work. Mirin is the sweet rice wine that is ubiquitous in Japanese cooking.

Black cod—sometimes called sablefish, butterfish, or Alaska cod—isn't actually a cod at all. It is a rich, mild white fish with sweet, soft flesh found in the waters of the north Pacific. It is reputed to have even higher levels of healthy omega-3 fatty acids than salmon. Substitute white sea bass or Pacific halibut if you can't find black cod.

Makes 6 servings

What to Drink: The sweet-salty flavors in this dish are perfectly paired with a fruity sake, a wine with a hint of sweetness such as many kabinett rieslings, or a cold beer. Or try it with Hula-va Saketini (page 23).

¼ cup loosely packed light brown sugar

¼ cup yellow miso

¼ cup mirin

¼ cup sake

Six 6-ounce black cod fillets

Olive oil to coat pan

Sesame Spinach, plus the dressing remaining from the recipe (page 220)

1. Heat the brown sugar with ¼ cup water in a small saucepan, stirring, until the sugar is completely dissolved. Cool for 10 minutes, then stir in the miso, mirin, and sake to make a smooth paste. Coat the black cod with the miso paste, cover, and refrigerate at least 2 hours, or as long as 2 days.

2. To cook, preheat the broiler to high with a rack set in the upper third of the oven. Place the marinated black cod on a lightly oiled baking sheet and broil until the fish is fully cooked and the surface is lightly browned, 10 to 15 minutes, depending on the thickness of the fish. (Alternatively, the fish can be baked in a preheated 450°F oven for 10 to 15 minutes.)

3. Center the fish on a serving plate, and place a small bundle of the sesame spinach to the side. Drizzle some of the remaining sesame dressing around the fish and plate.

SESAME CRUSTED SEARED AHI TUNA with STAR ANISE–GINGER SAUCE and SHIITAKE-CABBAGE STIR-FRY

I love the contrast of crunchy crust and soft inside. With delicate foods, chefs often crust just one side to keep the breading from overpowering the dish. Sesame seeds work beautifully in this way, especially with seafood and Asian-inspired sauces.

In this recipe, I apply a simple coating of sesame seeds (both black and white for visual appeal) and sear the fish quickly in olive oil to bring out the best in this sushi-grade (good enough to eat raw) tuna. The sauce is flavorful but won't overpower the fish, while the cabbage adds crunch and complements the sesame flavor.

Makes 4 servings

What to Drink: A medium-bodied Oregon pinot noir is a beautiful companion to the rich tuna and aromatic sauce.

1 cup black sesame seeds

1 cup white sesame seeds

Four 6-ounce Ahi tuna steaks, sushi grade

2 teaspoons olive oil

Shiitake-Cabbage Stir-Fry (page 217)

Star Anise–Ginger Sauce (page 198)

1. Put the black and white sesame seeds on separate shallow plates. Press the tuna into the white seeds to coat one side and the black seeds to coat the other. (It isn't necessary to coat the edges.) Heat the olive oil in a large heavy skillet over medium-high heat until the pan begins to smoke. Put the tuna into the pan for about 1 minute to sear one side, then turn and sear the other side for 2 minutes.

2. Remove the tuna to a cutting board and cut each steak crosswise at an angle into three large slices.

3. Mound the shiitake-cabbage stir-fry in the center of each serving plate. Fan a sliced tuna steak over the cabbage and spoon the star anise–ginger sauce over the tuna and cabbage, drizzling some onto the plate.

SULTRY POULTRY

P OULTRY HAS A BROAD FLAVOR RANGE, from mild chicken breast to gamey duck. Whatever poultry you are cooking, starting with a well-cared-for bird makes all the difference. I use farm-raised chickens when I can find them, preferably free-range, even better if they are organic. Purchase poultry from a reputable grocer and ask where it came from. Factory chickens, fattened up on cheap feed and chemicals, have given chicken a bad reputation, with bland flavor and often dry, mealy texture. Good poultry, cooked properly, will be plump and moist with a clean flavor that shines through in the finished dish. Likewise, buy fresh, local duck if you can find it. Frozen duck, thawed slowly in a refrigerator, can be delicious, too. I love the heirloom turkeys that show up in the markets around Thanksgiving. These endangered breeds with exotic names like Bourbon Red and American Bronze are more flavorful, with a higher proportion of dark meat to white than their oil-injected conventional hybrid counterparts.

Poultry strikes mid-range notes that make it versatile. It partners equally well with deep, earthy flavors like mushrooms and bright, treble flavors like citrus. (Lemon is my favorite citrus with chicken; orange with duck.) Because it works with so many flavors and so many styles of cooking, poultry is a favorite in most ethnic cuisines.

Mild chicken breasts are a great canvas for building complex flavors. The thighs are more robust, with enough fat to keep them moist after cooking, making them perfect for the intense heat of the grill. When roasted, chicken and duck deliver that coveted combination of succulent meat and crispy skin.

I love duck's distinctive flavor, assertive enough to support stronger flavors of chiles and fruit. Confit duck takes roasting a step further: First cured with salt and spices to allow the flavors to penetrate, the duck legs then go into the oven for a long roast, by the end of which the meat is tender to the point of falling off the bone. It's great on its own or as an ingredient in other dishes.

In this chapter, I show you how chefs unlock the texture and flavor of good poultry by matching it with the right cooking methods and complementary ingredients and techniques to make memorable dishes, from the simple to the sublime.

EASY
PREP

CHICKEN with ONION-GORGONZOLA SAUCE

The key to great restaurant chicken is crispy skin. Don't move the chicken during the first few minutes of cooking. After the skin browns and crisps, it will release easily from the pan without tearing way from the meat.

Northern Italy's sweet and youthful Gorgonzola dolce is worth seeking out in cheese shops and Italian food stores. It makes the creamiest, most perfectly balanced sauce for this dish. If you can't find it, substitute 3 ounces of mild, creamy-soft blue cheese and add a tablespoon of cream.

Makes 4 servings

What to Drink: Choose an unoaked, full-bodied Italian chardonnay with bright mineral flavors to cut through the richness of the dish. A citrusy sauvignon blanc with some body and richness, or a sparkling rosé, will also work.

4 boneless, skin-on half chicken breasts (about 10 ounces each)

Kosher salt and freshly ground black pepper

1 tablespoon extra-virgin olive oil

1 large yellow onion, quartered and cut into ¼-inch-thick slices

10 small cloves garlic, sliced as thin as possible

¼ cup plus 2 to 3 tablespoons chicken broth

4 ounces Gorgonzola dolce

2 to 3 teaspoons fresh lemon juice, to taste

Chopped flat-leaf parsley, for garnish

1. Preheat the oven to 375°F. Smooth the skin over the tops of the chicken breasts to remove wrinkles and cover the breasts as much as possible. Season the chicken liberally with salt and pepper. Set aside.

2. Turn on your kitchen exhaust fan. Heat the olive oil in a large heavy ovenproof skillet (cast iron works well) over medium heat until the oil is almost smoking. Lay the chicken breasts skin side down into the hot oil. Push down on the breasts with a spatula to make sure the skin is in good contact with the pan, and tilt the pan occasionally to distribute the oil, but do not move the chicken around during the first few minutes of cooking.

3. After the skins have browned and crisped, turn over the chicken breasts and sear lightly on the second side, about 1 minute. Remove the chicken breasts to a plate and drape loosely with aluminum foil to keep them warm. (The chicken will not be fully cooked.)

4. Increase the heat to medium-high and add the onions and garlic to the skillet, tossing to coat with the juices. Cook until they begin to color. Push them to one side and return the chicken to the pan, this time skin side up. Spoon the onions over the chicken.

5. Transfer the skillet to the oven until the chicken is cooked through, 15 to 20 minutes, depending on the size of the chicken breasts. They should feel firm but have a little give when you press them with your finger. Place a chicken breast on each of four warmed serving plates. Drape with foil to keep warm.

6. Return the skillet to medium heat and add the ¼ cup chicken broth, the Gorgonzola, and 2 teaspoons of the lemon juice. Stir with a whisk until the mixture is warm and smooth, adding a little more broth as needed to make a creamy sauce. Season with salt, pepper, and additional lemon juice to taste.

7. To serve, spoon the sauce and onions over the chicken breasts and sprinkle with parsley.

DON'T HOLD BACK ▪ MAKE IT YOURS

For a restaurant-style presentation, mound soft polenta (see "The Art of Polenta," page 238) in the center of each plate, top with a chicken breast to one side, and spoon the sauce and onions over the whole dish. Alternatively, place the chicken breast to one side of the plate and snuggle roasted new potatoes with rosemary or squares of grilled polenta to the side of the chicken.

PIMENTÓN CHICKEN with PIQUILLO PEPPER SAUCE

This recipe is a great example of bistro cooking, Spanish style. Chefs don't always work with the rarest, most expensive foods. They are also specialists in coaxing the most flavor from cuts of inexpensive poultry and meat. Roasting the meat on the bone is one way, and though an upscale restaurant might present the meat boneless on the plate, in the more casual bistro, it is served in this more rustic style. This recipe shows how to coax the most flavor out of one of the most affordable cuts of chicken.

Use a *picante* ("hot") pimentón for the spiciest dish, *dulce* ("sweet") for a mild one, or a mixture of the two or *agridulce* ("bittersweet") pimentón for something in between.

Makes 4 servings

What to Drink: A medium-bodied Spanish Rioja or tempranillo will have enough structure and spice to harmonize with the robust, smoky flavors of the dish.

½ cup sliced almonds

1¼ cups extra-virgin olive oil

3 tablespoons plus 2 teaspoons minced garlic

2 tablespoons plus 1 teaspoon pimentón

Kosher salt

2 teaspoons ground cumin

Freshly ground black pepper

4 bone-in, skin-on chicken leg-thigh quarters (about 3 pounds)

1 cup piquillo peppers or roasted red bell peppers, peeled, seeded, veins removed

2 tablespoons fresh lemon juice

4 stone-ground wheat crackers or saltines

Chopped cilantro or flat-leaf parsley, for garnish (optional)

CHEF'S TIP

Borrow a trick from Spanish chefs: Stir in crushed saltine crackers to thicken sauces without masking flavors.

1. Preheat the oven to 350°F. Spread the almonds on a baking sheet and toast for about 8 minutes, until fragrant and golden. Set aside to cool. Turn off the oven.

2. In a large bowl, stir together ¼ cup of the olive oil, the 3 tablespoons garlic, the 2 tablespoons pimentón, 1 tablespoon salt, the cumin, and 1 teaspoon pepper. Poke the skinless side of the chicken all over with a fork or paring knife. Coat the chicken with the spice mixture, cover, and refrigerate for at least 2 hours.

3. Remove the chicken from the refrigerator, allowing it to sit out for 15 to 30 minutes as you preheat the oven to 375°F. Place the chicken in a single layer on a rimmed baking sheet and bake until cooked through, about 50 minutes. (Cooking time will vary depending on the size of the pieces.) You should see the meat pulling away from the bone, with about an inch of bone visible at the drumstick. The skin should be crispy and golden brown. Transfer the chicken to a warm serving platter.

4. While the chicken cooks, make the sauce. Purée the remaining 2 teaspoons garlic, 1 teaspoon pimentón, the piquillo peppers, almonds, lemon juice, and crackers in a blender or food processor until nearly smooth. With the motor running, drizzle in the remaining 1 cup of oil until the mixture is well blended. Season to taste with salt and pepper.

5. Because this is a bistro dish, I like to serve it family style on a large platter. Spoon some of the pepper sauce over the chicken pieces and serve the rest in a bowl on the side. Garnish the chicken with chopped cilantro, if desired. Roasted new potatoes tossed with olive oil and sea salt make a great accompaniment.

DON'T HOLD BACK ▪ EXPLORE NEW FOODS

Used widely throughout the Basque region, the small red piquillo pepper is native to the village of Lodosa in the Ebro river valley in the north of Spain. The pointy-tipped pepper has a subtle bite. The peppers are fire-roasted over beech wood, hand peeled, and packed in their own juices. Look for jarred or canned piquillo peppers with the Spanish quality control label (denominación de origen) *in gourmet food shops. El Navaricco is a good brand. If you can't find them, substitute small roasted red bell peppers or mild red chiles.*

Pimentón is a flavorful paprika made from smoked piquillo chiles. It is a must for paella, but don't stop there. The secret is out—paprika isn't just for sprinkling on deviled eggs!

SPICY LEMON-BASIL CHICKEN

Chefs excel at combining ingredients in ways that produce layers of flavor that unfold as you eat. This chicken starts out bright with lemon and salty-briny capers. Then you notice the flavors underneath: garlic, honey, and toasty nuts. In between, the basil and chiles keep the dish full of flavor, from the first impression until long after swallowing. It's a simple recipe that makes for a special experience.

Makes 4 servings

What to Drink: A perfumed fiano di Avellino from Italy's Campania region will harmonize nicely with the chiles and lemon.

⅓ **cup pine nuts**

2 **tablespoons dried currants**

4 **medium boneless, skinless half chicken breasts (about 10 ounces each)**

2 **tablespoons extra-virgin olive oil, plus extra for the pan**

½ **cup fresh lemon juice**

1 **tablespoon minced garlic**

2 **teaspoons honey**

½ **to 1 teaspoon red chile flakes, to taste**

Kosher salt and freshly ground black pepper

1 **tablespoon capers, rinsed and drained**

1 **tablespoon unsalted butter**

¼ **cup fresh basil leaves, roughly chopped**

1. Preheat the oven to 350°F. Spread the nuts on a baking sheet and toast for about 8 minutes, until fragrant and golden. (Alternatively, you can toast them in a small dry skillet over medium heat.) Set aside to cool. Turn off the oven.

2. Soak the currants in warm water in a small bowl until plump, about 10 minutes. Drain well.

3. Put the chicken breasts in a gallon-size resealable plastic bag. Add the olive oil, lemon juice, garlic, honey, chile flakes, ½ teaspoon salt, and a few grindings of black pepper. Seal the bag and refrigerate for 30 minutes.

4. Preheat the oven to 375°F. Lightly coat an ovenproof skillet with olive oil and set it over medium heat. Remove the chicken from the bag, reserving the marinade in the bag. Lay the chicken in the skillet top side down (where the skin was) and sear for about 2 minutes. Transfer the skillet to the oven and cook until the chicken is just cooked through, about 10 minutes, depending on the size of the breasts. They should feel firm but have a little give when you press them with your finger. Transfer the chicken to a plate and drape loosely with foil to keep it warm.

5. Return the pan to medium-high heat and pour in the reserved marinade from the bag. Stir in the currants, capers, pine nuts, and butter. Simmer for a couple of minutes until the flavors are well blended and the sauce is slightly reduced. Return the chicken to the pan, turning the breasts in the sauce to coat. Stir in the chopped basil.

6. Place the chicken breasts presentation side up on four warmed plates. Spoon the sauce over the chicken, carefully distributing all the goodies with the flavorful sauce.

DON'T HOLD BACK ▪ EXPLORE NEW FOODS

Capers are a great way to add a bright high note to a dish. These immature flower buds are either pickled in vinegar or coated in salt. Their piquant-pungent, mustardy taste makes them a great accent flavor. Most commonly associated with the Mediterranean, where you will find capers used in many dishes, the bushy flowering plant also grows along the Atlantic Ocean and the Caspian Sea and the Black Sea. In antiquity, the Greeks and Romans are said to have used the berries for medicinal purposes, and we now know that they are high in bioflavonoids and antioxidants and, most important, in flavor. Capers are graded by their size, with the smallest, called nonpareils, considered the best. When I can find them, I prefer salt-packed capers for their full flavor and firm texture. Be sure to soak and drain them before using to remove excess salt, and watch the additional salt in the dish. Rinse and drain capers packed in vinegar before using.

DON'T HOLD BACK ▪ MAKE IT YOURS

A swirl of steaming spaghetti squash makes a pretty and tasty base for this dish. Cut the squash in half lengthwise, lay cut side down on an oiled baking sheet, and bake in a preheated 350°F oven until the inside is tender and can be easily pulled into strands with a fork, about 1 hour. Use a fork to pull apart the strands of squash, place in a bowl, then toss with butter, salt, and freshly ground black pepper to taste. Mound a swirl of the squash in the center of the plate and top with a chicken breast. Spoon the sauce over the chicken, drizzling it over the squash as well.

Baked sweet potatoes, such as the deep orange ones labeled "garnet yams," are another good option as a base for this dish. Scrape the cooked potatoes from their shells and use a fork to smash them with butter, salt, and pepper to taste.

TAMARIND-PECAN CHICKEN with DRIED CHERRIES

I first came upon whole tamarind pods on a shopping excursion in San Francisco's Mission district. Before that I had seen tamarind only in blocks or in jars of paste. Excited by my discovery, I brought some home to try. In this recipe I use the paste to make a tangy-fruity dressing to complement the sweet-tart dried cherries and crunchy toasted pecans in this nut-crusted chicken.

Makes 4 servings

What to Drink: A medium-bodied syrah or zinfandel will complement the tamarind and cherries. A pinot noir with bright cherry flavors is another good choice.

½ cup dried Bing or other sweet cherries

1 cup fresh orange juice

½ cup honey

½ cup cider vinegar

¼ cup Laxmi brand tamarind concentrate or 2 tablespoons tamarind paste dissolved in 2 tablespoons water (see "Explore New Foods")

2 tablespoons minced garlic

2 tablespoons minced shallots

4 medium boneless, skinless half chicken breasts (about 10 ounces each)

⅔ cup pecans, chopped medium-fine

¼ cup extra-virgin olive oil

4 cups tightly packed baby spinach, rinsed and spun dry

½ small red onion, quartered and cut into thin slices

Salt and freshly ground black pepper

1. Preheat the oven to 400°F with a rack set in the lower third of the oven. Soak the cherries in 1 cup warm water in a small bowl for 15 minutes, until plump. Drain well and set aside.

2. In a nonreactive saucepan over medium heat, stir together the orange juice, honey, vinegar, tamarind, garlic, and shallots. Simmer until the mixture is reduced by half, about 20 minutes, depending on the heat and size of the pot. Pour ½ cup of the tamarind glaze into a separate bowl and use it to brush the top (skin) side of the chicken breasts liberally. Let the rest of the glaze cool. Sprinkle the pecans generously over the glaze, pressing them gently to adhere.

3. Heat a large skillet over medium-high heat until it is very hot. Coat with 1 tablespoon olive oil, then place the chicken breasts into the pan pecan side up. Transfer the pan to the oven and cook until the nuts are golden brown and the chicken is cooked through, about 10 minutes. Let rest about 5 minutes before slicing the breasts crosswise on a 45-degree angle into about 5 pieces each. Drape the chicken loosely with foil to keep it warm.

4. In a large salad bowl, toss the spinach with enough of the reserved glaze to coat well. Just before serving, sauté the onions and drained cherries in the remaining 3 tablespoons olive oil over high heat until the onions soften and just begin to color. Immediately pour the hot mixture, including all the oil, over the spinach. Toss well to wilt the greens slightly. Season to taste with salt and pepper and drizzle in additional olive oil, if you like.

5. To serve, mound the spinach in the center of each of four plates and fan slices of one chicken breast half over each. Drizzle the chicken with any remaining glaze.

DON'T HOLD BACK ■ EXPLORE NEW FOODS

Tamarind adds a mysterious and alluring sweet-tart flavor to a dish. The tropical tamarind tree is an evergreen native to Africa, and the fruit is used widely in Asian, Latin American, Indian, and Caribbean cooking. What you are after is the soft pulp found alongside the hard seeds (discard these) inside large brown pods. The pulp is sour and acidic before it ripens and sweeter though still tart once ripe. Tamarind gives Worcestershire sauce its characteristic tang.

Look for tamarind in East Indian and Asian markets, where it can be found in jars of concentrated pulp (look for one without seeds), canned paste, dried bricks, or as a powder. To use the brick variety, cut off about 2 tablespoons' worth and soak it in ½ cup hot tap water until softened, about 30 minutes. Use your hands to break up and squish the pulp with the water to form a loose paste. Discard any seeds or tough fibers. Dissolve thick, sticky tamarind paste from a jar in an equal amount of warm water to soften and dilute it. One of my favorite "convenience foods" is jarred tamarind concentrate (I like Laxmi brand). The soft paste is already mixed with water, so it's ready to use straight from the jar.

QUICK SPICY CASHEW CHICKEN with GINGER-SCALLION RICE

American cooks can be intimidated by the unfamiliar ingredients and techniques used in Chinese restaurants. Actually, high heat, fast wok work, and great ingredients are all it takes to make great Chinese restaurant stir-fries at home.

When I was growing up, and still today, my favorite Chinese restaurant dish was Kung Pao Chicken. Over years of cooking I developed my own version of my favorite dish, substituting cashews for the classic peanuts. By making this dish at home, you, too, can have it your way.

Makes 4 servings

What to Drink: Beer is the perfect companion to this spicy, flavorful dish.

2 tablespoons hoisin sauce

2 tablespoons oyster sauce

2 teaspoons toasted sesame oil

1 teaspoon Chinese chili paste

3 to 4 tablespoons vegetable oil

1 pound boneless, skinless chicken, cut into 1-inch cubes (see "Chef's Tip")

½ small yellow onion, cut into 1-inch pieces (about ½ cup)

2 ribs celery, cut into ½-inch dice (about ½ cup)

½ cup roasted unsalted cashews

1 tablespoon minced garlic

A handful of cilantro leaves, coarsely chopped, or 1 scallion, sliced very thin on a sharp diagonal, for garnish

Ginger-Scallion Rice (page 232)

CHEF'S TIP

Thigh and leg meat are the most juicy, flavorful parts of the chicken, and also the least expensive. If you prefer breast meat, that works just as well here.

1. Stir together the hoisin sauce, oyster sauce, sesame oil, and chili paste in a small bowl. Set aside.

2. Heat a wok or skillet over medium-high heat. Add 2 tablespoons of the vegetable oil and the chicken. Leave the chicken for a minute or so to allow it to sear against the hot pan. Once the chicken easily releases, use a wok paddle or spatula to stir-fry another minute. Transfer the chicken to a plate.

3. Add 1 tablespoon of the vegetable oil to the pan along with the onions, celery, cashews, and garlic. Stir-fry until crisp-tender, about 2 minutes, adding more oil if needed. Add the sauce mixture and the chicken. Continue to stir-fry until the chicken is cooked through and the sauce thickens, 3 to 4 minutes longer.

4. To serve, mound the ginger-scallion rice in the center of a large platter or four warm dinner plates. Top with the chicken and sprinkle the cilantro over the top.

CHICKEN SALTIMBOCCA with BEURRE BLANC

I've borrowed the filling from veal saltimbocca, breaded the chicken à la cordon bleu, and then topped it all with a rich butter sauce. When you cut into the chicken, fontina cheese gently oozes out, carrying the aroma of prosciutto and sage along with it. It is very good even without the sauce.

Saltimbocca is Italian for "jumps in the mouth." You'll see that it's not at all difficult to reinvent a classic—or two—at home.

Makes 6 servings

What to Drink: The warm, Mediterranean climate of Italy's Umbria region gives Orvieto an earthy character that is perfect for this dish.

6 skinless, boneless half chicken breasts (about 10 ounces each)

6 thin slices fontina cheese (about 4 ounces)

6 paper-thin slices prosciutto (about 6 ounces)

12 fresh sage leaves, plus extra, for optional garnish

1 cup all-purpose flour

2 large eggs beaten lightly with 2 tablespoons milk

1½ cups panko or other bread crumbs

¼ cup freshly grated Parmesan cheese

Salt and freshly ground black pepper

3 tablespoons olive oil, plus extra for the optional sage leaves, if using

3 tablespoons unsalted butter

Parmesan Polenta (page 238)

Beurre Blanc (page 194)

Chopped flat-leaf parsley, for garnish (optional)

1. Pound each piece of chicken with a mallet to make a ¼- to ½-inch-thick rectangle. On one half of each piece, lay a slice of fontina, a slice of prosciutto, and 2 sage leaves. Fold the chicken in half to enclose the filling, pressing down to seal.

2. Put the flour, beaten eggs, and bread crumbs into three separate pie pans or broad shallow bowls and line them up in that order, left to right. Stir the Parmesan into the bread crumbs. Lightly season the flour with salt and pepper. Set a plate to the right of the pans to receive the breaded chicken.

3. Dredge each stuffed chicken breast in the flour, being careful not to lose the filling. Pat to shake off excess flour. Keeping one hand dry, use the other to dip each breast into the egg wash, then place the breast on top of the bread crumbs. Use your dry hand

to press bread crumbs onto both sides of the chicken. Place the breaded breast on the plate and repeat with the remaining chicken.

4. Let the breaded chicken rest for about 10 minutes or refrigerate, covered, for up to 2 hours. The three-step coating technique, along with the short rest, are the keys to a crust that stays on the chicken when you cook it.

5. Preheat the oven to 375°F. Combine the olive oil and butter, divide the mixture between two large heavy skillets and place over medium-high heat. (Alternatively, you can do this in two batches.) Add half the chicken to each pan without crowding. Cook until the coating begins to brown, 2 to 3 minutes. Turn and cook for 2 to 3 minutes on the other side.

6. Transfer the chicken to a rimmed baking sheet or pan and bake until the chicken is cooked through and the bread crumbs are golden and crispy, about 10 minutes.

7. If garnishing with the sage leaves, while the chicken is in the oven, heat the extra olive oil in a heavy skillet over medium-high heat until almost smoking. Gently slide in the leaves and press down to submerge them. Fry until they begin to crisp, just a few seconds. Carefully lift them out with tongs or a slotted spoon and drain on a plate lined with paper towels. They will crisp further as they cool.

8. To serve, mound the Parmesan polenta on each of six plates. Slice the chicken in half on a diagonal and place the two halves in opposite directions over the polenta. Spoon the beurre blanc over the chicken, drizzling a little onto the plates. Garnish with fried sage or chopped parsley, as desired.

DON'T HOLD BACK ■ EXPLORE NEW FOODS

Everyone loves crunch, and chefs know that bread-crumb coatings are a great way to make food crunchy without deep frying. The Japanese-style coating known as panko is prized by chefs for its light, crispy texture. It's made by grinding fresh bread and then drying it, rather than drying the bread first. The small shards make for a dramatic presentation and a satisfying crunch.

ROASTED DUCK with GINGER-ORANGE GLAZE

When my mom told me she wanted to be a guest on my show, I asked her, "What will you do?" Expecting some wacky concoction of cottage cheese, pineapple, and avocado that has become her form of South Florida Condo Cookery, she surprised me by replying, "Duck à l'Orange." When I asked her what she knew about this classic French preparation, she assured me she was quite familiar with it, having made it on many occasions. In fact, she insisted, I have had her duck dish and I liked it.

Turns out she knew what she was doing! My mother reintroduced me to that classic combination of duck and orange and I have not looked back. This version has my own spin: the addition of ginger. I love the way its bright, tangy flavor synchronizes with the orange to complement the duck's richness.

Crisp mahogany skin is everything when it comes to restaurant-quality roasted duck. The key is helping the bird release the thick layer of fat resting beneath its skin. Restaurant kitchens have many ways to do this, most of which are difficult, messy, or dangerous in a home kitchen. This recipe shows you how to turn out a reliably restaurant-crisp duck easily in your home kitchen. Give it a try.

Makes 4 servings

What to Drink: Pinot noir offers body and earthy flavors to stand up to the duck with enough acidity to balance the rich meat.

1 fresh or thawed frozen Long Island (Pekin) duck, 5 to 6 pounds

Kosher salt and freshly ground black pepper

Ginger-Orange Glaze (page 196)

2 tablespoons chicken broth

2 tablespoons (¼ stick) unsalted butter

CHEF'S TIP

Make the glaze while the duck roasts. Brushing it on after the duck is partially cooked assures that the sugars don't burn with the long roasting.

1. Preheat the oven to 350°F with an oven rack set in the lower third. Line a rimmed baking sheet with foil and place a metal rack (an ovenproof cake rack works well) over the foil.

2. Remove the duck neck and giblets and set aside for another use. (I like to sauté the liver as a chef's treat.) Remove any large pockets and flaps of fat from around the tail and neck ends. Pluck out any remaining feathers. Score or prick the duck all over using a sharp paring knife, being careful to penetrate the fat but not the meat. (See "Step Up Your Skills," page 154.)

3. Put the duck onto the rack breast side up. Season all over with salt and pepper. Roast for 90 minutes. If you see a lot of fat collecting on the foil, carefully remove the pan from the oven and spoon off as much fat as you easily can. (An empty can works well; discard it after the fat cools and solidifies.)

4. Simmer ¼ cup of the ginger-orange glaze with the broth and butter in a small saucepan over medium heat until it is slightly reduced, about 5 minutes. Set aside the remaining glaze to serve with the duck.

5. After 90 minutes, increase the oven temperature to 425°F and remove the duck from the oven. Brush the duck all over with the reduced glaze, then return it to the oven. Baste again after 15 minutes, then continue to roast until the skin is brown and crispy all over, 15 to 30 minutes longer. (Total roasting time will be 2 to 2¼ hours.) A meat thermometer should register 150°F when you insert it deeply into the thickest part of the leg without touching the bone. Transfer the duck to a carving board and let rest for 10 minutes before carving.

6. Carve the duck, place it on a platter, and serve the remaining glaze on the side.

DON'T HOLD BACK ■ MAKE IT YOURS

This basic roasted duck is meant to be a launching point for your creativity. Once you are comfortable roasting a duck, you can experiment with a variety of glazes and rubs. Some of my favorite rubs are Chinese five-spice, Cajun, or garlic and thyme. When using a rub, apply it after scoring the skin, then refrigerate the duck with the rub for 2 to 3 hours before roasting.

To prepare a duck for roasting, begin by cutting off any large pockets of fat. You'll find most of them near the two ends of the bird. Most of the feathers should have already been removed, but if you see any, you can grab them with a tweezers or needle-nose pliers. Pat the duck dry with paper towels. I don't truss my duck as I would a chicken.

Getting the duck to render as much of its fat as possible is the key to crispy skin. To help make that happen, you will want to cut through the skin and fat, stopping short of the flesh. I do this by scoring the skin in a crosshatch pattern. I start by cutting across one side of the breast with a sharp thin-bladed knife, making parallel cuts about 1/2 inch apart on a diagonal, starting at the tail end and moving toward the head. I then go back and cut across those cuts in a crosshatch pattern. Then I repeat the same thing on the other side. Finally, make cuts under the wings and on the thighs, where the duck tends to be fattiest.

If that all sounds like too much trouble, try polka dots instead of plaid. Just prick the duck all over with a fork or the tip of a sharp knife.

To carve the roasted duck, begin with the breast side up. Use a thin-bladed, sharp knife to cut down alongside the center bone until you reach the wishbone, then along the wishbone to one side. Continue to slide your knife, scraping it against the bone on the underside of the breast, until you can easily pull the breast from the bone. Repeat with the other breast.

Slice each breast on a diagonal into 4 to 5 pieces, about 1/2 inch thick.

Turn the duck over and cut out the oyster, that tender piece of meat near the leg end. Cut around the hip joint to release the leg and thigh. Leave together or cut the 2 pieces apart.

Fan the breast pieces out on a serving platter, then place the leg and thigh pieces beside them.

CONFIT DUCK with KABOCHA SQUASH SPAETZLE

Confit is French for "conserved." The term is used for preserving meat (most often duck) by cooking and storing it in its own fat. It is also used for fruits and vegetables conserved by cooking them with sugar until they are like a jam. Before refrigeration, the French used the technique for preservation, but we continue to use it for the incredibly tender and succulent meat it produces.

Curing and brining are favorite chefs' tricks for infusing flavor deeply into dense meats like duck. When the duck is then cooked in plentiful fat, the result is succulent, fall-off-the-bone texture, intense flavor, and duck meat that is preserved well enough to last a week or longer in the refrigerator for use in a variety of recipes. You can vary the curing process with other flavors, such as Chinese five-spice powder, Creole spices, dried chiles, or maple syrup.

The curing process keeps the meat moist and pink at the center, even after it is fully cooked. In this recipe, we allow 4 hours in the spice mixture so you can prepare and cook the duck the same day. If you have the time, cure it in the spice mixture for 24 to 48 hours for more intense flavor, cutting the salt in half to prevent the meat from getting too salty.

Once the duck fat is cool but still liquid, you can strain it to save in your refrigerator almost indefinitely to use again. The fat has a great flavor and many chefs love to sauté or fry with it, especially potatoes.

You may want to double the recipe and use the meat in other recipes, such as the Duck Cannelloni with Porcini Marsala Sauce (page 109). Just discard the skin and pull the meat from the bones with two forks or your fingers. If refrigerating the meat for longer than a day or two, cover it with the rendered fat to help preserve it.

Makes 6 servings

What to Drink: A lighter-bodied pinot noir will complement the duck's cured, slightly gamy flavors while also working with the sweetness of the squash.

2 tablespoons black peppercorns

1 tablespoon juniper berries

⅓ cup kosher salt

¼ cup sugar

2 tablespoons dried thyme

3 bay leaves, torn into a few pieces

6 duck leg-thigh quarters, trimmed of excess fat

Kabocha Squash Spaetzle (page 115)

1. Use the back of a skillet or the side of a cleaver to crush the peppercorns and juniper berries a bit to release their flavor. Combine them in a small bowl with the salt, sugar, thyme, and bay leaves. Sprinkle the mixture liberally on both sides of the duck legs, stacking the legs in a pan or bowl. Cover and refrigerate for 4 hours, or up to 48 hours. (If curing for more than 12 hours, reduce the salt to 3 tablespoons.)

2. When you are ready to cook the duck, preheat the oven to 300°F. Rinse the duck well, pat dry, and arrange in a single layer in a 2- to 3-inch-deep roasting pan. Cover with foil and bake for 2 hours. The duck is done when you can see about an inch and a half of the drumstick bone exposed, with the skin shrunk back. The meat should be very tender.

3. Carefully remove the pan from the oven and set on a heatproof surface to cool. When they are cool enough to handle, transfer the legs to a plate, taking care not to tear or push off the tender skin.

4. About 20 minutes before serving, preheat the oven to 450°F. Transfer as many duck legs as you will be serving skin side up to a nonstick ovenproof skillet, adding about a teaspoon of the rendered duck fat per leg. Roast in the oven until the skin is crispy, 15 to 20 minutes. (Alternatively, you can crisp the legs skin side down in the skillet over medium-high heat. Let the duck stand in the pan a few minutes off the heat before gently sliding a spatula underneath the skin to release it from the pan.)

5. To serve family style, mound the kabocha squash spaetzle on a large platter and top with the duck legs. Or plate individually, with the spaetzle in the center of the plate and a duck leg on top, falling to one side. I like to accompany the rich duck with something spiced and fruity, like my Apple-Mango Chutney (page 209).

COCOA-CHILE–RUBBED DUCK BREAST with CITRUS-MANGO SALSA

Chocolate, or more precisely cocoa, has been used in savory cooking since its discovery thousands of years ago. Its distinctive, sweet-earthy flavor adds an exotic nuance to savory foods. In this recipe, cocoa adds depth and richness to the spice blend.

For the most flavorful and aromatic rub, toast and grind the cumin seeds just before using them. (See "Step Up Your Skills," page 160.) If you can't find ancho chile powder, or to vary the flavor, substitute another mild to mildly hot, pure ground chile such as pasilla, guajillo, or red New Mexico varieties. If you use a super hot variety like chile de arbol or habañero, cut the quantity in half or less, depending on your heat tolerance. The Sweet Potato Purée (page 228) makes a great accompaniment.

Makes 4 to 6 servings

What to Drink: A medium-bodied pinot noir or syrah will have berry-cherry fruit flavors and spice to match this dish, along with earthiness to complement the cocoa and duck.

2 tablespoons unsweetened cocoa powder, preferably natural

2 tablespoons ancho chile powder

Kosher salt

1 teaspoon cumin seeds, toasted and ground

1 teaspoon garlic powder

Freshly ground black pepper

½ teaspoon cayenne pepper

4 boneless, skin-on Long Island (Pekin) half duck breasts (about 8 ounces each)

1 tablespoon extra-virgin olive oil, plus more for coating arugula

4 ounces arugula or watercress (4 big handfuls), rinsed and spun dry

Sea salt

Citrus-Mango Salsa (page 208)

1. Preheat the oven to 400°F.

2. Stir together the cocoa, chile powder, 2 teaspoons salt, the cumin, garlic powder, 1 teaspoon black pepper, and the cayenne in a small bowl.

3. If the duck is joined as whole breasts, cut each apart to make 4 separate pieces. Trim excess fat and score the skin with a sharp knife, making parallel cuts about ½ inch apart that go into the skin without cutting into the flesh. Make a second set of parallel cuts across the first to create a crosshatch pattern. Rub both sides of the duck breasts liberally with the cocoa-chile rub and set aside.

4. Heat 1 tablespoon olive oil in a large ovenproof skillet over medium heat. Lay in the breasts skin side down and cook until the skin renders its fat and turns golden brown, about 10 minutes. Leave the duck in one place during this time to allow it to form a crust that stays with the meat rather than sticking to the pan.

5. If too much fat has collected in the pan, transfer the duck to a plate and carefully pour off the fat into a heatproof container. Discard or save for another use. (I love it for sautéing potatoes.) Return the duck breasts to the skillet skin side down.

6. Put the skillet in the oven until the meat is medium rare and has an internal temperature of 140°F at the center of the breast, 4 to 6 minutes. (You may prefer to follow the USDA recommendation of cooking the duck to 170°F, but it won't be medium rare.) Remove from the oven and let rest in the skillet for 5 minutes.

7. Just before serving, toss the arugula with olive oil to lightly coat. Season with salt and pepper. Mound the arugula on six plates. Place the duck skin side down on a cutting board and slice crosswise at a 45-degree angle into thin strips. Fan about two thirds of a duck breast over the arugula and sprinkle lightly with sea salt. Tuck a large spoonful of the citrus-mango salsa next to the duck and serve the rest on the side.

DON'T HOLD BACK ■ STEP UP YOUR SKILLS

Spices are at their best when they are fresh. That means purchasing them in small quantities, storing them away from heat and light (beside the stove is not a good place!), and replacing them frequently. The same thing goes for toasted spices: For the best flavor, toast and grind them shortly before using.

A coffee grinder set aside only for spices is a convenient way to easily grind spices as you need them. To clean it, whirl a piece of fresh bread in the grinder after using it. The bread will collect all the remaining spice dust. Unless you like curried coffee, save your coffee grinder for coffee only.

To toast the spices, place them in a small dry skillet and shake gently over medium heat until you begin to smell their fragrance. Transfer to a small plate to cool.

MEAT MATTERS

GOOD RESTAURANT-STYLE COOKING is all about building layers of flavor that translate to simple pleasure in your mouth. Because of its big taste, meat is the perfect backdrop for layering flavors.

Meats with some fat generally taste best. That's because flavoring compounds are absorbed more readily into fat, making them accessible to your smell and taste receptors. Cook something in fat and you will immediately notice its great aroma, much more so than if you boil it in water, which tends to repel flavor molecules. Heat makes proteins contract, squeezing out moisture and making them dry. Fat helps to keep meat moist as it cooks. Unless you're on a doctor-prescribed diet, if you eat meat in moderation, don't worry too much about a little fat. Once it has done its job of helping the meat browning process and flavoring your food, you can drain or cut most of it away if you don't want to eat it. Or eat a smaller portion—flavor and fat, not quantity, are what make food satisfying!

One way to give meat flavor is by browning it. When meat hits heat, proteins on its surface combine with sugars naturally in the meat to turn the surface brown. The browning process creates all sorts of flavors and aromas. That's why the outside of a piece of meat often tastes best.

Although different types of meat have much in common, pork, beef, and lamb each has its own particular charms, which affect the ways chefs use them.

PORK has a naturally mild, meaty flavor that can be smoky or earthy, and it's a perfect match with sweet and spicy flavors. Many chefs consider pork among the most versatile of meats, and I agree.

Pork is easy to work with. People are often afraid of cooking it at home because of its reputation as a fatty meat. But these days I find pork is often too lean. I actually recommend choosing cuts with a little more fat to assure good flavor.

Small farms around the country are now raising heritage hogs—such as the marbled Kurobuta from Japanese Black Berkshire pigs—bred for their fattier, more flavorful meat. Although these breeds may cost more, chefs often choose them for their great taste, texture, and contribution to a sustainable food system that supports small local farms and ranches.

Beyond the pork recipes in this chapter, you'll find pork products used in other recipes throughout the book as an accent or flavor enhancer. Ask a chef how to make a dish taste better and I bet you that he or she will often say, "Add bacon!" Once you're used to cooking with pork, you, too, will be looking for new ways to add its alluring flavor to other recipes.

LAMB has a distinctive earthy flavor that some call gamy. I call it enticing. Whatever you call it, you will want to use this quality to your advantage by harmonizing it with ingredients that bring out its natural hearty flavor. I pair some of the boldest flavors with lamb, which can stand up to flavor combinations drawn from Middle Eastern, African, and Mediterranean cuisines.

BEEF falls between the adaptable canvas of pork and the assertive flavor of lamb. Make beef the predominant flavor in a dish and use sauces and side dishes to balance and embellish it. The meat itself doesn't require much manipulation. That's why you see steak on so many menus.

For the best flavor, look for beef from animals raised on a reputable ranch. In the finished dish, you will taste not only the meat, but also the diet the cattle was raised on. Grass-fed beef has a distinctive flavor and can sometimes be a little less tender than beef from cattle raised on corn or grain, but it is improving and gaining in popularity. As with cheese, the taste may even vary with the seasons. Some farmers raise their cattle on grass, then finish with corn for added fat and flavor. To support sustainable agriculture, I buy beef from small local farms.

Whatever meat you buy, search out purveyors who shy away from hormones and additives. If they raise their animals on organic feed, so much the better. The clean flavor of good meat will shine through.

PORK CHOPS with PORT-GLAZED FIGS and APPLES

Sometimes one element makes all the difference in a dish. Because pork is one of the mildest meats, it makes an ideal canvas for layering flavors. The pork sets the stage, but while it contributes its own flavor, it doesn't dominate the others. Pork is especially at home with sweet flavors. The sweet and savory combination of figs, apples, and long-cooked onions illustrates the point. This recipe introduces grains of paradise, the peppery seeds of a plant in the ginger family. Here, it adds another nuance to the ginger, while contributing its own aromatic flavor when ground in a pepper mill over the pork just before serving.

Paired with Sweet Potato Purée (page 228), this dish is my idea of elegant comfort food. The ginger in the fruit and potatoes creates a harmonious pairing.

I like Fuji apples in this dish for their firm texture and sweet-tart flavor, but you can substitute another variety with similar attributes. In California, we're blessed with abundant fresh figs that start in summer and follow with a second crop in fall. They add a hint of sweetness and concentrated flavor that make this dish addictive. Use whatever variety that's in season locally–dark purple Missions, Kadotas with their green skins and ruby-hued flesh, or the super size Brown Turkey. The figs should be ripe but not so soft that they will fall apart. Add softer figs closer to the end of the cooking time.

Port's ripe and dried-fruit flavors blend naturally with figs. Use something you would drink, but save your vintage Port for sipping after dinner. If figs aren't in season, reconstitute dried figs in the Port before adding them to the sauce.

Makes 6 servings

What to Drink: This dish offers many possibilities for pairing. A medium-bodied pinot noir will bring out the roasted flavors in the pork and caramelized fruit, while a zinfandel or syrah will stand up to the robust flavors.

6 bone-in, double-cut pork chops, approximately 1½ inches thick

Kosher salt and freshly ground black pepper

3 tablespoons extra-virgin olive oil

3 firm medium apples, peeled and cored

2 tablespoons (¼ stick) unsalted butter

1 tablespoon light brown sugar

2 tablespoons minced shallots or red onions

2 tablespoons finely chopped fresh ginger

1 pint fresh figs, stemmed and cut in half

1 cup chicken broth

1 cup ruby Port

¼ cup chopped chives or scallions

½ teaspoon grains of paradise (optional)

1. Season the pork chops liberally with salt and pepper. Heat half of the olive oil in a large skillet over medium-high heat. Cook half of the chops until well browned, 8 to 10 minutes per side, depending on their size. Transfer the chops to a plate and drape loosely with foil to keep them warm. Repeat with the remaining oil and chops. Drain off and discard the oil that has collected in the pan.

2. Cut the apples into large wedges, about 8 per apple. Return the skillet to medium heat, melt the butter, then stir in the brown sugar, scraping up any bits from the bottom of the pan. Add the apples and cook until they brown lightly, 1 to 2 minutes. Add the shallots, ginger, and figs and cook, stirring, for 2 minutes more. Add the stock and Port and simmer until reduced by half, about 15 minutes.

3. To serve, place a pork chop in the center of each plate and top with a few pieces of apple and fig. Drizzle with a few spoonfuls of the sauce, garnish with chives, and grind the grains of paradise, if using, in a spice grinder or pepper mill over the apples and figs just before serving.

DON'T HOLD BACK ■ MAKE IT YOURS

As you become more attuned to the blending and layering of flavors and learn the combinations that please you, you can begin to trust your palate and add variety to your meals. That's when cooking gets to be fun. In this recipe, consider substituting another fruit for the apples or figs: Fresh peaches or nectarines, for example, would add their characteristic sweet-aromatic flavors. Or play with the spices—consider swapping a cinnamon stick and a piece of vanilla bean for the ginger, or throw in a couple of star anise pods or Szechuan peppercorns as you begin to simmer the sauce for an exotic Asian accent. Strain out the spices before serving.

If you have the time, give the dish a flavor boost: Brine the pork chops before cooking them. In a large bowl or heavy resealable plastic bag, combine 2 quarts water, ½ cup kosher salt, and ½ cup granulated sugar. Add aromatics—I like a teaspoon of freshly ground black pepper, 2 bay leaves, ¼ cup fresh thyme sprigs, and a table-spoon of juniper berries. Or add subtle Asian nuances with star anise and sliced ginger. Stir to dissolve the sugar and salt, then submerge the pork chops in the brine, cover the bowl or seal the bag, and refrigerate for 1 hour. Pat the chops dry before cooking.

CHINESE BBQ SPARERIBS with SWEET and SPICY GINGER BBQ SAUCE

Since I was a kid, Chinese restaurant barbecued ribs have been my favorite "finger-lickin' good" food. Eventually, I couldn't resist the urge to try to replicate them in my own kitchen. The trick lies in a mélange of ingredients that comes together in just the right sweet-spicy balance for a compelling sauce that's not cloying, and in which no one flavor sticks out as dominant. With the formula uncovered, there's nothing at all difficult about making these at home.

Makes 4 appetizer servings or 2 entrée servings

What to Drink: Try a bold, earthy-spicy red wine such as an Australian shiraz or a California zinfandel. Too much tannin will clash with the spicy sauce.

2 tablespoons sesame seeds, for garnish (optional)

One 2-pound rack center-cut pork spareribs (ask your butcher to remove the membrane known as the fell from the inside of the rib bones)

Kosher salt and freshly ground black pepper

⅓ cup minced scallions

2 tablespoons minced fresh ginger

Sweet and Spicy Ginger BBQ Sauce (page 197)

1. Preheat the oven to 350°F with a rack positioned near the center. Line a rimmed baking sheet with foil and place a metal rack (an ovenproof cake rack works well) over the foil.

2. If using, spread the sesame seeds on a small baking sheet and toast for about 10 minutes, until fragrant and golden. (Alternatively, you can toast them in a small dry skillet over medium heat.) Set aside to cool.

3. Season the ribs lightly all over with salt and pepper. Place them on the rack meat side up and drape a sheet of foil over them. Bake until the meat begins to shrink back from the rib bones, 1½ to 1¾ hours, depending on the size of the ribs. Remove from the oven and set aside until the ribs are cool enough to handle.

4. Turn up the oven to 450°F (you will need it again soon).

5. Flip the ribs over and cut between them to make individual pieces. Remove the rack from the pan. If oil has collected on the foil liner, drain it off and discard. Place the ribs back onto the foil-lined sheet, pour half of the ginger BBQ sauce over them, and gently toss to evenly coat them. Spread out the ribs in a single layer and bake, uncovered, until nicely glazed, 10 to 12 minutes.

6. Place the ribs on a platter and scatter the scallions and ginger over them. Sprinkle with the toasted sesame seeds, if using. Serve the remaining sauce on the side.

SPICY MAPLE-GLAZED PORK TENDERLOIN with APPLE-MANGO CHUTNEY

I created this recipe for a caribou loin I was grilling in the snowy Minnesota wilderness after an afternoon of dogsledding. We were taping my Food Network show *Appetite for Adventure,* and we were showing our audience how to enjoy gourmet food in the great outdoors. I developed a sauce that was sweet but not cloying to tame the caribou's gamy flavor. Maple syrup seemed like the natural choice in this setting. I balanced the sweetness with spicy serrano chiles, red chile flakes, and ginger for a savory impression.

Not a lot of people cook caribou, so I translated the recipe to pork for my restaurant.

Makes 6 servings

What to Drink:
A gewürztraminer will complement the spicy glaze and tropical chutney, while a medium-bodied pinot noir will harmonize with the rich meat.

1 cup real maple syrup

2 tablespoons minced fresh ginger

1 large garlic clove, minced

¼ teaspoon red chile flakes

3 pounds boneless pork tenderloin, cut into 6 pieces, about 8 ounces each

Kosher salt and freshly ground black pepper

Canola or olive oil to coat the pan

½ cup veal stock or beef or chicken broth

4 tablespoons (½ stick) unsalted butter

Steamed, buttered spaghetti squash (optional)

Apple-Mango Chutney (page 209)

1. To make the glaze, in a deep medium-large nonreactive saucepan, stir together the maple syrup, ginger, garlic, and chile flakes. Bring to a simmer over medium heat, taking care not to let the mixture boil over. Continue to simmer gently until the glaze is reduced to approximately 1 cup, about 10 minutes. Remove from the heat, cover, and set aside.

2. Preheat the oven to 425°F. Lightly season the pork with salt and pepper. Heat about 1 tablespoon canola oil over medium-high heat in an ovenproof skillet large enough to hold the meat in one layer (or use two skillets). When the skillet is hot, add the meat and sear on one side, about 2 minutes. Turn the meat, brush liberally with the warm glaze, and place the skillet in the oven until the pork is medium rare, 7 to 10 minutes.

3. Turn the meat again, brush with the glaze, and continue to roast until the meat is pale pink in the center and has an internal temperature of 150°F, about 5 minutes longer. Transfer the tenderloins to a cutting board and drape loosely with foil.

4. Return the skillet to the stove top over medium heat and add the remaining glaze, along with the stock and butter. Whisk to combine as the butter melts, then simmer until the glaze has reduced and thickened. Season to taste with salt and pepper.

5. Slice the tenderloins thin on a diagonal. To serve, fan the tenderloin slices on the plate, or over the spaghetti squash, if using. Drizzle with the sauce and serve the apple-mango chutney on the side.

ANGRY PORK TENDERLOIN with BLACK BEANS and CILANTRO RICE

Restaurants often use marinades and sauces to boost the flavor of meats. Here, the marinade doubles as sauce, saving time in the kitchen. The marinade combines smoky-spicy chipotle chiles in adobo with sweet honey and brown sugar for a kick that sneaks up on you. The sauce is also great as a marinade and sauce for other cuts of pork and for grilled chicken.

This recipe is a lesson in blending Caribbean flavors, the eclectic mix of African, Latin, and Asian cuisines that began to mingle in the Caribbean centuries ago when the region's countries began trading throughout the Caribbean islands. At my Caribbean-inspired San Francisco restaurant, Miss Pearl's Jam House, I learned about the similarities among the flavor profiles of these cuisines that allowed them to merge so easily. Many chefs have embraced these equatorial cooking styles, incorporating them into other cuisines from French to Asian.

So, why is the pork angry? Well, how would you feel if you were marinated in a spicy, garlicky, acidic mixture and then grilled?

Makes 6 servings

What to Drink: Negra Modelo beer is a sure bet, but this dish is also good with syrah or other robust red wines. Too much alcohol or oak will fight with the spices.

⅔ cup fresh or "not-from-concentrate" orange juice

½ cup extra-virgin olive oil

3 tablespoons malt vinegar (see "Explore New Foods")

3 tablespoons fresh lime juice

1 tablespoon dark brown sugar

1 tablespoon honey

2 chipotle chiles in adobo plus 1 teaspoon sauce, plus more to taste

1 shallot, coarsely chopped

2 cloves garlic, coarsely chopped

2 teaspoons whole allspice berries or ½ teaspoon ground

2 whole cloves or ¼ teaspoon ground

Kosher salt and freshly ground black pepper

2 boneless pork tenderloins, about 12 ounces each, trimmed of excess fat and silverskin

Joey's Big, Bold Black Beans in Beer (page 239)

Cilantro Rice (page 231)

Salsa Cruda (page 203), sour cream, and warm flour tortillas, for serving (optional)

1. In a nonreactive skillet over medium heat, boil the orange juice to reduce it by half, about 5 minutes. Set aside to cool.

2. Combine the olive oil, vinegar, lime juice, brown sugar, honey, chipotle chiles, adobo sauce, shallots, garlic, allspice, cloves, 2 teaspoons salt, and ½ teaspoon pepper in a blender or food processor. Add the orange juice and purée until smooth. (If large spice pieces remain, strain before proceeding.) Season to taste with additional salt and pepper, as well as more chipotle or adobo for a spicier dish.

3. Arrange the tenderloins in a large baking dish and pour about one third of the marinade over them to coat them generously. Set aside the remaining marinade to use as a sauce for the finished dish. Let the meat stand for 1 hour at room temperature. Meanwhile, preheat a grill to medium-high or preheat the oven to 400°F.

4. Grill the tenderloins or bake them, turning every few minutes, until they are cooked to your preferred doneness–8 to 10 minutes on the grill or 20 to 30 minutes in the oven for medium, depending on the size of the tenderloins.

5. Allow the meat to rest for 10 minutes before cutting on a diagonal into ½-inch-thick medallions.

6. Serve the sliced tenderloins with the black beans, cilantro rice, and the remaining marinade. Serve bowls of salsa and sour cream, and a plate of warm tortillas as accompaniments, if you wish.

DON'T HOLD BACK ▪ EXPLORE NEW FOODS

Malt vinegar is a light amber vinegar made from malted barley. It has a lemony flavor favored by the British, who serve it with fish and chips. Look for it in the condiment aisle of your grocery store, or substitute white wine vinegar or lemon juice.

You can find chipotle chiles in adobo sauce (see page 10) in cans in the Latin foods section of many grocery stores. If you can't find them, substitute two dried chipotle chiles, toasted and seeded, and add ¼ cup water to the marinade.

YUCATÁN PORK STEW

One foggy San Francisco day, a young Scottish chef walked into my kitchen at Miss Pearl's Jam House. He was travel-working his way around the globe in search of adventure and experience. Many chefs had opened their kitchen doors to me when I was training, and I was happy to return the favor. The chef had just come up from the Yucatán, so when he offered to make the staff meal one day, he grabbed some pork shoulder and made this stew. It was such a hit with the crew that we soon featured it as a special. It's a recurring star today at my family get-togethers.

This recipe shows how simple techniques can lead to intricate flavors. Orange juice adds an elusive sweet-tangy aromatic note that combines beautifully with the bitterness of the beer and the heat of the chiles. Served over a steaming bowl of Corn Mash, this is the ultimate comfort food. The meat chunks are fork-tender and the polenta absorbs the rich juices.

Makes 6 servings

What to Drink: Choose a dry rosé or an albariño, pinot grigio, pinot blanc, or gewürztraminer. Or try a lighter red such as a pinot noir or Beaujolais. Mexican beer is also a good choice.

1 tablespoon canola oil

2½ pounds boned pork shoulder, trimmed and cut into 1-inch cubes

Kosher salt and freshly ground black pepper

1 yellow onion, cut into small dice

5 poblano chiles, seeded and cut into medium dice

1 habañero or 2 jalapeño or serrano chiles, seeded, veins removed, and chopped fine (optional)

10 large garlic cloves, smashed with the back of a knife and roughly chopped (about ½ cup)

1 pound fresh tomatillos, papery husks removed, washed, stemmed, and cut into quarters

1 cup fresh or "not-from-concentrate" orange juice

One 12-ounce bottle Negra Modelo beer or other medium-dark beer

¼ cup cilantro, coarsely chopped, plus sprigs for garnish

Corn Mash variation of The Art of Polenta (page 238)

1. Preheat the oven to 350°F with a rack positioned near the bottom. In a large heavy ovenproof saucepan over high heat, heat the canola oil until it just begins to smoke. Sear the pork cubes until lightly browned, seasoning them lightly with salt and pepper as they cook. Use tongs to remove the pork to a plate.

CHEF'S TIP

Save on prep time by purchasing peeled (not chopped) garlic cloves in a jar.

2. Add the onions, poblanos, habañero, and garlic, reduce the heat to medium-high, and cook, stirring frequently, to lightly caramelize the onions, about 10 minutes. As the onions exude their liquid, the liquid will soften the flavorful caramelized bits from the meat in the bottom of the pan. Use a wooden spoon to scrape this "love" into the mixture as it cooks.

3. Stir in the tomatillos, orange juice, beer, and a good pinch of salt and pepper. Add back the pork along with any juices that have collected. Bring the mixture to a simmer, stir, then place the saucepan, uncovered, in the oven. Cook until the mixture is thick and soupy, about 2 hours. If the stew is very liquidy, bring it back to the stove top and simmer until the juices have slightly thickened to a stew-like consistency, about 15 minutes. (To make ahead, cool the stew, then cover and refrigerate for up to 2 days. Reheat over medium-low heat or in a preheated 325°F oven.)

4. To serve, stir in the chopped cilantro and season with salt and pepper to taste. Ladle the stew over bowls of corn mash, decorating with a few sprigs of cilantro.

DON'T HOLD BACK ■ EXPLORE NEW FOODS

Poblano chiles are the large, dark green Mexican chiles typically used to make chiles rellenos. They vary widely from mild to hot. Sample them and adjust the type and amount of chiles to suit your taste. In the Yucatán, you might find the blazing hot habañero chile firing up this dish.

Tomatillos are another staple of Mexican cooking. Related to the cape gooseberry,

these small green orbs have a papery skin and sticky coating that are removed before cooking. They soften and release their flavor as they cook, imparting a tart, herbal accent. Purchase tomatillos that are firm and green; when they turn yellow they are past their prime. Look for tomatillos in specialty produce stores and Latin markets.

DRY-AGED STEAKS with SMASHED YUKON POTATOES and BUTTERED LEEKS

A good chef knows that less can be more. Treating a good ingredient simply is sometimes the key to unlocking great flavor. Here, I showcase the meat and vegetables by preparing each simply and combining them in a classic French bistro dish. The steak is front and center with the side dishes in a supporting role.

Bone-in, dry-aged New York strip loin steaks are the favorite of many chefs because of the extra flavor the bone gives to this already flavorful cut. The cut is made tender by fat marbling, and even more so by the aging process. I love them for this recipe.

Dry aging—leaving the meat to hang in a temperature- and humidity-controlled environment with good air circulation—gives the meat's natural enzymes time to break down its tough connective tissue. The controlled evaporation concentrates the meat's flavor while retaining enough moisture to keep it juicy. Chefs love to cook meat on the bone as it gives an extra flavor boost. Dry-aged steak is all the rage at steakhouses these days. The extra time, effort, and evaporation lead to higher costs, but chefs—and their customers—say it's worth it. Another personal favorite? Try this recipe with rib eye, or even bison steaks! Bison has become popular as it is lower in fat, incredibly tender, and flavorful.

The Balsamic-Roasted Mushrooms are a perfect additional accompaniment to this rustic, wintry dish. Yukon Gold potatoes are small, golden, and buttery even before you add butter (which makes them even better!). You can substitute other thin-skinned varieties such as German Butterball or Yellow Finn.

Makes 4 servings

What to Drink: This dish is for that special bottle of earthy cabernet. A Bordeaux blend, aglianico, Barolo, or Burgundy will also work.

1 pound Yukon Gold potatoes, unpeeled, cut in 2 or 3 pieces each if large

4 tablespoons (½ stick) unsalted butter

2 tablespoons extra-virgin olive oil

½ cup sour cream

¼ to ½ cup whole milk, warmed

Sea salt and freshly ground black pepper

1 pound leeks, roots and dark green tops trimmed

Two 10- to 12-ounce bone-in dry-aged strip loin steaks, about 1 inch thick

Balsamic-Roasted Mushrooms (page 219; optional)

1. Boil the potatoes in abundant salted water until they are soft, about 20 minutes (depending on the size). Drain and put them into a large bowl with 2 tablespoons of the butter, the olive oil, sour cream, and ¼ cup warm milk. Smash with a fork or potato masher until the potatoes are creamy but still have some texture, adding more milk if needed. Season with salt and pepper.

2. While the potatoes are boiling, cut the white part of the leeks in half lengthwise, then slice into thin half-moons. Rinse well in a colander under running water. Cook the leeks with the remaining 2 tablespoons butter in a skillet over low heat until they are very tender, about 15 minutes. Season with salt and pepper.

3. Season the steaks with salt and pepper. Grill, broil, or sauté to your preferred doneness, 5 to 7 minutes per side for medium-rare. Transfer the steaks to a plate and let stand for 5 minutes while you prepare the plates.

4. On each of four plates, mound the leeks in the center, using the back of a large spoon to form them into a ring. Mound the potatoes in the center. Cut the steaks crosswise into slices and arrange them over the top of the potatoes and leeks. Drape the mushrooms over the steak, if using.

BLACKENED RIB EYE with CHAYOTE and CORN SUCCOTASH and CHIPOTLE CHILE BUTTER

I love a dish that gives me a full-on sensory experience of deliciousness. So all too often, caught in a perfect food moment, I have a habit of announcing different recipes as "my favorite." (And it usually happens on my television show, so there are witnesses.)

Well, here it is in writing: This one really *is* my favorite steak dish. For my money, rib eye is the most flavorful and tender cut of beef. And here, the lively succotash provides crunch and a wonderfully sweet and fresh contrast to the crusty-spicy charred steak. Chipotle chile butter brings it all together with the perfect punch, waking up the dish without overwhelming it. I have served this dish in every restaurant where I have been chef and I have never tired of it. I warn you—it is addictive.

The steak rub is inspired by the flavors of a New Orleans–style spice blend. Chayote is another New Orleans favorite, where the vegetable goes by the name mirliton. You'll have more rub than needed for this recipe; store the remainder, tightly covered and away from heat and light, to use with chicken or other grilled or pan-seared meats.

Makes 6 servings

What to Drink: A medium-bodied cabernet sauvignon, cabernet franc, or merlot has the structure to tame this flavorful wild beast of a meal.

2 tablespoons chili powder

1 tablespoon ground cumin

1 tablespoon sweet paprika

1 tablespoon garlic powder

Kosher salt

1 teaspoon cayenne pepper

¾ teaspoon freshly ground black pepper

Six 10-ounce rib eye steaks, about 1 inch thick

2 tablespoons extra-virgin olive oil

Chayote and Corn Succotash (page 216)

Chipotle Chile Butter (page 193)

1. To make the steak rub, combine the chili powder, cumin, paprika, garlic powder, 2 teaspoons salt, cayenne, and black pepper in a small bowl. Rub the mixture generously on all sides of the steaks.

2. Turn on your kitchen exhaust fan. Heat two large heavy skillets over medium-high heat. (Alternatively, cook the steaks in two batches in one pan.) Add 1 tablespoon of the olive oil to coat each pan.

3. Lay 2 steaks into each pan and leave for about 2 minutes without moving them, to sear the outside. Turn the steaks to sear the second side, then reduce the heat to medium and cook the steaks until the crust is dark and the interior is your desired doneness, about 10 minutes total, or until they reach an internal temperature of 125°F to 130°F for medium-rare. Transfer the steaks to a cutting board and let stand for 5 minutes.

4. To serve, slice the steaks on a diagonal into ¼-inch-thick slices. Mound the warm chayote and corn succotash on four plates and lay the steak slices over it. Sprinkle the steak lightly with salt and top with a good-size dollop of the chipotle butter.

SEVEN-CHILE BARBECUE BEEF RIBS

While you can make a perfectly good barbecue sauce with just a couple of types of chiles, chefs know they can create a broader, more complex range of flavors that offers more than just heat by combining a variety of chiles, from mild to hot, and including fresh, dried, and smoked varieties. As you eat, the flavors just keep coming—some right up front, others in the background, still others evolving as you eat. Feel free to vary the chiles in the mix, but be sure to include at least a couple of mild varieties for balance.

Back ribs are the most tender rib choice. If you substitute the meatier short ribs, braise them until they are tender, then use the sauce as you would a barbecue sauce to coat them at the end of the cooking time. This sauce is also great with chicken, pork chops, and other meats. For a real "ribs joint" dinner, round out the plate with Snappy Apple Coleslaw (page 221) and corn bread or buttered dinner rolls.

Makes 6 servings

What to Drink: Beer is the perfect thirst quencher for this dish. If you prefer wine, choose a Beaujolais nouveau or a fruity zinfandel without a lot of alcohol or tannin, which may clash with the chile heat.

1 ounce each dried pequin, guajillo, cascabel, ancho, and New Mexican red chiles, seeds removed

1 large yellow onion, roughly chopped

¼ cup finely chopped fresh ginger

Extra-virgin olive oil

One 28-ounce can diced tomatoes

2 cups cider vinegar

1 cup dark brown sugar

¾ cup honey

10 large garlic cloves, smashed with the back of a knife and roughly chopped (about ½ cup)

6 fresh jalapeño chiles, seeded and veins removed

4 chipotle chiles in adobo, chopped, plus 1 teaspoon sauce

2 tablespoons ground cumin

1 teaspoon ground allspice

6 pounds beef back ribs

Kosher salt and freshly ground black pepper

1. Preheat the oven to 350°F with a rack positioned near the middle. Warm the dried chiles in the oven for a few minutes to soften them, then cut them open, remove the seeds, and pull out any large veins. Leave the oven on.

2. In a large nonreactive saucepan, sauté the onions and ginger in ¼ cup olive oil over medium-high heat until the onions begin to color. Add the tomatoes, vinegar, brown sugar, honey, garlic, jalapeños, chipotle chiles, adobo sauce, cumin, allspice, and the dried chiles. Simmer for 1 hour. Purée the mixture using an immersion blender, or carefully transfer to a traditional blender. The mixture should be almost smooth.

3. After the sauce has simmered for 30 minutes, coat the ribs lightly with olive oil and season with salt and pepper. Brown them meat side down in batches in a large skillet over medium-high heat until they begin to color, about 5 minutes. Transfer the ribs meat side up to the oven on a rimmed baking sheet. After you purée the sauce, spread it generously over the ribs and continue to bake, basting with additional sauce every 20 minutes, until they are tender, about 90 minutes total baking time. (To make ahead, cool the ribs, cover tightly, and refrigerate for up to 2 days. To reheat, put the ribs into a covered pan, top with sauce, cover, and warm in a preheated 325°F oven until hot, about 20 minutes.)

4. Transfer the ribs to a cutting board and cut between the ribs to serve.

GRILLED LAMB CHOPS with RED ONION JAM and CELERY ROOT PURÉE

Chefs pay constant attention not only to each ingredient, but also to the combination of flavors and textures on the plate. This restaurant-worthy composition starts with a rich Celery Root Purée, topped with juicy-thick lamb chops and Red Onion Jam as the crowning touch. Each of these elements can also be used in a variety of other preparations and presentations. Follow this suggestion or create your own masterpiece—the choice is yours!

When selecting lamb chops, you may find yourself faced with the choice of rib, loin, or sirloin chops. You can use any of these for this recipe. Rib chops are cut directly from the rack of lamb and have the characteristic long, protruding bone, making it easier to get at the meat. Loin chops have a T-bone, which requires a bit more carving. They are somewhat leaner—and more expensive—than rib chops. Rib and loin chops are both tender and flavorful. Sirloin chops come from the leg. They are slightly larger than loin chops, with a bit more marbling.

Makes 4 servings

What to Drink: Choose a red wine with some body to stand up to the grilled lamb. A cabernet or syrah are also good choices.

¼ cup extra-virgin olive oil, plus more for cooking chops

2 medium garlic cloves

1 medium shallot

1 tablespoon fresh rosemary

1 tablespoon fresh thyme

Kosher salt

1 teaspoon whole black peppercorns

Eight 4- to 5-ounce lamb chops, about 1 inch thick

2 medium red onions, cut in quarters and then lengthwise into ⅛-inch-wide slices

Freshly ground black pepper

1 tablespoon red wine vinegar

2 tablespoons balsamic vinegar

4 teaspoons unsalted butter

1 tablespoon pomegranate molasses

Celery Root Purée (page 230)

1. Combine 2 tablespoons of the olive oil in a food processor with the garlic, shallot, rosemary, thyme, 1 teaspoon salt, and the peppercorns to form a paste. It doesn't need to be completely smooth. Rub the paste on the lamb chops and allow them to rest, covered, at room temperature for 1 hour, or in the refrigerator for up to 24 hours. If you have refrigerated them, remove the chops from the refrigerator 30 minutes before cooking.

2. Combine the onions, the remaining 2 tablespoons olive oil, 1 teaspoon salt, and ½ teaspoon ground pepper in a large heavy skillet. Cook over medium heat, stirring frequently, until the onions begin to soften. Stir in the red wine vinegar, cover the skillet with a tightly fitting lid, reduce the heat to very low, and cook until the onions have a soft, jam-like consistency, about 30 minutes, stirring occasionally. Stir in the balsamic vinegar during the last 5 minutes of cooking. Season to taste with additional salt and pepper. Cover and set aside.

3. To cook the chops, scrape off excess marinade. Heat just a film of olive oil in a large heavy skillet over medium-high heat. Brown the chops, about 4 minutes per side. Add the butter and turn to coat the chops on both sides. Continue cooking until the lamb is medium-rare, just a minute or two longer, or to your desired doneness. Transfer the chops to a plate and brush liberally with the pomegranate molasses. Allow to rest for 5 minutes before serving.

4. To serve, spoon the celery root purée onto the center of each plate. Top with a lamb chop, and top the chop with a generous spoonful of red onions, using a fork to swirl them attractively. Spoon any juices that have collected in the pan or on the plate over and around the chops.

CARIBBEAN GRILLED LAMB SKEWERS with LONG BEANS

Intense spice rubs are popular with chefs who want to make a flavor statement. They are easy to prepare and quickly transform a simple cut of meat into something exotic and exciting. Wet rubs accomplish this by creating a tasty and attractive spice crust that coats and infuses flavor deep into the meat.

Believed to be of African origin, this Aruban dish known as *lambchi and boonchi* was a big hit at my Caribbean restaurant. Even those not partial to lamb loved the bold spicing and crunchy long beans—the type often found in Chinese restaurants. (Substitute green beans if long beans aren't available.)

In lieu of the couscous, you can serve this with steamed jasmine rice mixed with about a tablespoon each of chopped roasted peanuts, chopped cilantro, and butter.

Makes 6 servings

What to Drink: Pair with a medium-bodied South African red wine, such as a shiraz or pinotage.

¾ cup extra-virgin olive oil

⅓ cup fresh lime juice

2 tablespoons grated lemon zest (about 2 lemons)

6 garlic cloves, minced

1 tablespoon cumin seed

1 tablespoon chili powder

1 tablespoon curry powder

Kosher salt

1 teaspoon cayenne pepper

Freshly ground black pepper

2 jalapeño peppers, minced

3 pounds boneless lamb loin or well-trimmed leg, cut into 1-inch cubes

1 pound long beans, tips removed, left long or cut into 3-inch segments

2 teaspoons unsalted butter

Minted Couscous with Pomegranate Seeds (page 234; optional)

Tomato Chutney (page 210; optional)

Have on hand 12 wooden skewers

1. Put the skewers in a pan of water to soak for at least 20 minutes.

2. To prepare the lamb marinade, whisk together ½ cup of the olive oil, the lime juice, lemon zest, garlic, cumin, chili powder, curry powder, 2 teaspoons salt, cayenne, ¼ teaspoon black pepper, and jalapeños in a medium bowl. Taste and adjust salt, pepper, cayenne, and lime juice.

3. Put the lamb cubes and the marinade into a large glass baking dish and toss, rubbing the marinade all over the lamb. Thread 4 to 5 pieces of lamb onto each skewer. Place the skewers into the baking dish, cover with plastic wrap, and refrigerate for at least 1 and up to 4 hours.

4. While the lamb marinates, preheat a grill or broiler to medium-hot and prepare the beans. Sauté the beans in the remaining ¼ cup olive oil in a large skillet over medium-high heat, stirring frequently, until they are tender and begin to blister. Stir in the butter, 1 teaspoon salt, and ¼ teaspoon black pepper. When the butter just begins to brown, transfer the beans to a warm serving platter and drape with foil.

5. Grill the lamb, turning the skewers every few minutes, until medium rare (internal temperature of 130°F), about 6 minutes. (Alternatively, the skewers can be broiled until medium rare.) Transfer the skewers to a plate and let stand for 5 minutes.

6. To serve, mound the couscous, if using, in the center of each plate. Place long beans to the side and lay the skewers across the couscous and beans. Garnish with the tomato chutney, if desired, serving additional chutney on the side.

CHIANTI-BRAISED LAMB SHANKS with PORCINI MUSHROOMS and CANNELLINI BEANS

In the late 1980s, with the costs of business rising, neighborhood restaurants began seeking out less expensive cuts of meat to increase their profits. An inadvertent result was a trend toward more traditional, rustic cooking in high-end restaurants as chefs discovered the incredible flavor of these less-coveted cuts. Italian restaurants that once based their menus around pricey veal scaloppine and rack of lamb were suddenly showcasing veal breast and lamb shank. This still remains a favorite style of restaurant cooking when we go out; even though it's home-style food, restaurants seem to do it "better," with more finesse than many of us do at home.

Why were these dishes so flavorful? Where there is bone there is flavor. Major muscles like the shoulder and leg get a lot of flavor from the blood that flows through them. Lamb shank packs a double punch: This well-exercised muscle has a big bone. In this Italian-style preparation, we play the lamb's heartiness off of earthy porcinis and tangy tomatoes and wine. Make this when you want to feel like you've tucked into a table at a Tuscan farmhouse.

Makes 4 servings

What to Drink: Try serving with the same Chianti or sangiovese you used in the dish.

Four 12- to 14-ounce lamb shanks, silverskin and tendons trimmed away

Sea salt and freshly ground black pepper

1 ounce dried porcini mushrooms

One 750 ml bottle Chianti or other red wine

½ cup extra-virgin olive oil

1 large yellow onion, cut into ¼-inch dice

2 medium carrots, cut into ¼-inch dice

1 large rib celery, cut into ¼-inch dice

10 large whole garlic cloves, plus 5 medium garlic cloves, minced

One 14-ounce can diced tomatoes

One 14-ounce can cannellini beans, drained

1 bay leaf

1 tablespoon chopped fresh thyme

1 tablespoon chopped fresh rosemary

Soft polenta from The Art of Polenta (page 238)

¼ cup chopped flat-leaf parsley, for garnish

1. Preheat the oven to 325°F. Season the lamb shanks generously with salt and pepper. Rinse the porcini and soak them in 2 cups of the wine.

2. Heat ¼ cup of the olive oil in a large (7-quart) Dutch oven or heavy ovenproof saucepan over medium heat. Brown the lamb shanks on all sides, then transfer to a plate.

3. Add the onions, carrots, and celery to the pot, adding more olive oil, if needed. Cook, stirring occasionally with a wooden spatula, until they begin to brown, about 5 minutes. Add the whole and minced garlic and cook, stirring, for another 2 minutes.

4. Remove the mushrooms from the soaking wine, squeeze, and chop into medium pieces. Add them to the pot along with the soaking wine, the remaining red wine, the tomatoes, cannellini beans, bay leaf, thyme, and rosemary. Season lightly with salt and pepper.

5. Return the shanks to the pot, cover, and transfer to the oven. Cook until the shanks are very tender and the meat has shrunk back to expose an inch of bone, 2 to 2½ hours, turning every 30 minutes. Remove from the oven and season again to taste. Remove the bay leaf and skim fat from the sauce. (To make ahead, cool the shanks, then cover and refrigerate for up to 2 days. Reheat before serving.)

6. To serve, mound polenta on each plate, top with a shank, smother with sauce, and sprinkle with chopped parsley.

MOROCCAN-SPICED LAMB STEW with CHICKPEAS and DRIED APRICOTS

Going out to dinner can be like a mini vacation, offering exotic tastes that transport you to another part of the world with each bite. That's what this Moroccan-inspired stew does for me. The blend of sweet and savory and the aromatics add up to something exotic and adventurous. Preparing meat with fruit and spices can be tricky. The key is getting the balance of sweet and savory right, so that neither overpowers the dish and so that they let the natural flavor of the lamb shine through.

This recipe's broad palette of spices results in a nonstop parade of flavors with each bite. But don't be afraid of the long ingredient list. You can collect and mix the spices in advance to save time and effort.

I keep two spice grinders: one for coffee, the other reserved only for spices. If you don't have one, use a small food processor bowl fitted with a metal blade, or a mortar and pestle, to grind the spices. I like to use a mix of California and Turkish dried apricots in this dish. The California variety are tart and chewy with a bright flavor. The Turkish apricots are plump, soft, and sweet. If you can find both, the combination adds complexity, but any dried apricots will do.

Cilantro and mint in the stew are mirrored in the yogurt and couscous to bring the many elements in the dish together into a harmonious whole.

DON'T HOLD BACK ■ EXPLORE NEW FOODS

Harissa is a fiery Tunisian condiment made by puréeing chiles with spices and flavorings, typically garlic and cumin, and sometimes coriander, caraway, olive oil, and tomato paste. It is used beyond Tunisia in Moroccan, Algerian, and other North African cuisines. Harissa is available in tubes, which make it easy to dispense just as much as you need. Store the tightly capped tube in the refrigerator to use on sandwiches and in couscous (its classic use), pastas, soups, and stews. Look for harissa in the ethnic foods aisle of your grocery, in specialty shops, and in Middle Eastern markets. If you can't find it, substitute Indonesian sambal or a red chili paste with garlic.

3 pounds bone-in lamb stew meat, trimmed and cut into 2- to 3-inch pieces

1 tablespoon cumin seeds

2 teaspoons kosher salt

2 teaspoons loosely packed saffron threads

1 teaspoon hot paprika

1 teaspoon coriander seeds

1 teaspoon ground cinnamon

1 teaspoon ground ginger

½ teaspoon turmeric

½ teaspoon whole allspice berries

½ cup chopped fresh mint leaves

3 tablespoons extra-virgin olive oil

1 large onion, cut into ½-inch dice

2 tablespoons minced garlic

One 15-ounce can chickpeas (garbanzo beans), drained, or 2 cups cooked

One 14-ounce can diced tomatoes, with juice

⅔ cup dried apricots

¼ cup raisins

2 tablespoons harissa

1 cup plain whole-milk yogurt

½ cup chopped cilantro

3 tablespoons minced red onions

2 teaspoons sumac or za'atar blend (optional)

Minted Couscous with Pomegranate Seeds (page 234)

1. Put the lamb into a large glass bowl or baking dish. Use a spice grinder to grind the cumin, salt, saffron, paprika, coriander, cinnamon, ginger, turmeric, and allspice. Add the spice mixture and half of the mint to the lamb, tossing to coat the meat evenly. Cover with plastic wrap and refrigerate for at least 1 hour or as long as overnight.

2. Heat the olive oil in a large (7-quart) Dutch oven or heavy ovenproof saucepan over medium heat. Add the onions and sauté until they have softened and turned transparent. Add the garlic and lamb and cook, stirring often, until the meat is browned on all sides and any juices it has exuded are reduced by about half.

3. Stir in the chickpeas, tomatoes, apricots, raisins, harissa, and 2 cups water. Cover and adjust heat to simmer slowly, stirring occasionally, until the meat easily falls off the bone when coaxed with a fork, about 2 hours.

4. While the stew simmers, stir together the yogurt, ¼ cup of the cilantro, the red onions, and sumac, if using, to combine well. Cover and refrigerate until serving time. About 30 minutes before serving, make the minted couscous.

5. To serve, mound couscous in shallow bowls. Ladle the stew over the couscous, being sure to include plenty of the chickpeas, fruits, and sauce. Drizzle with the yogurt and sprinkle with the remaining cilantro and mint. Serve the remaining yogurt on the side.

ALL DRESSED UP

CHEFS KNOW that a sauce is more than a mere embellishment to a piece of fish or meat. At times, it is the accent that makes the dish memorable, catapulting a simple dish from ordinary to extraordinary.

A good sauce pulls together the elements of a dish into a harmonious whole. It is the tie that completes the suit; the scarf or piece of jewelry that perfectly pulls together the outfit. It dresses up the dish and prepares it to go out in style, whether from the restaurant kitchen to the dining room, or from your own kitchen to your family table.

Most sauces aren't difficult to make, but some people consider them a level of fussiness that's beyond their patience at home. With these recipes, you will learn that even a simple sauce can transform a dish, giving it "bling" that raises the bar on the usual home-cooked meal.

Please don't save sauces for company. I've included compound butters, simple dipping sauces, chunky chutneys and salsas, and others that you can throw together in minutes and keep on hand for the right moment and the right dish. There is almost nothing complicated in these sauces, which can turn a perfectly acceptable dinner into a big "Wow!" from your family and friends.

The recipes in this chapter don't include beverage pairings because the choice will depend on the dish you embellish with the sauce. Look for pairings in the main dish recipes in which the sauces are used.

Get your dishes dressed and take them out for a spin!

COMPOUND BUTTERS

Salt and fat are two of the greatest flavor conductors in the kitchen. I think of melting butter as the amplifier that turns up the volume on taste. Mixing softened butter with spices, herbs, and other flavorful ingredients is a simple technique for adding bold flavor to grilled or pan-roasted meat and fish. Easy to make and great to have on hand, flavored butters can transform an ordinary grilled steak, chicken breast, or fish fillet into a restaurant-quality dining experience. Shape leftover butters into a log, cover with plastic wrap, and refrigerate for up to a week or freeze for up to a month, cutting off thick slices or "coins" as needed.

CHIPOTLE CHILE BUTTER

Each butter makes about ½ cup

Use this butter to give grilled foods a Southwestern flair.

¼ pound (1 stick) unsalted butter, softened

2 chipotle chiles in adobo, minced, plus 2 teaspoons adobo sauce

4 teaspoons fresh lime juice

Kosher salt

Use a fork or small whisk to mix the butter with the chipotle chiles and adobo sauce until well blended. Slowly drizzle and stir in as much of the lime juice as the butter will absorb. (Alternatively, combine the ingredients in a food processor.) Season to taste with salt.

GINGER-SCALLION BUTTER

This butter is a great way to build on flavors often found in Asian dishes.

¼ pound (1 stick) unsalted butter, softened

1 to 2 tablespoons fresh lime juice

2 tablespoons chopped fresh ginger

2 scallions, coarsely chopped

Kosher salt and freshly ground black pepper

In a food processor fitted with a metal blade, process the butter with 1 tablespoon lime juice, the ginger, and scallions until combined into a smooth paste. Add salt and pepper to taste, as well as additional lime, if desired.

BEURRE BLANC

This simple wine and butter sauce adds richness and elegance to any dish. It is perfect with grilled chicken or fish. Add a tablespoon of capers to the vegetables for a briny, mustardy accent with sautéed fish. For the wine, use a sauvignon blanc or lighter-bodied chardonnay with little or no oak.

Makes 1 cup

½ small onion, cut into ⅛-inch dice (½ cup)

1 small carrot, cut into ⅛-inch dice (½ cup)

1 rib celery, cut into ⅛-inch dice (½ cup)

1 tablespoon finely chopped fresh sage

2 cups dry white wine

½ cup chicken broth

4 tablespoons (½ stick) unsalted butter, cold, cut into 8 pieces

Kosher salt and freshly ground black pepper

1. Simmer the onions, carrots, celery, and sage in the wine and broth in a medium sauce-pan over medium heat until the liquid is reduced to about half of its original volume (about 1 cup). Whisk in the cold butter just until it is incorporated. Season to taste with salt and pepper.

2. Cover and place on a warm part of the stove, but not directly over a flame or hot burner, until serving time.

CUMIN-LIME CREAM

Simple sauces like this one give chefs an easy way to give a dish a surprising dimension of flavor and richness. This one is great with Mexican food, or wherever a little cumin and lime would add punch. For more intense flavor, lightly toast cumin seeds in a small skillet, let cool, then grind them in a coffee grinder before adding them to the sour cream. For a lighter touch, swap plain whole-milk yogurt for some or all of the sour cream. Taste and adjust the lime, as the yogurt will be more tart than the sour cream.

Makes about ½ cup

½ cup sour cream

1 tablespoon finely grated lime zest (about 1 lime)

2 tablespoons fresh lime juice

½ teaspoon paprika, sweet or hot, your choice

½ teaspoon ground cumin

Kosher salt and freshly ground black pepper

1. Stir together the sour cream, lime zest, lime juice, paprika, and cumin in a small bowl. Add salt and pepper to taste.

2. Use immediately, or cover tightly and refrigerate for up to 2 days.

GINGER-ORANGE GLAZE

This is a great glaze to have on hand for making richly lacquered roasted poultry or meats.

Makes about 2 cups

2 cups fresh orange juice

½ cup soy sauce

2 tablespoons minced fresh ginger

2 tablespoons minced shallots

1 tablespoon minced garlic

1 chipotle chile in adobo, minced, or ½ teaspoon chipotle chile powder

1 cup honey

⅓ cup dark brown sugar

1. Stir together the orange juice, soy sauce, ginger, shallots, garlic, chipotle chile, honey, and brown sugar in a wide nonreactive saucepan over medium heat. Boil, stirring occasionally, until the glaze is thickened and reduced by half, 20 to 30 minutes.

2. Use immediately, or cover tightly and refrigerate for up to 1 week.

SWEET and SPICY GINGER BBQ SAUCE

This is the sauce that finally unlocked the secret to my restaurant-quality Chinese BBQ Spareribs (page 168). It's also great with grilled chicken or crispy fried catfish or bass.

Plum and hoisin sauces add a complex sweetness to the marinade. My favorite brands are Koon Chun, Lee Kum Kee, Dynasty, and Kikkoman.

Makes 1¼ cups

¼ cup Chinese plum sauce

¼ cup hoisin sauce

2 tablespoons minced fresh ginger

2 tablespoons minced scallions

2 tablespoons minced garlic

2 tablespoons sambal oelek or red chili paste

2 tablespoons sesame oil

2 tablespoons rice wine vinegar

⅛ teaspoon freshly ground black pepper

1. Whisk together the plum and hoisin sauces, ginger, scallions, garlic, sambal oelek, sesame oil, vinegar, and pepper in a medium bowl until smooth.

2. Use immediately, or cover tightly and refrigerate for up to 1 week.

DON'T HOLD BACK ▪ STEP UP YOUR SKILLS

In this sauce, the ginger is minced rather than grated to create crunchy little explosions of flavor in the mouth. Slice a 2-inch length of ginger lengthwise as thin as possible, then stack the slices and cut the long way into strips. Finally, cut across the strips to finely dice the ginger. Use young ginger if you can find it—it's very tender and doesn't need peeling.

STAR ANISE–GINGER SAUCE

Unusual combinations like star anise and ginger make familiar foods taste new all over again. Star anise can be found at upscale grocery stores, in Asian markets, and at shops that sell spices in bulk. You can substitute regular anise seed in a pinch, about a quarter teaspoon per pod.

I was inspired to make this sauce by my chef friend Scott Bryan, of New York City's Veritas restaurant. Scott made the sauce when he worked with me at Miss Pearl's Jam House. I was blown away by the synergy of red wine, ginger, spice, and chiles. Like a gospel choir, the different voices combine in a soulful harmony that makes the hairs sway on the back of my neck.

I developed this adaptation of Scott's recipe for my Sesame-Crusted Seared Ahi Tuna (page 136). It would also be great over grilled salmon or roasted duck.

Makes about 1 cup

1 cup chicken broth

1 cup dry red wine

¼ cup soy sauce

¼ cup rice wine vinegar

4 star anise pods

2 tablespoons dark brown sugar

2 tablespoons finely chopped fresh ginger

2 tablespoons finely chopped shallots

2 tablespoons finely chopped garlic

½ teaspoon red chile flakes or 1 teaspoon Sriracha sauce

¼ pound (1 stick) unsalted butter, at room temperature

1. Combine the broth, wine, soy sauce, vinegar, star anise, brown sugar, ginger, shallots, garlic, and chile flakes in a large nonreactive saucepan over medium heat. Bring to a slow boil and cook until the liquid is reduced to about ¾ cup, about 30 minutes. (You can make the sauce ahead up until this point, then cool, cover tightly, and refrigerate for up to 2 days before continuing.)

2. Continue to simmer the sauce as you whisk in the butter, 1 tablespoon at a time, to create a silky sauce. Strain the sauce through a fine mesh strainer into a small pitcher and keep warm for up to an hour until serving time.

EMERALD SAUCE

This Asian-inspired pesto is just the kind of back-pocket sauce a chef loves to have on hand to perk up a variety of dishes. I toss it with capellini and top with Thai Grilled Prawns (page 124), but you could just as easily use it to top grilled chicken or fish, or toss it with any type of Asian or Italian noodle as a cold or hot lunch.

The recipe makes enough sauce for a pound of cooked pasta, with enough remaining sauce to toss with grilled seafood or chicken to serve on top. Garnish with strips of red bell pepper and sprinkle with additional chopped peanuts and cilantro.

Makes about 3 cups

½ cup peanut or vegetable oil

¼ cup toasted sesame oil

½ cup fresh lime juice

¼ cup rice wine vinegar

¼ cup roughly chopped fresh ginger

6 small to medium cloves garlic

3 jalapeño peppers, stemmed and seeded

2 tablespoons sugar

2 teaspoons kosher salt

1 cup packed cilantro, stems included (about ½ bunch)

½ cup packed fresh mint, tough stems removed

½ cup packed fresh basil leaves

½ cup roasted peanuts

1. Put the ingredients into a blender jar in the order listed—first the oils, lime juice, vinegar, then the aromatics (ginger, garlic, jalapeños), the sugar and salt, and finally the herbs (cilantro, mint, basil) and ¼ cup of the peanuts. Blend, stopping occasionally to scrape down the jar with a spatula, until the mixture is quite smooth. Taste and adjust salt to your liking. Add the remaining ¼ cup peanuts and pulse a few times to roughly chop them for a bit of crunch in the sauce.

2. Use immediately, or cover tightly and refrigerate for up to 2 days.

POBLANO-BANANA SAUCE

In the United States we think of the banana mostly as a cereal topping. Few of us would consider it as a sauce thickener, and we would hardly think of pairing bananas with poblano chiles. In other parts of the world, however, the fruit plays a more prominent culinary role, showing up in savory recipes, especially spicy ones. Sometimes bananas are used unripe, when they are more starchy than sweet. Ripe or not, you'll find them in Indian chutneys and yogurt raitas, Mexican and Latin American salsas, and a number of Southeast Asian dishes. Chefs have caught on to this as they find that sweet and heat are a match made in heaven. This sauce benefits from the banana's buttery texture and a sweet flavor. What's more, it's a great conversation starter!

Makes about 2 cups

1 small poblano chile pepper

2 ripe medium bananas

3 scallions, trimmed, green part only

¼ cup fresh lime juice

2 cloves garlic, coarsely chopped

1 tablespoon minced fresh ginger

¼ teaspoon cayenne pepper

1 cup olive oil

Kosher salt and freshly ground black pepper

1. Hold the poblano chile with tongs over a gas flame, or broil it at high heat, until it is blackened on all sides. Transfer to a plate or cutting board and cover with a bowl for about 5 minutes to steam. Pull and scrape most of the charred skin from the poblano. (Do not rinse under running water; that will wash away all that good grilled flavor.) Pull out and discard the stem and seeds.

2. Put the poblano into a blender or food processor along with the bananas, scallions, lime juice, garlic, ginger, and cayenne. Blend or process until smooth, pushing the ingredients down occasionally with a spatula. With the motor running, slowly drizzle in the olive oil through the top until all of it is incorporated. Season to taste with salt and pepper. Serve the sauce at room temperature.

3. Use immediately, or cover tightly and refrigerate for up to 1 day. Remove from the refrigerator about 30 minutes before using.

QUICK-and-EASY TOMATO SAUCE

Plenty of olive oil gives this fresh-tasting sauce richness and great flavor. Use good-quality San Marzano tomatoes. Or use one of my favorites–Muir Glen Fire Roasted Tomatoes–for a hint of smoky roasted flavor.

Makes about 4 cups

1 large onion, cut into ¼-inch dice

6 medium cloves garlic, thinly sliced

¼ cup extra-virgin olive oil

One 28-ounce can whole peeled Roma tomatoes

½ teaspoon red chile flakes

2 bay leaves

Kosher salt and freshly ground black pepper

1. Sauté the onions and garlic in the olive oil in a medium nonreactive saucepan over medium heat until they are tender but not browned. Stir in the tomatoes, chile flakes, and bay leaves. Simmer until the flavors are well blended, about 5 minutes. Purée the sauce with an immersion or traditional blender until it is nearly smooth. Season to taste with salt and pepper.

2. Use immediately, or cover tightly and refrigerate for up to 3 days before reheating to use.

RANCHERO SAUCE

Sauces often make the difference between bland and exciting. This hearty sauce, with its great depth of flavor from roasted poblano chiles, can form the basis for a vegetarian dish—just add tortillas and rice. Use it to perk up grilled chicken or quesadillas, or to transform a couple of simply prepared eggs into a warming supper. I use this for Joey's Huevos Rancheros (page 56).

Makes about 4 cups

2 tablespoons vegetable or olive oil

1 small yellow onion, cut into ⅛-inch dice (about 1 cup)

3 cloves garlic, minced

2 jalapeño peppers, seeded and minced

1 chipotle chile in adobo, minced, and 1½ teaspoons sauce

1 teaspoon cumin seeds, toasted

1 teaspoon chili powder

One 15-ounce can diced tomatoes (fire roasted, if available)

One 15-ounce can black beans, drained and rinsed, or 1½ cups cooked

2 poblano chiles

3 small fresh tomatoes, chopped (no need to peel or seed)

¼ cup chopped cilantro, for garnish

Kosher salt and freshly ground black pepper

1. In a large heavy nonreactive saucepan over medium-high heat, heat the vegetable oil and sauté the onions until they soften, about 4 minutes. Add the garlic, jalapeños, chipotle chile, adobo sauce, cumin, and chili powder and cook for 2 to 3 minutes longer, stirring. Add the canned tomatoes and the beans, reduce the heat to a simmer, and cook for about 10 minutes longer, stirring occasionally.

2. While the sauce simmers, hold the poblano chiles with tongs over a gas flame, or broil it at high heat, until blackened on all sides. Transfer to a plate or cutting board and cover with a bowl for about 5 minutes to steam. Pull and scrape most of the charred skin from the poblano. (Do not rinse under running water; that will wash away all that good grilled flavor.) Pull out and discard the stem and seeds. Cut the poblanos in half lengthwise, then crosswise into thin strips.

3. Stir the fresh tomatoes and poblano strips into the sauce. Add about ¼ cup water if needed to keep the mixture saucy. Cook a couple of minutes longer. Stir in the cilantro and season to taste with salt and pepper.

4. Use immediately, or cover tightly and refrigerate for up to 3 days. Reheat before serving.

SALSA CRUDA

Salsa cruda simply means "uncooked salsa." Typically, it is made with chopped tomatoes, onions, and chiles, with lemon or lime juice, cilantro, and other ingredients often added, as I have here. This simple fresh tomato salsa is sometimes known as *pico de gallo,* or "rooster's beak," and there are as many colorful stories about how the condiment relates to the bird's beak as there are versions of the salsa. In Mexico, the term is used for a whole range of salads and condiments made from fruits or vegetables, with or without chiles. I use this versatile version to accent many different dishes. It's best used within an hour or two of when it is made.

Makes approximately 2 cups

6 Roma tomatoes, cored, halved, seeded, and diced

½ medium red onion, diced (about ½ cup)

¼ cup fresh lime juice

¼ cup gently packed chopped cilantro

1 tablespoon extra-virgin olive oil

2 jalapeño peppers, stemmed, seeded, and finely diced

Kosher salt and freshly ground black pepper

Stir together the tomatoes, onions, lime juice, cilantro, olive oil, and jalapeños in a medium bowl. Season to taste with salt and pepper.

PORCINI MARSALA SAUCE

Most chefs will tell you that fresh is best. That's usually true...except when it comes to dried mushrooms. Dried porcinis have a more intense flavor than their fresh counterparts. Hydrated and used in sauces, they add a bold, penetrating mushroom flavor.

The earthy flavors in this rich sauce pair beautifully with pasta and duck. I developed it for my Duck Cannelloni (page 109), but you could also serve it over linguine with a dusting of freshly grated Parmigiano-Reggiano cheese.

Makes about 4 cups

2 cups dried porcini mushrooms

¼ cup minced shallots

Kosher salt

4 tablespoons (½ stick) unsalted butter

2 tablespoons minced garlic

1 cup brandy

2 cups duck stock or chicken broth

1 cup heavy cream

½ cup Marsala wine

Freshly ground black pepper

1. While you are assembling the ingredients, put the porcini mushrooms into 4 cups warm water and set aside to soak for 10 minutes. Strain, saving the liquid, and chop the mushrooms into ¼- to ½-inch pieces.

2. Sauté the shallots with a pinch of salt in the butter in a wide shallow saucepan over medium-high heat until they just begin to soften, about 1 minute. Add the garlic, brandy, and chopped porcinis. Cook, stirring, until the mixture is nearly dry, 3 to 4 minutes. Pour in the mushroom soaking liquid through a fine mesh strainer. Add the duck stock and cream, bring to a boil, and continue to cook until the mixture is reduced by about half, about 30 minutes. Stir in the Marsala and season to taste with salt and pepper.

3. Use immediately, or cover tightly and refrigerate for up to 3 days before reheating to use.

ROASTED POBLANO HOLLANDAISE

Flavor variations are the fuel for ever-changing restaurant menus. In this twist on a classic, I flavor hollandaise sauce with roasted poblano chiles for a sauce that kicks back. The sauce is great over poached eggs or drizzled over quesadillas. It's the perfect addition to Crab Cakes (page 54).

Makes about 1½ cups

1 medium poblano chile

3 large egg yolks

½ pound (2 sticks) unsalted butter, cut into 16 tablespoons, at room temperature

2 tablespoons fresh lemon juice

Kosher salt and freshly ground black pepper

1. Hold the poblano chile with tongs over a gas flame, or broil it at high heat, until it is blackened on all sides. Transfer to a plate or cutting board and cover with a bowl for about 5 minutes to steam. Pull and scrape most of the charred skin from the poblano. (Do not rinse under running water; that will wash away all that good grilled flavor.) Pull out and discard the stem and seeds. Cut the chile into ⅛-inch dice.

2. Whisk the egg yolks with 1 tablespoon water in a medium metal mixing bowl. Place the bowl over a saucepan of just-simmering water. The bowl should not be touching the water. Whisk continuously until the yolks are frothy. Add the butter 1 tablespoon at a time, continuing to whisk until the mixture thickens into a creamy-thick sauce. (You may not need all of the butter.) Whisk in the lemon juice. Remove the bowl from the saucepan and stir in the roasted poblano. Season to taste with salt and pepper.

3. This sauce is best used immediately. To hold for up to 30 minutes, cover tightly and set in a shallow saucepan of warm water.

DON'T HOLD BACK ■ EXPLORE NEW FOODS

Chile terminology can be confusing. The fresh peppers labeled "pasillas" in your market in California may actually be poblanos. True pasillas are dried chilaca peppers. Poblanos are called ancho chiles when dried. Confused? You can recognize a fresh poblano as the one you've enjoyed in chiles rellenos.

AVOCADO SALSA with ROASTED CORN

I love adding a twist to a familiar favorite, breathing in new life while retaining the qualities that made it popular in the first place. Here, roasted corn adds crunchy texture and toasty taste to an already flavorful guacamole-salsa hybrid. An added bonus is the way the corn harmonizes with the (corn) chips. (It's great without the corn, as well.)

Enjoy as a chip dip or as a garnish with any Mexican meal.

Makes about 2 cups

1 ear of corn, husk and silk removed

1 avocado, peeled, pitted, and cut into ¼-inch dice

1 Roma tomato, halved, seeded, and cut into ⅛-inch dice

¼ cup minced red onions

2 tablespoons fresh lime juice

1 jalapeño pepper, seeded and finely minced

¼ cup minced cilantro

Kosher salt and freshly ground black pepper

1. Heat a grill or stovetop grill pan to medium-high. Grill the corn, turning occasionally, until the kernels are lightly charred on all sides, about 10 minutes. Remove and leave to cool while you prepare the other ingredients.

2. When the corn is cool enough to handle, cut off the kernels (see page 19). Use the back of the knife to scrape the remaining corn from the cob.

3. Stir together the corn, avocado, tomatoes, onions, lime juice, jalapeño, and cilantro in a small bowl. Add salt and pepper to taste, and more lime juice, jalapeño, or cilantro, if you like.

A little-known fact: Avocados come equipped with a secret window to their freshness. Pull off the nub at the stem end and look beneath it. If it is green inside, the avocado should be a good one. If it is brown, that's what you are likely to find inside. Quietly place it to the back of the mound and check out the next one—but don't let the produce clerk catch you! (And don't overdo it either.) When ripe, the avocado should yield to your gentle squeeze, but it should not be completely soft and certainly not mushy.

To easily cut an avocado, use a sharp paring knife to cut it in half lengthwise. Twist the two sides in opposite directions to separate them. Press the blade of a sharp knife into the pit and twist; it should come out easily. Finally, use a butter knife to cut the avocado in a cross-hatch pattern, then scoop the flesh out by running a spoon between it and the shell to release the diced fruit.

CITRUS-MANGO SALSA

Salsas are a great way to showcase fruits' savory side. You know that spicy tomato sauce you scoop up with a tortilla chip is not the only salsa, right? *Salsa* is Spanish for "sauce," and this fruit-based version has a bright, fresh flavor with just the right kick. Olive oil mellows the mix. Besides the Cocoa-Chile–Rubbed Duck Breast (page 151), this salsa makes a refreshing addition to grilled chicken or fish. It's pretty darned good with chips, too.

Makes about 2½ cups

1 navel orange, peeled, seeded, and cut into ⅛-inch dice

1 mango, peeled and cut into ⅛-inch dice

2 red Fresno or jalapeño chiles, seeded and minced

¼ cup extra-virgin olive oil

2 tablespoons minced red onion

2 tablespoons minced cilantro

2 tablespoons minced chives (optional)

2 tablespoons fresh lime juice

1 tablespoon rice wine vinegar

Kosher salt and freshly ground black pepper

Combine the orange, mango, chiles, olive oil, onions, cilantro, chives, if using, lime juice, and vinegar in a medium bowl. Season to taste with salt and pepper. Use immediately, or cover tightly and refrigerate for up to 2 days.

DON'T HOLD BACK ■ EXPLORE NEW FOODS

Mangoes are the most consumed fruit in the world. With more than 143 varieties, how can you choose? Two common varieties are Haden and Manila. Originating in India, Hadens, with their orange-red skins tinged with yellow and green, tend to be large, juicy, and sweet, with classic mango flavor. The smaller, flatter Manila mango of the Philippines has a thin yellow skin, creamy texture, and a floral perfume.

When choosing a mango, a sniff at the stem end should reveal an exotic fragrance. Place underripe mangoes in a closed paper bag at room temperature for a day or two. Refrigerate ripe mangoes, but eat them at room temperature.

To cut a mango, hold the fruit with its narrow side on the cutting board and cut one "cheek" (broad side) away from the flat central pit. Repeat with the second cheek, then cut the two smaller pieces from the pit. A classic way to remove the flesh from the large cheeks: use a paring knife to cut a grid across the fruit, then turn the cheek inside out. The cut squares will pop out and are easily cut off. Alternatively, peel the mango before cutting, then cut into chunks.

APPLE-MANGO CHUTNEY

This chutney is one of my favorites, and it's easy to make. Use firm, tart apples such as Fuji, Granny Smith, or pippin varieties.

Makes about 2½ cups

2 cups cider vinegar

½ cup dark brown sugar

½ small red onion, cut into thin strips (about 1 cup)

One 2-inch piece ginger, cut into thin strips

2 cloves garlic, sliced thin

1 cinnamon stick, about 2 inches long

1 teaspoon coriander seeds

3 whole allspice berries

1 whole clove

3 firm tart apples, peeled and cut into quarters, then cored and cut into medium dice

2 mangoes, peeled, cut off the pit, and cut into medium dice

2 serrano chiles, seeded and minced, plus more to taste

6 tablespoons fresh lime juice, plus more to taste

Kosher salt and freshly ground black pepper

1. In a medium-large nonreactive saucepan, stir together the vinegar, brown sugar, onions, ginger, garlic, and cinnamon. Crush the coriander seeds and allspice berries with the back of a cast-iron skillet, then add to the saucepan along with the clove. Bring to a simmer.

2. Add about one third of the apples and simmer for 15 minutes, stirring occasionally to prevent sticking or scorching. Add another third of the apples and half of the mangoes, stir again, and simmer for another 10 minutes. Add the remaining apples and mangoes, along with the serrano chiles and lime juice. Stir well and continue to simmer until the fruit has softened and most of the juices have evaporated, about 15 minutes longer.

3. Transfer the chutney to a bowl to cool. Season to taste with salt, pepper, and additional chiles or lime juice. Use immediately, or cover tightly and refrigerate for up to 3 days.

TOMATO CHUTNEY

A chutney is a piquant condiment made with cooked or raw fruits or vegetables, together with vinegar, sugar, and spices. Chutneys range from sweet to sour and from mild to spicy hot. This version is a great way to use off-season tomatoes. Though they may be bland on their own, they cook up into a rich, flavorful chutney that's just right with warm autumn and winter flavors, from Mediterranean to Indian to African.

Makes about 2 cups

4 large Roma tomatoes

1 small red onion

One 2-inch piece fresh ginger, peeled and cut into thin strips

5 cloves garlic, sliced thin

¼ cup dark brown sugar

½ cup malt vinegar, cider vinegar, or red wine vinegar

2 teaspoons coriander seeds

2 teaspoons mustard seeds

2 teaspoons anise seeds

2 teaspoons fennel seeds

One 14-ounce can diced tomatoes

2 tablespoons fresh lime juice

2 jalapeño peppers, seeded and cut into small dice

¼ cup loosely packed chopped cilantro, stem ends removed

Sea salt and freshly ground black pepper

1. Blanch the fresh tomatoes in boiling water for 1 minute; drain. When the tomatoes are cool enough to handle, use a paring knife to pull off the skin. Cut the tomatoes in half lengthwise, push out the seeds with your fingers (discard), squeeze out any juices into a small bowl, and cut the tomatoes into ¼-inch dice, reserving any juice with the tomatoes in the bowl. Set aside.

2. Cut the onion into quarters lengthwise, then into long, very thin slices.

3. Bring the onions, ginger, garlic, brown sugar, vinegar, coriander, mustard, anise, fennel, and canned tomatoes with their liquid to a boil in a large, wide nonreactive saucepan. Reduce to a lively simmer and cook, stirring occasionally, until most of the liquid has evaporated, about 20 minutes. Stir in the lime juice, jalapeños, cilantro, and the chopped fresh tomatoes. Bring back to the boil, stirring, then remove from the heat. Season with salt and pepper to taste. Serve slightly warm or at room temperature.

4. Use immediately, or cover tightly and refrigerate for up to 2 days. Remove from the refrigerator 30 minutes before using.

ROUNDING OUT THE PLATE

SIDE DISHES GIVE CHEFS A CHANCE to balance all the elements on a plate. While they used to be a restaurant afterthought—overcooked vegetables and your choice of rice or potatoes with every entrée—that is no longer the case. Accompaniments are now equal partners with the main course. Whether a starch, vegetable, or other embellishment, the right side dish should complement and contrast with what's in the center of the plate to keep the meal exciting to the last bite.

With side dishes listed alongside each main course on the menu, we often use them to decide which dish to order. In the mood for Celery Root Purée and meltingly soft Red Onion Jam? Go for the Grilled Lamb Chops (page 182). Just reading the names of those dishes whets your appetite for the chops.

Some restaurants list side dishes separately on the menu so that diners can pick and choose. I do the same for my family and friends by serving a selection of side dishes family style on large platters in the middle of the table. I choose side dishes that offer variety and that will taste good together. It's hard to make a mistake.

This chapter includes side dishes that are paired with specific recipes in the book along with other favorites, so you can suit your own taste. Whether you are serving a simple grilled piece of fish or a more complicated entrée, you will find just the right thing to round it out without robbing it of its glory.

Note: The recipes in this chapter don't include beverage pairings because the choice will depend on the main food flavors that you will be eating. Look to the main course recipes for suggestions.

ASPARAGUS with MINT and GARLIC

Fresh mint, garlic, and a squeeze of lemon harmonize with asparagus to make them sing "spring." This formula also works well with other spring vegetables. Try it with fava beans, zucchini, or English peas plucked from the pod.

Many people believe that the thinnest asparagus are best. I like the medium ones for their fuller flavor and texture. Meyer lemons are a bit sweeter than common lemons. If they aren't available in your area, substitute ordinary lemons. It's worth splurging on your best olive oil here—its fruity, herbal, and peppery flavors will shine through in this dish.

Makes 4 servings

1 pound medium asparagus

¼ cup extra-virgin olive oil

3 medium cloves garlic, minced

1 tablespoon unsalted butter

¼ cup finely chopped fresh mint leaves

1 tablespoon fresh lemon juice

Kosher salt and freshly ground black pepper

1. Snap off and discard the tough ends of the asparagus. Cut the top 2 inches from the tips on a diagonal and set aside. Cut the rest of the asparagus on a diagonal into 1-inch segments.

2. Heat the olive oil in a medium skillet over medium heat. Add the garlic and toast for 1 minute, stirring, just until very lightly golden. Add the asparagus and cook for 1 minute longer, tossing the pieces with tongs to coat them with the oil. Add ¼ cup water, increase the heat to high, and cook, uncovered, until the water evaporates.

3. Add the butter, mint, and lemon juice, tossing to combine and melt the butter. Add salt and pepper to taste and toss again.

4. Transfer the asparagus to a platter. Serve warm or at room temperature.

SAUTÉED ZUCCHINI with ALMONDS

Chefs look to side dishes to lend distinction to the plate. This quick dish is inspired by the Italian trattoria, known for using vegetables in simple and delicious ways as *contorni,* or "side dishes," to add interest to the meal. Although the recipe is easy, there's nothing simple about it. The presentation is elegant and the flavors are satisfying.

This dish is the perfect accompaniment to a simple piece of sautéed fish with butter and a squirt of lemon, or a grilled chicken breast.

Makes 4 to 6 servings

3 medium zucchini, ends trimmed

2 tablespoons extra-virgin olive oil

2 tablespoons (¼ stick) unsalted butter

½ cup sliced almonds

Kosher salt and freshly ground black pepper

1 ounce Parmigiano-Reggiano or other good-quality Parmesan cheese (optional)

1. Cut the zucchini into ¼-inch julienne with a mandoline (see "Step Up Your Skills"). To cut it by hand, use a sharp chef's knife to cut off a thin lengthwise strip, then place the zucchini cut side down on a cutting board. Cut the zucchini lengthwise into ¼-inch planks, then cut across the planks to make thin batons.

2. Heat the olive oil and butter in a medium skillet over medium-high heat. Add the almonds and sauté until they are lightly browned. Add the zucchini and season with salt and pepper to taste. Sauté until the zucchini is just tender, about 1 minute.

3. Transfer the zucchini and almonds to a platter. Use a vegetable peeler to shave Parmesan over the top, if desired. Serve immediately.

I love music, but when I suggest using a mandoline, I'm not talking about the pear-shaped stringed instrument. The one you want for this recipe is the kitchen version, the one that effortlessly slices your vegetables paper thin. You use a hand protector to grab the vegetable and move it across a super sharp blade to cut thin slices or strips. The best mandolines are adjustable so that you can vary the thickness of the cut. Most can also be used to cut vegetables into perfect julienne like we're looking for in this recipe. Some make other fancy cuts.

The advantage of perfectly cut vegetables is that they cook evenly. They're also more elegant, and can be nicer to eat. The most expensive mandolines are French and typically are made from stainless steel, but I love my plastic V-slicer, with a V-shaped blade that makes perfect slices every time.

CHAYOTE and CORN SUCCOTASH

Succotash may be old news, but you can make it new all over again by adding a different ingredient. Chayote is a pear-shaped vegetable (botanically, it's actually a fruit) in the same family as cucumbers, melons, and summer squash. If you can't find it, substitute zucchini.

Makes 6 servings

1 chayote squash	**2 tablespoons minced garlic**
2 ears of corn, husks and silk removed	**2 tablespoons (¼ stick) unsalted butter**
1 medium red onion, sliced into ½-inch rounds	**1 red bell pepper, seeded and diced**
5 scallions, roots trimmed	**1 yellow bell pepper, seeded and diced**
Extra-virgin olive oil	**1 teaspoon chili powder**
Kosher salt and freshly ground black pepper	**½ cup chicken or vegetable broth**

1. Heat a grill or stovetop grill pan to medium-hot. Slice the chayote lengthwise into ¼-inch-thick slabs. (No need to cut out the edible seed in the center.) Lightly coat the chayote slices, corn, onions, and scallions with olive oil and sprinkle with a little salt and pepper. Grill the vegetables until they show grill marks and the onions have softened.

2. Transfer the vegetables to a cutting board. When they are cool enough to handle, cut the chayote and onions into ¼-inch dice, cut the scallions into ¼-inch slices, and cut the kernels from the ears of corn (see page 19).

3. Sauté the garlic in the butter in a large skillet over medium heat until it softens; it should not brown. Increase the heat to medium-high and add the grilled vegetables, the bell peppers, chili powder, 1 teaspoon salt, and ¼ teaspoon pepper. Sauté until the vegetables are tender, about 5 minutes.

4. Add the chicken broth and cook over high heat, stirring occasionally, until only enough broth remains to coat the succotash. Adjust salt and pepper to taste.

5. To make ahead, cool then refrigerate in a covered container for up to 1 day. Reheat in a skillet with a little chicken broth or serve cool or at room temperature.

SHIITAKE-CABBAGE STIR-FRY

This dish is simple to prepare, lovely to look at, and delightful to eat, even if you think you're not a fan of cabbage.

Makes 4 servings

1 head green cabbage, quartered, cored, and shredded

Kosher salt

1 cup sliced shiitake mushrooms

2 tablespoons (¼ stick) unsalted butter

2 tablespoons toasted sesame oil

Freshly ground black pepper

1. Blanch the cabbage in a large pot of salted boiling water for a minute or two to soften it. Drain.

2. Sauté the mushrooms in the butter in a large skillet over medium heat until they are tender and cooked through, about 5 minutes.

3. Add the steamed cabbage, drizzle with the sesame oil, and toss over the heat for a minute to combine the flavors. Season to taste with salt and pepper.

BALSAMIC-ROASTED MUSHROOMS

Chefs know that roasting vegetables is a great way to concentrate their flavors. Tomatoes, small onions, and mushrooms are roasting favorites. Here, sweet-tangy balsamic vinegar balances the earthy flavor of the mushrooms. You can use accompaniments like this one to dress up simple pan-roasted or grilled meats. As an added bonus, this can be made up to two days in advance, refrigerated tightly covered, and warmed just before serving.

When possible, I like to combine at least three varieties of farmed and wild mushrooms in this dish for the most complex, woodsy flavor.

Makes 4 servings

1 pound assorted wild or farmed mushrooms

3 to 4 tablespoons olive oil

Sea salt

2 tablespoons minced shallots

2 tablespoons minced garlic

2 teaspoons fresh thyme

2 to 3 tablespoons balsamic vinegar

2 tablespoons flat-leaf parsley, chopped

1 tablespoon unsalted butter

Freshly ground black pepper

1. Brush any dirt from the mushrooms. Pull off and discard any tough stems. Chop large mushrooms into thick slices; leave small ones whole. Heat the olive oil in a large skillet over medium-high heat. Add the mushrooms, sprinkle with a little salt, and sauté for 2 to 3 minutes, until they begin to soften, adding a little more olive oil if needed.

2. Add the shallots, garlic, and thyme and continue to cook until the mushrooms are tender. By this time they should have exuded their juices and begun to caramelize as some of the moisture evaporates and the mushrooms reabsorb the rest.

3. Stir in the balsamic vinegar to taste and cook a minute or two longer. Stir in the parsley and butter and season with salt and pepper.

SESAME SPINACH

This is my version of the sushi bar favorite *Goma-ae*. The secret is to infuse aromatics into the spinach as it cooks, then squeeze all the liquid from it to form a compact bundle of spinach that's full of flavor. The sesame dressing is the perfect complement.

Makes 4 to 6 servings

3 tablespoons sesame seeds

¼ cup peanut oil

¼ cup toasted sesame oil

¼ cup light soy sauce

¼ cup fresh lime juice

2 tablespoons rice wine vinegar

2 shallots, minced

4 cloves garlic, minced

1 tablespoon minced fresh ginger

1 teaspoon sugar

2 tablespoons extra-virgin olive oil

8 cups loosely packed spinach leaves, rinsed and spun dry

Kosher salt and freshly ground black pepper

1. Toast the sesame seeds in a small skillet until fragrant. Stir together the peanut and sesame oils, the soy sauce, lime juice, sesame seeds, vinegar, half of the minced shallots, half of the minced garlic, the ginger, and the sugar in a small bowl. Set aside, or refrigerate in a covered container for up to 3 hours.

2. Heat the olive oil in a large skillet over medium-high heat. Add the remaining shallots and garlic, stirring for a few seconds, then the spinach, moving it around to quickly stir-fry until it is completely wilted. Season lightly with salt and pepper. Set aside to cool.

3. When it is cool enough to easily handle, press the spinach between your hands to squeeze out as much liquid as you can. Put in a bowl and cover with plastic wrap and refrigerate until cold or for up to 6 hours.

4. To serve, put the spinach in a ceramic serving bowl and drizzle the dressing generously over it. You will have leftover dressing, which can be drizzled over the dish you serve the spinach with, or used as a dressing or dipping sauce.

SNAPPY APPLE COLESLAW

This recipe shows why knife skills matter: Chefs know that the way in which an ingredient is cut makes a difference in how you experience it in your mouth. The finely shredded vegetables offer plenty of surface area, and that means more flavor. It also allows all the elements in the salad to be coated evenly with dressing, and to mingle comfortably in your mouth as you eat it. If you have one, make easy work of cutting the cabbage and apples using a mandoline.

Green apples give this colorful salad a sweet-tart contrast and refreshing crunch that make it a great complement to spicy meat and seafood dishes.

Makes 8 servings

1 small green cabbage	**2 teaspoons Colman's dry mustard**
¼ small red cabbage	**1 teaspoon kosher salt**
2 Granny Smith apples, unpeeled	**1 teaspoon celery seeds**
1 medium carrot	**Freshly ground black pepper**
2 scallions	**½ cup mayonnaise**
3 tablespoons cider vinegar	**1 tablespoon Dijon mustard**
2 tablespoons sugar	

1. Cut the green cabbage into quarters, cut out the core, and slice very thin crosswise to make about 4 cups of finely shredded cabbage. (Reserve the remaining cabbage for another use.) Cut the red cabbage in the same way. Cut the apples into thin slices and then crosswise into thin strips (julienne). Shred the carrot. Cut the scallions into thin slices on a diagonal. Toss together the cabbages, apples, carrot, and scallions in a large salad bowl.

2. In a small bowl or 2-cup glass measure, whisk together the vinegar, sugar, dry mustard, salt, celery seeds, and pepper until the sugar and salt dissolve. Whisk in the mayonnaise and Dijon mustard.

3. Add enough of the dressing to the vegetables to liberally coat them. Toss until everything is well coated, then set aside for 20 minutes to allow the flavors to mingle. Toss one more time, adjust the seasonings to taste, and serve, or refrigerate in a tightly covered container for up to 1 day.

CAULIFLOWER COUSCOUS

A different cooking method can reinvent an ingredient's personality. Inspired by San Francisco chef James Ormsby, this recipe shares a simple technique that reveals a whole new side to cauliflower.

Here, I share his secret for making "couscous" out of grated cauliflower. It's a fun and satisfying replacement for potatoes or rice. Try using it as a staple for soaking up sauces and curries.

Makes 6 servings

1 medium head cauliflower

1 tablespoon unsalted butter or extra-virgin olive oil, or a combination of the two

Kosher salt and freshly ground black pepper

1. Remove the outer leaves and large central core from the cauliflower. (Discard or save for another use.) Cut the cauliflower into large pieces, then pulse them in a food processor fitted with a metal blade until the cauliflower looks like grated cheese. (Alternatively, you can grate the cauliflower using a box grater.)

2. Heat the butter in a large skillet over medium-high heat. Add the cauliflower, sprinkle with salt and pepper, and cook, stirring and tossing frequently, until it is cooked through, 3 to 5 minutes. Adjust salt and pepper to your liking, then transfer to a warm shallow bowl to serve.

DON'T HOLD BACK ■ MAKE IT YOURS

For a pristine presentation, watch carefully as you cook the cauliflower so that it does not brown. Alternatively, allow the cauliflower to brown in spots for a more caramelized, roasted flavor. For variety, fold in a handful each of toasted sliced almonds, drained and rinsed capers, and plumped raisins just before serving.

FRESH BASIL RATATOUILLE

MAKE AHEAD

Taking a little extra time with individual ingredients coaxes the best from each. The result is an exciting dish with lots of flavor variation in every bite. Careful cutting turns this home-style, rustic stew into a company-worthy mosaic. If you're a little less casual in your cuts, it will still taste great, but aim for pieces of approximately equal size for even cooking. Fresh basil at the end adds bright, fresh flavor.

Ratatouille makes a great accompaniment for roasted chicken, or as a vegetarian entrée served over a steaming bowl of polenta (see "The Art of Polenta," page 238). Look for fire-roasted diced tomatoes for added complexity.

Select a small to medium eggplant with firm, smooth, shiny skin. Unlike many other fruits (yes, eggplant is a fruit), eggplants should be light for their size. Purchase the eggplant no more than a day or two before cooking as it can become bitter with time. Some people believe that eggplants with a dash-shaped mark on the blossom end have fewer seeds—and therefore are less bitter—than those with a round mark; others disagree.

Makes 8 servings

1 medium-small globe eggplant (about ¾ pound)

1 medium green zucchini

1 medium golden zucchini or crooked-neck squash

1 medium red onion

1 medium red bell pepper

6 tablespoons extra-virgin olive oil, plus more, if needed

Kosher salt

1 heaping tablespoon minced garlic

One 14-ounce can diced tomatoes

½ cup roughly chopped or torn fresh basil

Freshly ground black pepper

1. Cut the eggplant, green and golden zucchini, and onion into ¼-inch dice, placing each in a separate bowl. (You can combine the two types of zucchini.) Cut the top and bottom off the red bell pepper, cut in half top to bottom, and remove the seeds. Lay each half skin side up on a cutting board and give it a good whack with the flat side of a cleaver or chef's knife to flatten it. Turn it over and, holding the knife almost parallel to the red pepper and work surface, carefully skim off the internal veins. Cut the pepper into ¼-inch dice.

2. Heat ¼ cup of the olive oil in a large skillet or wok over medium-high heat. I like to use a nonstick pan for this–it allows the vegetables to brown nicely without excessive oil or sticking. When the olive oil is hot, add the eggplant and sprinkle it with 1 teaspoon salt. Wait a minute or two before stirring to allow the eggplant to begin to take on some color. Alternate stirring and leaving it to sit a minute or so until the eggplant softens and is lightly browned all over. Remove the eggplant to a large serving bowl and set aside.

3. Add the remaining 2 tablespoons olive oil to the pan, then add the onions and garlic. When the onions are softened and light golden, add the red peppers. Sauté another minute to soften them, and then add the zucchini and 1 teaspoon salt. Add more olive oil as needed to keep the vegetables from sticking. When they are finished cooking, the vegetables should be tender but not at all mushy.

4. Return the eggplant to the pan and add the tomatoes with their juices. Stir and sauté to heat everything through and combine it well. (To make ahead, cool then refrigerate in a tightly covered container for up to 1 day. Reheat in a skillet over medium heat, stirring frequently, or serve cool or at room temperature.)

5. Stir in the torn basil and season with pepper and additional salt to taste before transferring to the serving bowl.

HONEY-ROASTED ROOT VEGETABLES

Great chefs have the talent for turning simple, seasonal ingredients into spectacular dishes. This is one way I have learned from my chef-colleagues and *Bay Café* guests to turn humble root vegetables into an explosively delicious and vibrant dish. Reducing the honey to a caramelized glaze and using it as the sole cooking medium results in vegetables with a rich, creamy texture and an earthy flavor with a hint of sweetness.

Use small, young vegetables for the best flavor. The vegetables should all be cut to about the same size (½- to ¾-inch dice) for even cooking and stylish presentation. Vary the dish by substituting sweet potatoes and celery root for part of the vegetables, if you like.

Makes 6 to 8 servings

1 cup honey

4 medium carrots, cut into ½-inch dice

3 small-medium parsnips, peeled and cut into ½-inch dice

2 medium turnips, peeled and cut into ½-inch dice

2 small-medium rutabagas, peeled and cut into ½-inch dice

1 medium or 2 small red onions, cut into 8 wedges

1 tablespoon unsalted butter

1 tablespoon fresh lemon juice

1 teaspoon fresh thyme or rosemary, chopped medium-fine (optional), plus large sprigs, for garnish

Kosher salt and freshly ground black pepper

1. Preheat the oven to 400°F. Cook the honey in a large heavy skillet over medium heat until it is thick and dark with large bubbles, about 10 minutes. Stir in the carrots, parsnips, turnips, rutabagas, and onions and cook until the vegetables are deeply glazed, 8 to 10 minutes.

2. Transfer the skillet to the oven and roast until the vegetables are tender and well caramelized, 15 to 20 minutes. (Alternatively, continue cooking and tossing the vegetables on the stove top until they are tender and well glazed, about 25 minutes.)

3. Stir in the butter, lemon juice, and thyme, if using. Season to taste with salt and pepper. (To make ahead, cool then refrigerate in a covered container for up to 2 days. Reheat in a skillet over medium heat, stirring frequently to prevent scorching.)

4. Transfer to a warm platter and decorate with large sprigs of the thyme, if you wish.

SWEET POTATO PURÉE

Zingy ginger and creamy sweet potatoes are a great foil for a meaty pot roast, baked ham, or turkey. This colorful purée is a welcome change from mashed potatoes.

You can make these ahead and keep them warm for up to an hour, or refrigerate and reheat them in a microwave oven. Use light-fleshed sweet potatoes or the moister orange-fleshed ones labeled "yams" in most U.S. markets. (True yams are a starchy white-fleshed tuber.) Butternut or acorn squash also work well in this recipe.

Makes 6 to 8 servings

4 tablespoons (½ stick) unsalted butter

1 medium yellow onion, coarsely chopped

3 medium sweet potatoes (about 2 pounds), peeled and cut into 1-inch chunks

1 cup chicken broth

1 cup heavy cream or half-and-half

4 teaspoons minced fresh ginger

Kosher salt and freshly ground black pepper

1. Melt the butter and sauté the onions in a heavy saucepan over medium heat for 5 minutes, stirring frequently, until they are lightly browned. Add the sweet potatoes, chicken broth, cream, and ginger and bring to a simmer. Cover, reduce the heat, and simmer slowly until the potatoes are tender, about 45 minutes.

2. Purée the mixture until it is as smooth as you like (see "Step Up Your Skills"). Season to taste with salt and pepper. Serve hot.

The technique you use to purée will depend on the equipment available in your kitchen and the food you are puréeing. The following will help you to choose.

An immersion blender makes easy work of blending hot liquids. It reduces the risk of burns as there is no need to transfer the hot liquid to a blender or food processor. It's also convenient and makes for easy cleanup. It's my top choice for this dish.

To purée the potatoes in a food processor, carefully strain off and reserve the liquid and add just enough to the processor to

purée the mixture. This helps to avoid splashing. Stir in the remaining liquid after the mixture has been puréed.

If your kitchen is equipment challenged, transfer the sweet potatoes to a bowl and whip them by hand or with an electric mixer. As above, carefully strain off and reserve the liquid before whipping and stir it back in afterward.

Blenders are not well suited to thick mixtures, which can tax the motor and result in a lumpy purée. Save your blender for mixtures no thicker than a milk shake.

CELERY ROOT PURÉE

This play on classic mashed potatoes uses an unexpected ingredient to turn a tried-and-true comfort dish into a special event. Substitute this flavorful purée for mashed potatoes at home and, voilà, restaurant cooking. Sometimes it's just that simple.

Makes 4 to 6 servings

1 tablespoon unsalted butter

2 celery roots (about 1½ pounds), peeled and cut into small chunks

1 cup whole milk

½ cup heavy cream or additional whole milk

Sea salt

½ teaspoon freshly ground black pepper

1. Melt the butter in a large saucepan over medium heat. Add the celery root and sauté for a minute or two. Add the milk, cream, and 1 teaspoon salt and bring just to a boil. Reduce the heat and simmer slowly, partially covered, until the celery root is tender, about 30 minutes. Keep an eye out as the milk has a tendency to boil over.

2. Purée until smooth, either using an immersion blender directly in the pot or by transferring to a traditional blender. Add the pepper and additional salt to taste. (To make ahead, cool then refrigerate in a covered container for up to 2 days. Reheat in a saucepan over medium heat, stirring frequently.) Serve hot.

RICE THREE WAYS

Rice is among the simplest foods to prepare. But that doesn't mean it has to be boring. Adding just a few flavorings will give your rice plenty of punch. Because rice makes such an easy and satisfying side dish, I am sharing three options, each made a slightly different way. In Cilantro Rice, the flavorings are stirred into freshly cooked rice. In Ginger-Scallion Rice, the rice is cooked and cooled before stir-frying it with flavoring ingredients. (You can save a step by picking up steamed rice at your local Chinese restaurant.) In Red Pepper Rice, the flavorings and rice are cooked together.

You should have no trouble finding one to pair with your favorite fish, chicken, or meat entrées. Better yet, borrow from these techniques and add your own favorite flavor enhancers. You can vary the flavor further by using fragrant jasmine or basmati rice.

When shopping for rice, look for whole grains with few if any broken pieces. Long-grain rice has less starch than its shorter relatives. To enhance its naturally fluffy quality, rinse and shake the rice in a colander under cool running water before cooking to remove the excess starch that can make the grains stick together after they're cooked.

CILANTRO RICE

Each recipe makes about 4 cups of cooked rice for 6 servings

1½ cups long-grain white rice, rinsed and drained

Kosher salt

2 tablespoons (¼ stick) unsalted butter

2 cloves garlic, minced

½ cup minced cilantro

1. Bring the rice and 2¾ cups water to a boil in a medium saucepan. Add 1 teaspoon salt, reduce to a simmer, then cover and cook until the rice is tender and most of the liquid has been absorbed, about 20 minutes. Remove from the heat and let stand, covered, for 10 minutes.

2. Melt the butter in a small skillet over medium heat. Add the garlic and sauté until it softens.

3. Transfer the rice to a large bowl and gently stir in the cilantro and sautéed garlic, scraping in all the butter from the skillet with a spatula. Adjust salt to taste and keep covered in a warm place until ready to serve.

GINGER-SCALLION RICE

Kosher salt

1½ cups long-grain white rice, rinsed and drained

1 teaspoon black or white sesame seeds (optional)

2 tablespoons vegetable oil

1 cup finely chopped scallions

2 tablespoons minced fresh ginger

1 tablespoon toasted sesame oil

Freshly ground black pepper

1. Bring a large pot of generously salted water to a boil. Add the rice and cook, uncovered, as you would cook pasta, until tender, about 20 minutes. Drain, then spread out the rice on a baking sheet to cool, about 30 minutes.

2. If using, toast the sesame seeds in a small skillet until fragrant. Set aside. Heat a wok or large skillet over high heat until it is very hot. Add the vegetable oil, scallions, ginger, and sesame oil. Use a metal wok paddle or wooden spatula to stir-fry the vegetables for 1 minute to soften them. Add the cooled rice and sesame seeds, if using, and continue to stir-fry for another 2 minutes to thoroughly combine and heat everything through. Season to taste with salt and pepper.

DON'T HOLD BACK ■ STEP UP YOUR SKILLS

Here's my favorite way to cook rice that will be used in another dish. Thoroughly rinse long-grain white rice in a colander under cool running water. Put the drained rice in a saucepan with abundant water, as you would to cook pasta. Boil, uncovered, until the rice is tender, about 20 minutes. Drain, then spread the rice on a baking sheet to cool, about 30 minutes, for the best consistency in your stir-fry. The rice will be in distinct grains, and it won't be gummy from excess starch.

RED PEPPER RICE

2 tablespoons (¼ stick) unsalted butter

1 tablespoon olive oil

2 small red bell peppers, halved, stemmed, seeded, and cut into ⅛-inch dice

1 small yellow onion, cut into ⅛-inch dice

3 small cloves garlic, minced

1½ cups long-grain white rice, rinsed and drained

Kosher salt and freshly ground black pepper

1. Heat the butter and olive oil in a heavy saucepan over medium-high heat. Add the red peppers, onions, and garlic, and sauté, stirring occasionally, until the vegetables soften, about 5 minutes. Add the rice, cooking and stirring for another 2 minutes. Stir in 3 cups water and 1 teaspoon salt. Bring to a boil, then reduce the heat and simmer, covered, until the rice is tender and has absorbed the water, about 20 minutes.

2. Uncover and fluff the rice with a fork. Season to taste with salt and pepper. Replace the cover until serving time.

MINTED COUSCOUS with POMEGRANATE SEEDS

Couscous makes an easy, elegant platform for grilled chicken, pork chops, lamb, shrimp, or other main dish foods. Mint gives this version bright flavor, and pomegranate seeds add jeweled color and crunch.

For seasonal variety, add freshly shelled English peas and toasted pine nuts in spring; diced peeled peaches and toasted hazelnuts in summer; diced Fuyu persimmons and toasted almonds in autumn, or tangerines and carambola (star fruit) with toasted macadamia nuts or toasted coconut in winter. Mint will work with any of these combinations. Olive oil adds richness and flavor. If you prefer, you can use less oil and the recipe will still work well.

Makes 4 to 6 servings

¼ cup extra-virgin olive oil

Sea salt

1 cup couscous

¼ cup minced red onions

¼ cup pomegranate seeds

¼ cup fresh spearmint leaves, chopped

2 tablespoons fresh lemon juice, or to taste

Freshly ground black pepper

CHEF'S TIP

Toast couscous in a dry skillet to bring the natural oils and flavor to the surface and help it to absorb the liquid.

1. Bring the olive oil, 1 teaspoon salt, and 1 cup water to a boil in a 1½-quart saucepan. Heat the couscous in a dry skillet over medium-high heat, gently shaking the pan, until the couscous begins to exude a toasty aroma, about 3 minutes. Remove the saucepan of boiling water from the heat, stir in the toasted couscous, cover, and let stand until the water is absorbed, 15 to 20 minutes.

2. Use a fork to fluff the couscous into individual grains. (To make ahead, cool then refrigerate in a covered container for up to 1 day. Reheat in a covered casserole in a preheated 350°F oven until warm, about 15 minutes.) Just before serving, stir in the onions, pomegranate seeds, mint, and 1 tablespoon of the lemon juice. Add salt, pepper, and additional lemon juice to taste.

Turn a pomegranate flower end down and you'll see a natural star pattern of ridges going top to bottom around the fruit. Score along those lines with a sharp knife and, working over a large bowl of water, carefully pull the thick skin apart to separate it into five or six sections.

With your hands under the water, pull the seeds off of the membranes. Small pieces of membrane will rise to the top, while the seeds will sink. After pulling off all the seeds, discard the large pieces of skin and membrane, pull the floating membrane pieces off the water, then scoop out the seeds with your hands into a small bowl.

Alternatively, look for plastic containers of the seeds, all ready to go, in the produce section of your supermarket.

SPOON BREAD, with VARIATIONS

Chef's love to embrace the past while cooking in the present by giving simple recipes creative makeovers with unexpected ingredients. This tender Southern spoon bread rises like a soufflé but isn't nearly so fussy. Cooking the cornmeal into a porridge before adding the other ingredients and baking it results in a smooth, custardy spoon bread that tastes much richer than its humble ingredients might suggest. This recipe is a palette for your creativity. See "Make It Yours" for suggestions.

Makes 4 to 6 servings

¾ teaspoon kosher salt

½ cup stone-ground cornmeal

1 tablespoon unsalted butter, plus more for the pan

2 large eggs

½ cup buttermilk or whole milk

¼ cup heavy cream

¼ cup shredded Cheddar cheese

2 tablespoons freshly grated Parmesan cheese

1. Preheat the oven to 425°F with a rack in the lower third. Butter an 8-inch square glass baking pan.

2. Bring 1¼ cups water to a boil with the salt in a medium nonreactive saucepan. Slowly whisk in the cornmeal, stirring to prevent it from clumping. Reduce the heat to medium-low and cook, stirring occasionally, until the mixture is a thick porridge and begins to pull away from the sides of the pan, about 5 minutes. Stir in the 1 tablespoon butter until incorporated. Transfer the mixture to a bowl and set aside for at least 10 minutes to cool slightly.

3. Whisk together the eggs, buttermilk, and cream in a small bowl, then stir them into the cooled cornmeal. Stir in the Cheddar and Parmesan. Pour the batter into the prepared pan and bake until the spoon bread is golden brown and a toothpick or knife comes out clean when tested an inch from the center, about 35 minutes. Let rest for 5 minutes before spooning the hot "bread" onto plates as a side dish, or into small bowls. (To make ahead, cool then cover and refrigerate for up to 2 days. Cover with foil and reheat in a preheated 350°F oven until hot, about 20 minutes.)

Once you have cooked the cornmeal "porridge" and added the eggs, buttermilk, and cream, think like a chef and add flavorings to suit the season, your mood, and the meal you will serve it with. Try these variations:

- Add crumbled bacon and chives to the spoon bread and serve with eggs for breakfast.

- Substitute blue cheese for the Cheddar and Parmesan and serve with a grilled steak.

- In autumn, add cremini mushrooms sautéed in a little butter and strips of roasted poblano chiles.

- And at the height of spring, stir in blanched, peeled fava beans and sautéed morels.

THE ART OF POLENTA

This highly adaptable dish can be used as a flavor-absorbing backdrop for a number of recipes in this book, including the Yucatán Pork Stew (page 174). It's also a great comfort food on its own.

For an Italian breakfast, tuck a piece of Taleggio cheese under the hot polenta and top with a poached egg. The melting cheese and oozing yolk add up to a rich and satisfying experience. As a late-night snack, season polenta with salt and pepper and top with butter and grated Parmesan cheese. For dessert or Sunday breakfast, drizzle a bowl of hot polenta with real maple syrup and cream.

Makes 4 to 6 servings

1 cup whole milk

Kosher salt

½ cup polenta

2 tablespoons (¼ stick) unsalted butter

Freshly ground black pepper

CHEF'S TIP

For the creamiest polenta, keep the heat low. Place the saucepan of polenta into a cast-iron skillet to diffuse the heat.

In a medium saucepan over medium heat, bring the milk and 2 cups water to a boil. Stir in 1 teaspoon salt, then whisk in the polenta in a steady stream. Simmer, stirring frequently, until the polenta is creamy, 10 to 20 minutes. (Look at package directions for guidance; coarser polenta will take longer than finer grinds.) Stir in the butter until it melts, season with salt and pepper, then cover and keep warm until serving time.

DON'T HOLD BACK ■ MAKE IT YOURS

For Corn Mash, cut the kernels from one ear of corn (see page 19), scraping the cob with the back of the knife to extract the corn milk. Use a blender to process the corn with the water and milk in the recipe. It needn't be perfectly smooth. Bring the liquid to a boil and continue as above.

For Parmesan Polenta, follow the instructions above, stirring in ⅓ cup grated best-quality Parmesan cheese during the last few minutes of cooking.

To make firm polenta for grilling or sautéing as a side dish, use 5 parts liquid to 1 part polenta rather than the 6-to-1 ratio used in this recipe. I add a big handful of grated Parmesan cheese to the hot polenta for extra flavor. Make it your way by adding sun-dried tomatoes, pesto, sautéed mushrooms, or other tasty bits. Pour out the hot polenta onto a rimmed baking sheet and smooth the surface with a spatula. When it is cool and firm, cut the polenta into squares and grill or sauté until it is hot and crusty.

JOEY'S BIG, BOLD BLACK BEANS in BEER

This recipe shows how a good chef is very much a craftsperson. Cooking and caramelizing the vegetables and spices before adding the beans builds a solid foundation of complex flavors, spice, and heat into these full-flavored beans.

If you can find them, build additional flavor by using fire-roasted diced tomatoes; I like the Muir Glen brand. Beer is another secret ingredient. I like the bold flavor of Negra Modelo, a dark beer from Mexico's Yucatán Peninsula.

When using dried beans, you can reduce the cooking time and facilitate even cooking by covering the beans with plenty of water and soaking overnight in the refrigerator. Rinse and top with new water before cooking. But don't fret if time is short. Here, I show you how to cook them without soaking.

Serve with grilled chicken, beef, or pork, Cilantro Rice (page 231), warm tortillas, and your favorite condiments, or in a large bowl topped with sour cream and cilantro.

Makes 6 to 8 servings

2 cups dried black beans or 4 cups cooked black beans, rinsed and drained

2 tablespoons vegetable oil

1 yellow onion, cut into small dice

4 medium cloves garlic, minced

1 tablespoon chili powder

1 teaspoon whole cumin seeds or ½ teaspoon ground

1 chipotle chile, finely chopped, plus 1 teaspoon adobo sauce

One 12-ounce bottle dark beer

One 14-ounce can diced tomatoes

1 bay leaf

Kosher salt and freshly ground black pepper

1. If using dried beans, pick through the beans, removing any small rocks or other debris. Rinse the beans in a colander under cool running water, then place them in a heavy saucepan large enough to cover them with 4 inches of water. Cover the pan and gently boil until they are tender and fully cooked, about 1 hour and 15 minutes, adding more water if it falls below the top of the beans. (If you presoaked the beans, begin checking after 45 minutes.) Drain the beans, saving a couple cups of the cooking liquid.

2. Heat the vegetable oil in a large saucepan over medium heat. Add the onions and cook, stirring frequently, until they begin to soften and caramelize. Add the garlic, chili powder, cumin, chipotle chile, and adobo sauce and cook until the onions are well browned. Stir in the beer and cook for 2 minutes, then add the tomatoes, bay leaf, and drained beans. Season to taste with salt and pepper.

3. Bring the mixture to a boil, then reduce the heat to a slow simmer and cook, uncovered, for 30 minutes, stirring occasionally to keep the beans from sticking. If the beans begin to look dry, add some of the reserved cooking liquid or a little water. The beans are done when the juices have gone from being very soupy to forming a rich sauce. (The beans will thicken further as they sit.) (To make ahead, cool then cover and refrigerate for up to 2 days. Reheat in a saucepan over medium heat, stirring frequently.)

SAVE ROOM FOR DESSERT

LIKE THE LAST SONG IN A CONCERT, a perfect dessert forms the lingering impression you take home from a meal. Some restaurateurs play on this by offering handmade chocolates or miniature pastries at the end of the meal. Some send you off into the night with a "souvenir" treat to enjoy the following day.

In this chapter, I share my favorite desserts. I must admit that I don't have the patience of the typical pastry chef. It requires a type of scientific precision that just isn't my style. But I do love a good dessert, and over the years I've developed several that are special without being overly fussy. These are the desserts I've created in my restaurants so that I don't find myself in the weeds when the pastry chef calls in sick at the last minute. They're also the ones I use to add a sweet touch without a lot of hassle to a meal I'm cooking at home.

With these relatively simple desserts, I'll teach you a few basic techniques and show you how to keep the flavors bold, all the way to the last bite of the meal. Most important, they are desserts that you will remember, and that your dinner guests will ask you to make, again and again.

BANANAS FOSTER

This dessert creates great drama and delight as you make it, then delivers on its promise with great taste. Bring your guests into the kitchen to watch you flame the rum, or for the most dramatic presentation—and only if you are experienced and comfortable doing this—bring the skillet into the dining room, place it on a nonflammable heatproof surface, and ignite the rum with a long match. (Do not attempt this after drinking large quantities of wine with dinner!)

Makes 4 servings

What to Drink: The caramelized bananas are a great match for botrytis, the deliciously funky "noble rot" that develops naturally on some late-harvest grapes. The classic one is Sauternes. A rum-spiked, sweet coffee would also be good.

4 tablespoons unsalted butter

1 cup packed dark brown sugar

½ cup coarsely chopped pecans

4 medium bananas, cut on a diagonal into ¾-inch-thick slices

¾ cup dark rum (I like Myers's in this recipe)

1 pint premium vanilla ice cream

1. Melt the butter in a large skillet over medium heat. Stir in the brown sugar and pecans and cook for 3 to 4 minutes. Add the bananas and continue to cook until they begin to brown. Add the rum, carefully tipping the skillet away from you to ignite it in the pan. (If you are using an electric stove, use a long-handled lighter or long match to light the rum.) Allow the alcohol to burn off until the flame has completely died down.

2. Have two scoops of ice cream ready in each of four shallow serving bowls. Divide the bananas and sauce over the ice cream and serve immediately.

MARGARITA GRANITA

This icy dessert is all about fun. Is it a cocktail or a dessert? Chefs love to play tricks on food and diners. A granita couldn't be easier to make, yet it's a special occasion food. Now, that's my kind of a dish. This also makes a refreshing palate cleanser between courses.

Granitas are as flavorful as ice creams, but they're lighter, more refreshing, and easier to make—even easier than sorbet. Both sugar and alcohol lower the freezing point, keeping the mixture from freezing into a rock-hard block of ice. Too much of a good thing, however, and the liquid won't freeze enough to scrape up into a granita or will melt too quickly when you serve it.

You can make granitas in so many wonderful flavors. Besides this one, some of my favorites are mixed berry, mango, and espresso. The last is lovely served in a tall glass, layered with slightly sweetened whipped cream. It's a sweet ending to a meal that won't weigh you down.

You don't have to use your most expensive tequila for this, but do use a tequila you like well enough to drink. A fruity silver or white (clear) tequila, or the oak-aged, mellower añejo, will work well.

Makes 8 servings

What to Drink: This one stands on its own as a cocktail, palate cleanser, or dessert.

1 cup sugar

½ cup tequila

6 tablespoons fresh lime juice

¼ cup fresh orange juice

¼ cup Cointreau

Mint sprigs, for garnish (optional)

1. Heat the sugar with 2½ cups water, stirring, until the sugar is completely dissolved. Remove from the heat and stir in the tequila, lime and orange juices, and Cointreau until well mixed.

2. Pour the mixture into a 13 by 9-inch glass baking pan or covered plastic container, and clear a flat space in the freezer for the pan. Freeze until slushy, about 3 hours, then break up the mixture by running the tines of a fork through it several times. Repeat every 2 hours or so until the granita is icy throughout, about 8 hours. (It will not freeze hard, as alcohol has a very low freezing temperature.) At the end, you will have piles of fine slivers of very flavorful ice that melt when they hit your tongue. Pack the granita loosely in a covered plastic container and freeze for up to 3 days.

3. To serve, scoop the granita into martini glasses and garnish with a sprig of mint or mint leaves cut into thin ribbons, if desired. Serve quickly—it melts fast!

CHOCOLATE CRACKLE COOKIES

These cookies are a perennial favorite. What makes them restaurant special is the walnut oil, which subtly enhances the flavor of the walnuts in the cookies.

Purchase nut oils in small quantities and store in the refrigerator to keep them from going rancid. If the oil has an off taste, discard it. The off taste would only become magnified in the recipes you make with it.

Makes about 30 cookies

What to Drink: Enjoy with a glass of milk, a cup of coffee, or, for the mint version, mint tea. A sweet oloroso Sherry or Malmsey Madeira pairs beautifully with the nuts and brown sugar.

8 ounces semisweet chocolate, chopped

1 cup packed light brown sugar

⅓ cup walnut oil

1 cup all-purpose flour

1 teaspoon baking powder

½ teaspoon fine sea salt

¼ cup walnuts, chopped medium-fine

2 large eggs

1 teaspoon pure vanilla extract

¼ cup powdered sugar, for rolling

1. Melt the chocolate, brown sugar, and walnut oil together in a double boiler over but not touching simmering water or in the microwave. Stir with a whisk until the chocolate is melted and smooth. The sugar does not have to be completely dissolved. If the chocolate is not completely melted, continue heating in 20-second increments, stirring between, until it is smooth. (Alternatively, you can heat the mixture in a small saucepan over low heat, or in a double boiler over but not touching boiling water, whisking frequently, until the chocolate is melted and smooth.) Allow to cool until the mixture is barely warm.

2. Stir together the flour, baking powder, and salt in a medium bowl. Stir in the walnuts. Set aside.

3. Whisk the eggs into the cooled chocolate until well blended. Whisk in the vanilla. Use a spatula to fold the chocolate mixture into the dry ingredients until everything is just combined.

4. Refrigerate the dough until it is firm, about 1 hour, or put it into the freezer for 10 to 15 minutes.

5. Preheat the oven to 350°F. Line two baking sheets with parchment paper or silicon baking mats. Sift the powdered sugar into a broad shallow soup bowl. Scoop out table-spoon-size nuggets of dough, roll them between your hands to make balls (don't worry about making them perfectly round), and drop them into the powdered sugar. Toss them in the sugar until they are well coated on all sides. Transfer the balls to the baking sheets, leaving about 1 inch between them.

6. Bake for 8 minutes for soft, chewy cookies, or 10 minutes for cookies with a crisp exterior. Use a spatula to transfer the cookies to a rack to cool. Store the completely cooled cookies in an airtight container for up to 4 days.

DON'T HOLD BACK ■ MAKE IT YOURS

You can substitute another nut oil such as hazelnut or almond to vary the flavor. Or for mint chocolate crackle cookies, use ¾ teaspoon peppermint extract in place of the vanilla.

These cookies are fantastic in little ice cream sandwiches. Flatten the dough balls slightly with the palm of your hand before baking. While the baked cookies are cooling, slightly soften your favorite ice cream. Place a scoop of ice cream onto the bottom of one cookie and top with a second cookie. Press gently to make an even layer of ice cream between the cookies. Individually wrap the sandwiches in waxed paper and place into a flat container. Freeze until firm.

BUTTERMILK PANNA COTTA

Panna cotta is Italian for "cooked cream." This recipe shows that, with the right ingredients and techniques, something as uncomplicated as basic gelatin can be made as sophisticated and creamy as crème brûlée. The silky, molded cream dessert has only a few ingredients, is simple to make, and takes well to creative variations. A touch of gelatin stabilizes the cream so that it can be molded for an attractive plated dessert. It's a restaurant favorite that's perfectly suited to making at home.

In this version, I add buttermilk for tang. For exotic flavor, infuse the milk and cream with herbs and spices, or add a few squirts of one of the flavoring syrups now available in many supermarkets and liquor stores. (I like Torani and Monin brands.) Serve the panna cotta with fresh berries, drizzle it with warm honey, or top with strawberries tossed with the best balsamic vinegar you can find and a twist of black pepper for a classic Italian flavor pairing.

Makes 6 servings

What to Drink: Pair this rich, tangy dessert with a refreshing moscato d'Asti, a slightly fizzy wine from Italy.

Vegetable oil, for the molds

1 cup whole milk

2 teaspoons granulated gelatin (slightly less than one ¼-ounce packet)

1 cup heavy cream

½ cup sugar

Half 4-inch vanilla bean or
1 teaspoon pure vanilla extract

1 cup buttermilk

Fresh berries or other fruit and mint sprigs, for garnish (optional)

1. Coat six 4-ounce molds very lightly with vegetable oil. Pour ¼ cup of the milk into a wide shallow bowl and sprinkle the gelatin over to distribute it evenly over the surface. Let stand without stirring for 5 minutes to soften.

2. While the gelatin softens, put the remaining ¾ cup of the milk, the cream, and sugar into a small saucepan. Cut the vanilla bean, if using, in half lengthwise, scrape the seeds into the saucepan, and drop in the pod. Cook over medium heat until very warm, with small bubbles just beginning to form around the edges of the pan. (If the liquid is boiling hot, let it cool a minute before adding the gelatin.)

3. Remove from the heat and stir in the softened gelatin, stirring continuously for a full 2 minutes to assure that it is completely dissolved. Stir in the vanilla extract, if using, and the buttermilk.

4. Pour the mixture through a fine mesh strainer into a 4-cup measure or bowl with a pouring spout. Discard the vanilla pod, if you used it.

5. Fill the molds with the mixture and allow to cool to almost room temperature before refrigerating until set, for at least 3 hours or up to 2 days. (The panna cotta will become a bit firmer over the next few hours.) To avoid condensation, do not cover until the panna cotta is well chilled.

6. To serve, carefully dip the molds into very warm water up to the fill line for 5 to 10 seconds, being careful not to get any water into the panna cotta. Wipe the outside of the molds with a towel before inverting onto a plate. Garnish with fruit and mint sprigs, if desired, before serving.

DON'T HOLD BACK ■ STEP UP YOUR SKILLS

Gelatin comes granulated in small packets or in sheets, also known as leaves. Chefs often prefer the sheets found in specialty baking shops because they can be softened without adding water to the recipe, which might dilute its flavors. Home cooks tend to prefer the granulated type because it's easily found in most supermarkets and it softens more quickly.

A ¼-ounce packet contains about 2¼ teaspoons of granulated gelatin. It's worth measuring as the packets can vary slightly, and in panna cotta, a small varia-tion can mean the difference between a thick and creamy molded pudding and rubbery milk gelatin. One tablespoon of granulated gelatin is equal to 4 sheets of leaf gelatin.

To use the leaves, lay them over a bowl of cool water and leave for about 15 minutes. When ready, the sheets will look like a wrinkly-skinned Shar-pei dog. Pull the sheets from the water and transfer them to the warm milk, discarding the soaking liquid. You will need three sheets for this recipe.

LEMON-LIME PARFAIT with RASPBERRIES

The lemon-lime curd can be prepared up to a day ahead, making for quick-and-easy assembly at serving time. It's easy and elegant, rich yet light–the perfect ending to a special meal.

Makes 4 servings

What to Drink: Pair with a sweet Vouvray made from chenin blanc grapes in France's Loire Valley. A sweet sparkling wine would also pair well.

2 large eggs, lightly beaten

¼ pound (1 stick) unsalted butter, cut into 8 pieces, at room temperature

½ cup sugar

1 tablespoon freshly grated lemon zest

1 tablespoon freshly grated lime zest

2 tablespoons fresh lemon juice

2 tablespoons fresh lime juice

1 cup very cold heavy cream

1 pint (2 cups) fresh raspberries, gently rinsed and laid out to dry on paper toweling

1. To make the lemon-lime curd, combine the eggs, butter, sugar, lemon and lime zests, and lemon and lime juices in a heavy nonreactive saucepan over medium-low heat. Cook, whisking constantly, until the mixture is thick enough to hold the mark of the whisk after you drag it through the curd, 8 to 10 minutes. Pour the curd through a fine mesh strainer into a bowl and let cool to room temperature. Cover with plastic wrap, pressing it directly against the curd, and refrigerate for at least 1 hour.

2. Just before serving, whip the cream to soft peaks. Layer the curd, whipped cream, and raspberries in that order in four parfait glasses, repeating the layers two more times to make three layers of each.

PEAR-GINGER CRISP

Crisps, cobblers, crumbles, buckles, and other fruit-based desserts are a great, homey, and satisfying way to take advantage of whatever is in season. The classic finish is a scoop of rich vanilla ice cream.

Pears and ginger are a classic pairing. I like Bosc pears in this recipe for their firm texture that stands up to long baking. Anjou, French Butter, Comice, or your favorite pears will be delicious, too. Use fruit that is ripe but not too soft.

Makes 6 servings

What to Drink: Complement the pear and ginger with an ice wine from Germany or Canada's Niagara Lake region.

¼ pound (1 stick) plus 1 tablespoon cold unsalted butter, diced

1 cup plus 1 tablespoon packed dark brown sugar

¼ teaspoon baking powder

¼ teaspoon baking soda

¾ cup all-purpose flour

1½ cups rolled oats

½ cup sliced almonds

⅓ cup finely ground almonds (almond meal or almond flour)

Kosher salt

6 large firm-ripe pears (about 3 pounds), cored and cut into 1-inch dice

2 tablespoons finely grated fresh ginger

CHEF'S TIP

Sauté fruit briefly before putting it into a crust to coax out juices and sweetness and to enhance flavor.

1. To make the topping, use your fingers to rub together 1 stick of the butter with 1 cup of the brown sugar. Stir the baking powder and baking soda into the flour, then add to the butter mixture along with the oatmeal, sliced and ground almonds, and a generous pinch of salt. Continue to rub together with your fingertips until the dry ingredients are well coated. You should be able to form clumps when you squeeze the mixture in your hands. Refrigerate until needed.

2. Preheat the oven to 350°F. Sauté the pears and ginger with the remaining 1 tablespoon butter and the 1 tablespoon brown sugar in a medium skillet over medium heat, stirring, until the fruit is well coated and begins to release its juices, about 3 minutes.

3. Transfer the pears to a 13 by 9-inch baking pan, scraping the syrupy juices from the pan with a spatula. Sprinkle the topping over the fruit using your hands to make small clumps with some of the topping.

4. Bake until the topping is deep golden brown and the fruit is bubbling, about 50 minutes. Let cool for 15 minutes before spooning the crisp into shallow bowls to serve. (To make ahead, cool then cover and refrigerate for up to 2 days. Warm in a 350°F oven for 10 minutes, if desired.)

MIXED BERRY CROSTATA

A crostata is a rustic Italian fruit tart, and rustic is in. Why? Because in our fast-paced high-tech world, it's nice to enjoy something simple, seasonal, and authentic. With its craggy crust and open center, this tart that looks and tastes as if it could have come from Nana's oven brings us a warm sense of nostalgia.

The dough is rolled out in a single large round, the filling mounded on top, edges tucked over, then into the oven it goes. No need for meticulous fitting of top and bottom crusts. No fancy lattice work required. Just all the great flavor of seasonal fruit and buttery crust in a presentation that looks great with a fraction of the effort.

This dessert lends itself to seasonal variations: nectarine and blueberry, pear and ginger sprinkled with sliced almonds, peaches and fresh ginger. But that's between you and your local market.

Makes 10 to 12 servings

What to Drink: Pair with a sweet pink sparkling wine such as brachetto d'Acqui from Northern Italy, or a black muscat or ruby Port.

1 pint strawberries, rinsed, tops removed, and quartered

½ pint each raspberries, blueberries, and blackberries, gently rinsed and blotted dry

1 cup granulated sugar

1 tablespoon cornstarch

Fine sea salt

2 cups all-purpose flour, plus more for the work surface

¼ cup almond meal or very finely ground almonds

10 tablespoons cold unsalted butter, cut into about 10 chunks

2 whole eggs

1 egg yolk

1 tablespoon finely grated orange zest

1 tablespoon finely grated lemon zest

¼ cup turbinado sugar or other coarse sugar, for garnish (optional)

Whipped cream, crème fraîche, or vanilla ice cream (optional)

1. Combine all the berries with ½ cup of the granulated sugar, the cornstarch, and a pinch of salt in a medium bowl. Set aside.

2. In a food processor fitted with a metal blade, pulse together the 2 cups flour, the almond meal, the remaining ½ cup granulated sugar, and ½ teaspoon salt to combine them. Add the butter and pulse just until the butter pieces are the size of small peas. Add 1 egg, the egg yolk, and the orange and lemon zests and pulse until the dough is well combined and begins to ball up around the blade.

3. Transfer the dough to a work surface that has been liberally dusted with flour. Using your well-floured hands, gently form the dough into a ball, flatten it into an 8-inch disk, wrap in plastic wrap, place on a baking sheet, and refrigerate for at least 30 minutes.

4. Twenty minutes before baking, preheat the oven to 350°F with a rack set at the lower middle position. Unwrap the dough and place it on the floured work surface.

5. Dust a rolling pin with flour and roll the dough into a 14-inch round. (If the dough is too cold and stiff, leave it for a few minutes and try again.) Move the dough frequently with a large spatula or metal bench scraper to keep it from sticking to the work surface. Don't worry if it breaks in places—just patch it together. This is a forgiving dough.

6. Line a flat baking sheet with parchment paper or invert a rimmed baking sheet and drape parchment over the top. This will make it easier to move the crostata after it is baked. Use a pastry brush to gently brush excess flour from the surface of the dough. Place the rolling pin across the dough circle a few inches from the top and gently roll the dough around the pin. Use the pin to carefully lift the dough and unroll it onto the center of the sheet.

7. Use a slotted spoon to give the fruit a stir, then pile it in the center of the dough, leaving behind the juices that have collected in the bowl. Distribute the fruit evenly over the crust, leaving a 3-inch band of dough around the edge.

8. Carefully lift the edges of the dough over the filling, tucking and ruffling to fit. Lightly beat the remaining egg with 1 tablespoon water and brush it over the exposed surface of the dough. Liberally sprinkle the dough with coarse sugar, if using.

9. Bake until the pastry is a deep, golden brown and the fruit is bubbling, about 45 minutes. Transfer to a rack to cool for at least 30 minutes or up to 4 hours before sliding the crostata onto a large platter.

10. Serve wedges of the crostata warm or at room temperature, topped with whipped cream, crème fraîche, or vanilla ice cream, if desired.

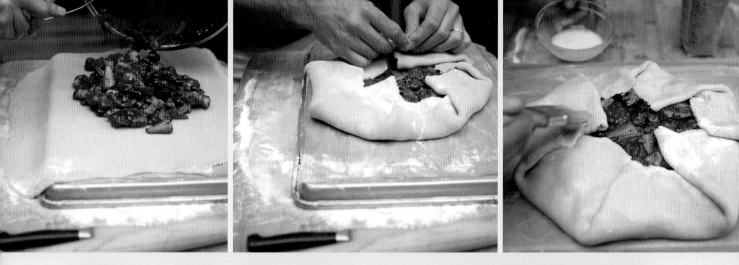

OOZING CHOCOLATE CAKE

MAKE AHEAD

Some variation of this cake with a lava-like center appears on countless restaurant menus. It's no wonder why—the cake is rich and satisfying, and it couldn't be easier to make. These cakes are at their oozy best immediately after baking, but leftover cakes can be reheated in a 325°F oven for about 4 minutes. Use a good-quality chocolate with a high percentage of cacao solids, 68 to 72 percent.

Makes 6 servings

What to Drink: Go for a chocolate-friendly wine such as vintage Port, black muscat, or late-harvest zinfandel. A cup of bitter espresso is another good choice.

8 ounces bittersweet chocolate

¼ pound (1 stick) unsalted butter

3 large eggs, separated

½ cup sugar

Nonstick vegetable oil cooking spray

1 pint premium vanilla ice cream (optional)

CHEF'S TIP

For oozing centers, refrigerate the batter before baking. The outside bakes through while the cold center stays insulated—it warms but doesn't set.

1. Melt the chocolate and butter together in the top of a double boiler over—but not touching—simmering water. Set aside to cool.

2. In a medium bowl, whisk the yolks with ¼ cup of the sugar until they are pale and light, about 5 minutes.

3. Whip the whites in a large, clean, dry bowl until they are thick and frothy, then add the remaining ¼ cup sugar and continue whipping until they form soft peaks. They should not be at all stiff or dry.

4. Fold the yolks into the melted chocolate, then fold the mixture into the whites. Cover and refrigerate for at least 1 hour or up to 2 days.

5. About 20 minutes before baking, preheat the oven to 400°F with an oven rack set in a lower middle position. Cut six 3-inch squares of parchment paper and arrange them on a rimmed baking sheet. Spray six 2½-inch stainless-steel ring forms with cooking spray and set them on top of the parchment squares. (Alternatively, you can bake and serve these in 6-ounce ramekins.) Divide the batter among the six molds.

6. Bake the cakes until they are set around the outside but are still quite runny when you poke a toothpick into the center, about 15 minutes. Run a paring knife around the inside edge of the molds to loosen the cakes, then gently slide a spatula between the mold and the parchment and transfer the cakes to individual dessert plates. Carefully lift off the rings. Serve two small scoops of vanilla ice cream on the side of each cake.

CHOCOLATE CRÈME BRÛLÉE

This crackly-topped custard always creates excitement, its burnt sugar crust delicately shattering to reveal the cool, smooth custard beneath.

When preparing this, I use a wooden spoon to stir the ingredients for the creamiest texture and no air bubbles.

Chocolate liqueur intensifies the chocolate in this custard. My favorite for this recipe is Godiva brand, but you could also use a clear or dark crème de cacao. You can vary the flavor by substituting Vandermint chocolate mint liqueur, Bailey's Irish Cream, Kahlúa, Chambord, or Grand Marnier. Or omit the alcohol and increase the cream by ¼ cup.

Makes 8 servings

What to Drink: Try a Banyuls or Maury from the south of France, a vintage Port, or a late-harvest zinfandel. A strong cup of espresso works just as well.

1½ cups heavy cream

4 ounces semisweet or bittersweet chocolate, finely chopped

½ cup, plus about 3 tablespoons sugar, for caramelizing

8 large egg yolks

¼ cup chocolate liqueur

CHEF'S TIP

Use cream that is not ultra-pasteurized and has no additives for the most reliable set of the custard.

1. Preheat the oven to 250°F with a rack placed in the center position and no rack above it. Fold a clean kitchen towel to fit the bottom of a baking dish that is at least 2 inches deep and place eight 4-ounce ramekins or crème brûlée dishes into the pan. (You may need to use two pans to hold all the ramekins.)

2. Heat the cream to a slow simmer in a medium saucepan over medium heat. Add the chocolate, let stand a minute, then stir until the chocolate is completely melted.

3. Use a wooden spoon to mix ½ cup of the sugar with the yolks in a large bowl just until they are thoroughly combined. Slowly add about one third of the cream mixture to the yolks, stirring continuously to prevent them from scrambling. Stir in the remaining cream until everything is evenly combined. Stir in the chocolate liqueur.

4. Pour the mixture through a fine mesh strainer into a 4-cup measure or a bowl with a pouring spout.

5. Divide the mixture equally among the ramekins. Place the pan of ramekins onto the oven rack, then pour in hot water from a kettle to reach about halfway up the sides of the ramekins. Bake the custards until they are set around the edges but still a bit quivery in the center when shaken, 60 to 75 minutes. (Deeper ramekins will take longer than shallow ones.)

6. Carefully lift out and transfer the ramekins to a rack to cool to room temperature. Refrigerate for at least 6 hours or up to 3 days. To avoid condensation, wait until they are completely cold before covering them with plastic wrap.

7. Just before serving, have ready a kitchen torch or preheat the broiler with a rack at the highest setting. Working with one custard at a time, blot any liquid from the surface of the custard and sprinkle it evenly with a teaspoon of the remaining sugar, tilting and shaking the ramekin to coat it evenly. (You may need to use a little more depending on the size of the ramekin.)

8. Move the torch flame steadily over the surface about 2 inches above the custard until the sugar melts and bubbles slightly. You are looking to caramelize the sugar without heating the custard any more than necessary.

If you are using a broiler, put the sugar-coated ramekins on a rimmed baking sheet and place under the preheated broiler until a crust forms, 3 to 5 minutes, watching carefully to see that it doesn't burn. Remove immediately from the baking sheet.

9. Leave the crèmes brûlées for a few minutes to allow the sugar crust to harden before serving.

BLACK-and-WHITE TIRAMISÙ

Restaurants are often the setting for celebrations and have at least one show-stopping dessert on the menu for a grand finale.

Here's my contribution on this front—I know you can do it, and it will wow any crowd you're cooking for. My philosophy here: If it's worth doing, sometimes it's worth overdoing! A lot of steps? Sure. Worth it? You bet!

Tiramisù is typically made with a strong coffee syrup and mascarpone cheese, often whipped with Marsala wine. The coffee and wine together account for the name, which is Italian for "pick me up." In this version, I add a layer of dark chocolate mousse and spike the syrup for an adult version that's sure to lift your spirits.

Use a good-quality bittersweet chocolate with 60 to 70 percent cacao solids. (The higher levels will make a denser mousse.) Callebaut, El Rey, Ghirardelli, Guittard, Scharffen Berger, and Valrhona are all good brands.

Makes 12 servings

What to Drink: Coffee or coffee liqueur will highlight the coffee flavor and complement the chocolate. Banyuls, Maury, Port, or the Spanish Dulce Monastrell will each bring out different nuances.

6 ounces good-quality bittersweet chocolate, roughly chopped, plus an additional small chunk (at least 1 ounce) for making chocolate shavings, for optional garnish

3 tablespoons unsalted butter, at room temperature

3 eggs, separated (you will have 1 leftover white)

1 cup sugar

¾ cup heavy cream

¼ cup plus 1 tablespoon Kahlúa or other coffee liqueur

1 teaspoon pure vanilla extract

1 pound mascarpone cheese

1 cup strong, hot brewed coffee

⅓ cup brandy or rum, or a combination of the two

36 ladyfingers, purchased or homemade (see "Step Up Your Skills")

Shaved chocolate or cocoa powder, for garnish (optional)

1. To make the dark chocolate mousse, melt the 6 ounces chocolate and the butter in the top of a double boiler over, but not touching, barely simmering water. Heat and stir until the chocolate is melted and smooth. Set aside until it is near room temperature but still fluid.

2. Whip 3 egg yolks with 2 tablespoons of the sugar in a standing mixer using the whip attachment at medium speed until the mixture is pale and light, about 5 minutes. Fold in the cooled chocolate.

3. Whip ¼ cup of the heavy cream with the 1 tablespoon Kahlúa to medium peaks. Gently fold into the chocolate mixture.

4. In a large, clean, dry bowl, whip 2 egg whites with 2 tablespoons of the sugar until they just begin to hold a stiff peak but are not at all dry. Gently fold into the chocolate mixture. Cover with plastic wrap and refrigerate until thickened and spreadable, at least 1 hour.

5. To make the mascarpone cream, whisk together the remaining ½ cup cream, ½ cup of the sugar, and the vanilla in a medium bowl until the sugar dissolves. Add the mascarpone, whisking until the mixture is smooth and thick. Set aside. (Refrigerate if not using immediately.)

6. To make the coffee syrup, stir together the coffee and brandy with the remaining ¼ cup sugar and the ¼ cup Kahlúa until the sugar is completely dissolved.

7. To assemble the tiramisù, put 12 ladyfingers into a small (10 by 7-inch) glass or ceramic baking dish or serving dish, cutting them as needed to (mostly) cover the bottom of the dish. Use a pastry brush to soak the ladyfingers with coffee syrup, using about one third of the syrup and painting them a couple of times as the syrup absorbs into the cookies.

8. Dollop and spread half of the mascarpone cream evenly over the ladyfingers. Top with another 12 ladyfingers and brush them generously with the syrup.

9. Dollop and spread all of the dark chocolate mousse evenly over the ladyfingers. Top with the final 12 ladyfingers and brush them with the remaining syrup.

10. Use a grater or sharp knife to shave about 1 ounce chocolate into small pieces. Fold the chocolate into the remaining mascarpone cream, then dollop and spread the mixture evenly over the ladyfingers to form the top layer.

11. Lightly press a piece of waxed paper over the tiramisù, then wrap the dish with plastic wrap and refrigerate for at least 2 hours or up to 2 days.

12. To serve, cut the tiramisù with a sharp knife dipped in warm water and wiped with a clean towel. Carefully lift the pieces onto dessert plates with a small, flexible spatula. Top with additional chocolate shavings or sifted cocoa, if desired.

DON'T HOLD BACK ■ STEP UP YOUR SKILLS

You can make your own ladyfingers. It's not difficult, and they will be better than any you will purchase at the store—light, moist, and ready to soak up that wonderful coffee syrup that makes tiramisù such a great pick-me-up. Ladyfingers are traditionally dusted with powdered sugar before baking, but that's not needed here.

For the tiramisu, prepare the chocolate mousse first so that it can chill while you make the ladyfingers. Mix the mascarpone cream and coffee syrup while the ladyfingers cool and you will be all ready to assemble the dessert.

LADYFINGERS

4 large eggs, separated

⅔ cup granulated sugar

½ teaspoon pure vanilla extract

¾ cup plus 2 tablespoons all-purpose flour

1. Preheat the oven to 325°F with a rack set in the lower center position. Line two baking sheets with silicone baking mats or buttered parchment paper.

2. Whip the egg whites in a large, clean, dry bowl until they are foamy, then gradually add the sugar, continuing to beat until they just begin to hold a stiff peak but are not at all dry. Beat the yolks in a separate bowl with the vanilla until they are light and pale. Gently fold the yolks into the whites until they are almost combined but still streaky. Sift in the flour, gently folding it in until it is just combined.

3. Transfer about half of the mixture to a pastry bag fitted with a standard round tip, or to a resealable plastic bag. If using the plastic bag, force the mixture into one corner, twist the bag at the corner to close it off, then snip off the corner to form about a ¾-inch round opening. Pipe the batter onto the prepared baking sheets in 3-inch-long fingers, continuing with the remaining batter, to form 36 cookies.

4. Bake until the cookies just barely begin to color, about 15 minutes. Transfer the pan to a rack to cool until the cookies can easily be peeled from the mat or paper.

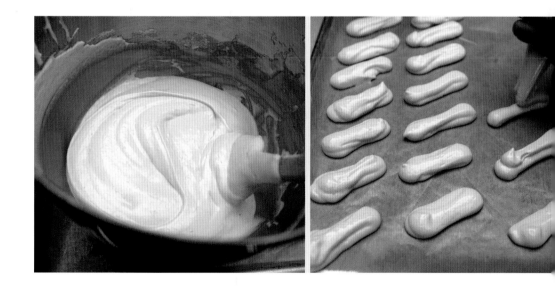

MENUS

Casual Autumn Get-Together

Mixed Greens with Roasted Pears, Blue Cheese, and Spiced Pecans (page 61)

Pork Chops with Port-Glazed Figs and Apples (page 165)

Honey-Roasted Root Vegetables (page 226)

Mixed Berry Crostata (page 253)

Cooking with Friends

Pomegranate Sangria (page 31)

Panino of Brie, Figs, Prosciutto, and Arugula (page 35)

Oven-Roasted Beet and Orange Salad (page 67)

Cauliflower and Roasted Garlic Soup with Parmesan Croutons (page 87)

Perfect Carbonara (page 104)

Chocolate Crème Brûlée (page 258)

Quick-and-Easy Dinner

Strawberry Spinach Salad (page 65)

Grilled Lamb Chops with Red Onion Jam and Celery Root Purée (page 182)

Cauliflower Couscous (page 222)

Asparagus with Mint and Garlic (page 213)

Family Dinner

My Favorite Caesar (page 77)

Stuffed Shells with Fun-Tina and Tomato Sauce (page 106)

Sautéed Zucchini with Almonds (page 214)

Pear-Ginger Crisp (page 252)

Cocktails, Anyone?

Assorted "Cocktail Hour" Cocktails

Ahi Tuna Poke with Wonton Crisps and Wasabi Cream (page 41)

Curried Chicken in Radicchio Cups (page 39)

Pancetta-Wrapped Sea Scallops with Ginger-Citrus Butter Sauce (page 48)

Salt and Pepper Shrimp (page 46)

Spicy Lamb Sliders with Cilantro-Cumin Yogurt Sauce (page 52)

Cinco de Mayo Party

The Desert Rose (page 26)

Avocado Salsa with Roasted Corn (page 206) with chips

Prawns with Ancho Chile, Tequila, and Lime (page 44)

Yucatán Pork Stew (page 174)

Margarita Granita (page 244)

Entertaining with Exotic Flavors

Sweet and Spicy Watermelon Salad (page 72)

Pad Thai My Way (page 117)

Spicy Lemon-Basil Chicken (page 114)

Bananas Foster (page 243)

Sunday Brunch

Bloody Maria (page 28)

Island Gazpacho (page 81)

Joey's Huevos Rancheros (page 56)

Buttermilk Panna Cotta (page 248)

Elegant Dinner Party

Hula-va Saketini (page 23)

Crab-Stuffed Avocado with Spicy Citrus-Mango Salad (page 69)

Butternut Squash Soup with Tamarind-Glazed Confit Duck (page 89)

Seared Halibut with Quinoa, Arugula, and Meyer Lemon–Ginger Vinaigrette (page 131)

Oozing Chocolate Cake (page 257)

Mochatini (page 25)

Picnic in the Park

Grilled Steak Texarkana Hand Rolls (page 50)

Chinese Chicken Salad (page 75)

Chocolate Crackle Cookies (page 246)

Backyard Barbecue #1

Super Summer Sipper (page 29)

Caribbean Grilled Lamb Skewers with Long Beans (page 185)

Tomato Chutney (page 210)

Minted Couscous with Pomegranate Seeds (page 234)

Lemon-Lime Parfait with Raspberries (page 250)

Backyard Barbecue #2

Joe-Hito (page 32)

Arugula Salad with Grilled Peaches, Goat Cheese, and Marcona Almonds (page 63)

Blackened Rib Eye with Chayote and Corn Succotash and Chipotle Chile Butter (page 178)

Spoon Bread (page 236)

Chocolate Crackle Cookies (page 246) with ice cream

SOURCES

Chefs spend a lot of time developing relationships with purveyors to source the best ingredients for their menus. They are out there pounding the pavement, looking for the best products at their local farmers' markets, in ethnic neighborhoods, and in the aisles of specialty food stores. This time-consuming process is essential to their work. The following sources will make it a little easier for you to find those things you may not be able to locate in your own community. It's my way of showing you a little love.

Ingredients

CHOCOLATE

CHOCOSPHERE
877-992-4626
www.chocosphere.com

ETHNIC INGREDIENTS

THE CMC COMPANY
800-262-2780
www.thecmccompany.com

THE ETHNIC GROCER
630-860-1733
www.EthnicGrocer.com

GUSTIAMO (ITALIAN)
718-860-2949
www.gustiamo.com

LATIN MERCHANT
206-223-9374
www.LatinMerchant.com

THE SPANISH TABLE
206-682-2827
www.spanishtable.com

FLAVORING SYRUPS

MONIN
800-966-5225
www.monin.com

TORANI
800-775-1925
www.torani.com

FLOUR AND GRAINS

KING ARTHUR FLOUR
800-827-6836
www.kingarthurflour.com

GENERAL INGREDIENTS

ZINGERMAN'S MAIL ORDER
888-636-8162
www.zingermans.com

SPICES

PENZEYS SPICES
800-741-7787
www.penzeys.com

QUICK SPICE
323-728-4762
www.quickspice.com

Wine

K&L WINE MERCHANTS
877-559-4637
www.klwines.com

ZACHYS WINE ONLINE
866-922-4971
www.zachys.com

Kitchen Equipment

BRIDGE KITCHENWARE
212-688-4220
www.bridgekitchenware.com

BROADWAY PANHANDLER
866-266-5927
www.broadwaypanhandler.com

SUR LA TABLE
800-243-0852
www.surlatable.com

WILLIAMS-SONOMA
877-812-6235
www.williams-sonoma.com

INDEX

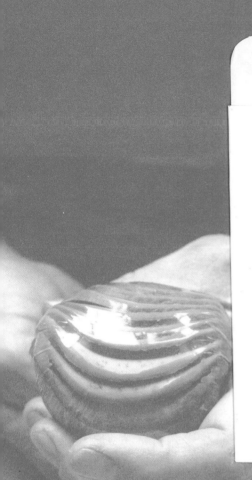